SPECIFICATION AND PROOF IN REAL-TIME CSP

Distinguished Dissertations in Computer Science

Edited by
C.J. van Rijsbergen, University of Glasgow

The Conference of Professors of Computer Science (CPCS) in conjunction with the British Computer Society (BCS), selects annually for publication up to four of the best British Ph.D. dissertations in computer science. The scheme began in 1990. Its aim is to make more visible the significant contribution made by Britain - in particular by students - to computer science, and to provide a model for future students. Dissertations are selected on behalf of CPCS by a panel whose members are:

M. Clint, Queen's University, Belfast
R.J.M. Hughes, University of Glasgow
R. Milner, University of Edinburgh (Chairman)
K. Moody, University of Cambridge
M.S. Paterson, University of Warwick
S. Shrivastava, University of Newcastle upon Tyne
A. Sloman, University of Birmingham
F. Sumner, University of Manchester

SPECIFICATION AND PROOF IN REAL-TIME CSP

Jim Davies
University of Oxford

CAMBRIDGE
UNIVERSITY PRESS

Published by the Press Syndicate of the University of Cambridge
The Pitt Building, Trumpington Street, Cambridge CB2 1RP
40 West 20th Street, New York, NY 10011-4211, USA
10 Stamford Road, Oakleigh, Melbourne 3166, Australia

First published 1993

Printed in Great Britain at the University Press, Cambridge

Library of Congress cataloguing in publication data available

A catalogue record for this book is available from the British Library

ISBN 0 521 45055 1

To my parents, for their love and support
&
to Alice, for everything

CONTENTS

PREFACE

REAL-TIME SYSTEMS

As computing devices become faster and more powerful, we find ourselves increasingly dependent upon systems which are difficult to understand and prone to failure. The failure of a commercial banking system or a company database may be expensive and inconvenient. The failure of an aircraft control system or a railway signalling network may result in injury or death. As the consequences of system failure become ever more severe, we must find ways to make these applications of computing technology safer and more reliable.

Over the past twenty-five years, mathematical techniques have been developed for the specification and implementation of computing systems. Formal methods have been used in the design and analysis of transformational systems—in which results are computed from a given set of inputs—and have been shown to reduce design costs and improve reliability. However, many of the systems in which safety is a primary concern are real-time systems, and cannot easily be viewed in a transformational setting.

Real-time systems maintain a continuous interaction with their environment and are often subject to complex timing constraints. They may also be required to perform several tasks concurrently. To reason about such systems we require a mathematical formalism that supports a treatment of timed concurrency. In this thesis we explore and extend one such formalism, the theory of Communicating Sequential Processes, first introduced by Hoare (1985).

We are working towards a formal method for the specification and refinement of real-time systems, based upon the denotational semantic models proposed by Reed and Roscoe (1987). This method should support both formal and rigorous reasoning at every stage of system development—from initial specification to final implementation—and be applicable to systems of a realistic size. It is our hope that the results of this research may be used to improve the safety and reliability of computing systems.

OUTLINE OF THE THESIS

The thesis begins with a brief introduction to the theory of Communicating Sequential Processes. We introduce the algebraic language of processes, and discuss the existing semantic models. In the second chapter we extend the language of processes and provide a timed semantics for each construct. In the third chapter we discuss the definition of processes by mutually-recursive sets of equations. We deduce a set of semantics-preserving rules for rewriting these equation sets, and obtain a useful test for the validity of a recursive definition.

In our denotational semantic model each language construct is identified with a set of possible behaviours. In the fourth chapter we show that informal requirements upon a system may be captured as behavioural specifications—predicates upon an arbitrary system behaviour—and that the notation of the model gives rise to a formal specification language. This language may be used to capture safety and liveness requirements, and to formalise assumptions about the operating environment.

Once a set of system requirements have been formalised, the language of processes may be used to suggest an implementation. In the fifth chapter we present a complete proof system for relating specifications and implementations, using the a simple notion of satisfaction. This proof system is compositional: properties of a compound process can be deduced from the external specifications of its components. This is essential if the proof system is to be employed in the development of large, complex systems.

A formal specification of a real-time system will include many requirements that can be established without recourse to timing information. In this case we may use the untimed semantic models to simplify our proof obligations. A substantial part of the fifth chapter is devoted to a simple theory of timewise refinement, which relates untimed safety conditions in the timed failures model to behavioural specifications in the traces model. The research described in this chapter is a continuation of research carried out jointly with Steve Schneider.

If we wish to produce a readable specification of a large system, then we must take care to present our description in a clear, structured fashion. In the sixth chapter we show how the hiding operator may be used to structure specifications, and present a simple proof rule for abstraction which allows us to separate the concerns of concealment and scheduling. We then introduce a macro specification language—a first-order logic with time—which makes it easier to formalise system requirements.

The seventh chapter is a case study, in which we show how the research described in the previous chapters may be applied to the specification and verification of a real-time system. A local area network protocol is described at two levels of abstraction, and the language of processes is used to suggest an implementation. The case study employs a general method for structuring CSP descriptions of layered protocols; this method is described at the beginning of the chapter.

In a description of a real-time system, it is sometimes convenient to include events that are not synchronisations: this can make it easier to describe and analyse certain aspects of behaviour. In chapter eight we show how the timed failures model may be extended to include a treatment of broadcast concurrency, in which output events may occur without the cooperation of the environment. The resulting semantic model is then used to complete the implementation of the protocol presented in chapter seven.

In the final chapter we discuss the results of the research presented in the the thesis. We then consider alternative approaches to the specification and development of real-time systems, paying particular attention to other timed process algebras. The chapter ends with a discussion of future research directions.

ACKNOWLEDGMENTS

I am indebted to my supervisor, Jim Woodcock, for his guidance, encouragement, and good taste. Also to Steve Schneider, whose concurrent approach to the subject has led to many enjoyable discussions and collaborative results. The research described in this thesis is founded upon earlier work by Mike Reed and Bill Roscoe; I am very grateful to them for their insight and friendship.

I wish to thank Jeremy Gibbons, Michael Goldsmith, Tony Hoare, Dave Jackson, Alan Jeffrey, Geraint Jones, Mathai Joseph, Andrew Kay, Quentin Miller, Joy Reed, and Phil Richards for their friendly advice and invaluable suggestions. Thanks also to Jacqui Thornton for her constant encouragement and support. Finally, I would like to acknowledge the financial assistance of BP International, the Royal Signals and Radar Establishment, and the Science and Engineering Research Council.

GLOSSARY

MATHEMATICAL SYMBOLS

$\mathbb{P}$	powerset operator	$\{\}$	the empty set
$\mathbb{F}$	set of all finite subsets of	$\equiv$	semantic equivalence
seq	set of all finite sequences of	$\widehat{=}$	defined to be equal to
$\mathbb{N}$	set of natural numbers	$\preceq$	a partial order
$\mathbb{Z}$	set of integers	seg	initial segment
$\mathbb{Q}$	set of rational numbers	$\underline{v}$	vector v
$\mathbb{R}$	set of real numbers	dom	domain of a function
$m \,..\, n$	integers from m to n	ran	range of a function

OBSERVATIONS

$\langle\rangle$	the empty trace	*first*	first event
$\frown$	catenation of traces	*last*	last event
$\leqslant$	trace prefix	*begin*	start time
$\dot{-}$	time shift	*end*	end time
$-$	time shift	*head*	first timed event
$\downarrow$	count of events	*foot*	last timed event
$\upharpoonleft$	before	*times*	time values present
$\uparrow$	during	*tstrip*	strip time values

$\upharpoonright$	after	σ	events present
$\downharpoonleft$	restrict	$\cong$	trace equivalence
$\backslash$	hiding	$CL_{\cong}$	closure under $\cong$

SYNTAX

$\perp$	divergence	$STOP$	deadlock
$SKIP$	successful termination	$;$	sequential composition
$WAIT$	delayed termination	$\fatsemi$	δ sequential composition
$\rightarrow$	prefix	$\backslash$	hiding
$\rightarrowtriangle$	instant prefix	$f(P)$	direct image
$\xrightarrow{t}$	delayed prefix	$f^{-1}(P)$	inverse image
$\Box$	deterministic choice	$\sqcap$	nondeterministic choice
$\parallel$	lockstep parallel	${}_A\parallel_B$	alphabet parallel
$\interleave$	interleaving	$\underset{A}{\parallel}$	sharing parallel
$\overset{t}{\rhd}$	timeout	$\underset{e}{\nabla}$	event interrupt
$\lightning$	untimed interrupt	$\underset{t}{\lightning}$	timed interrupt
$\mu X \bullet P$	delayed recursion	$\mu X \circ P$	immediate recursion
$P[Q/X]$	substitution	Θ	timed abstraction

SEMANTICS

tr	untimed trace	Σ	all events
s	timed trace	UT	all untimed traces
ref	untimed refusal	TE	all timed events
X	timed refusal	TT	all timed traces
α	stability value	TR	timed refusal sets

ρ	environment	$\mathcal{O}_{TF}$	all timed failures
δ	delay constant	$\mathcal{S}_{TF}$	all sets of timed failures
$\checkmark$	termination event	d	distance metric
η	non-event	$M(X, P)$	mapping for $\mu X \circ P$
VAR	process variables	$M_\delta(X, P)$	mapping for $\mu X \bullet P$
ENV	environments	$\rho[Y/X]$	environment over-riding
$TIME$	the time domain $[0, \infty)$	$\mathcal{S}^I_{TF}$	product space
TI	half-open time intervals	$\mathcal{M}^I_{TF}$	product model
RT	refusal tokens	$\underline{d}$	vector metric

SEMANTIC FUNCTIONS AND MODELS

$\mathcal{F}_{UT}$	traces	$\mathcal{M}_{UT}$	traces model
$\mathcal{F}_{US}$	stabilities	$\mathcal{M}_{US}$	stabilities model
$\mathcal{F}_{UF}$	failures	$\mathcal{M}_{UF}$	failures model
$\mathcal{F}_{UFS}$	failures-stabilities	$\mathcal{M}_{UFS}$	failures-stabilities model
$\mathcal{F}_{TT}$	timed traces	$\mathcal{M}_{TT}$	timed traces model
$\mathcal{F}_{TS}$	timed stabilities	$\mathcal{M}_{TS}$	timed stabilities model
$\mathcal{F}_{TF}$	timed failures	$\mathcal{M}_{TF}$	timed failures model
$\mathcal{F}_{UFTS}$	untimed failures-timed stabilities	$\mathcal{M}_{UFTS}$	untimed failures-timed stabilities model
$\mathcal{F}_{TFS}$	timed failures-timed stabilities	$\mathcal{M}_{TFS}$	timed failures-timed stabilities model

SPECIFICATION

sat	satisfies
$\mathbf{sat}_\rho$	satisfies in environment ρ
Φ	abstraction mapping for trace specifications
act_A	active for every event in set A
$\setminus\!\!\setminus$	whenever these events are active

1 THE LANGUAGE OF CSP

1.1 COMMUNICATING SEQUENTIAL PROCESSES

The theory of Communicating Sequential Processes, introduced by Hoare (1985), is a mathematical formalism for reasoning about patterns of communication in distributed systems. Systems and components are represented by behaviour patterns called *processes* which evolve and interact through a series of atomic actions called *events*. Each event is an instantaneous communication, acting as a synchronisation between two or more communicating processes.

The language of CSP is a process algebra; the terms representing processes may be rewritten in accordance with certain algebraic laws. These laws are justified by a number of semantic models, in which each term is associated with a set of possible observations. In the simplest of these models, the *traces* model, each term is associated with a set of traces: sequences of observable events. The other models include more information in the semantic set and allow us to draw finer distinctions between processes.

The syntax includes primitive operators for parallel composition, concealment, and nondeterministic choice. The result is an elegant notation in which the problems of concurrency, abstraction, and nondeterminism can be addressed separately. The syntax also provides constructs for modelling sequential composition, deadlock, and recursion:

$$\begin{aligned} P \quad ::= \quad & \mathit{STOP} \mid \mathit{SKIP} \mid a \to P \mid P \,;\, P \mid P \,\Box\, P \mid P \sqcap P \mid P \parallel P \mid \\ & P \interleave P \mid f(P) \mid f^{-1}(P) \mid P \setminus A \mid \mu X \bullet F(X) \end{aligned}$$

This grammar—with a wide variety of operators—contrasts with those defined in purely algebraic approaches to concurrency, in which much emphasis is placed upon obtaining a minimal set of operators.

The semantic models can be used to specify process behaviour. In each model, processes are associated with sets of observations, and predicates upon observation sets may be used to formalise process requirements. As an example, we may use the traces model to capture the requirement that a process P never performs a visible action; we

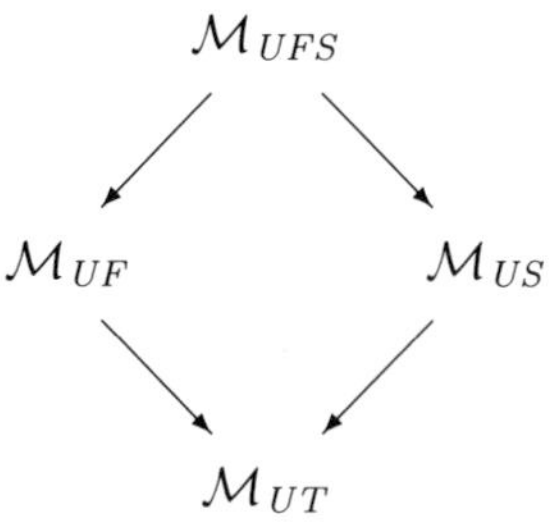

Figure 1.1 Reed's untimed models

have only to insist that any trace of P must be equal to the empty trace:

$$\forall\, tr \in traces(P) \bullet tr = \langle\rangle$$

In this semantic model, the broken process $STOP$ is associated with the singleton set $\{\langle\rangle\}$ and is thus a suitable candidate for process P.

The traces model $\mathcal{M}_{UT}$ is sufficient for the capture and analysis of untimed *safety* requirements; these are constraints that proscribe certain events or sequences of events in the history of a process. However, if we wish to ensure that a synchronisation event is offered to the environment, we must include either readiness or *refusal* information in our semantic model. In the failures model $\mathcal{M}_{UF}$ we associate each trace of a process with the set of events that may be refused afterwards. If the failure (tr, ref) is present in the semantic set of process P, then P may perform trace tr and then refuse to engage in any event from ref.

In Hoare's book, another aspect of behaviour is considered: the *divergences* of a process. A trace of process P is a divergence if it may be followed by an unbounded sequence of internal events, during which P may refuse to communicate with its environment. Reed's thesis (1988) contains an alternative treatment of divergence; in the stability model $\mathcal{M}_{US}$, each trace of a process is associated with a stability value of ∞ or 0, depending on whether or not the process may diverge after engaging in that trace. These models can be arranged in a simple hierarchy, illustrated in Figure 1.1.

Reed's failures-stability model $\mathcal{M}_{UFS}$ corresponds to the failures-divergences model introduced by Hoare (1985). In Reed's model each process is associated with a set of triples (tr, α, ref); a stability value α, chosen from the set $\{0, \infty\}$, is attached to each failure. If α is zero, then the process is known to be stable after performing trace tr: it cannot diverge. If α is infinity, then internal activity may continue indefinitely. The arrows in the diagram correspond to projection mappings between the four untimed models; observational results established in one model remain valid in models lower in the hierarchy.

1.2 TIMED MODELS

The models of CSP presented by Roscoe (1982), Brookes (1983), and Hoare (1985) do not include timing information. By considering only the sequence of observable events and the subsequent refusal sets, we obtain simplified semantic models with a number of convenient algebraic laws. However, if the logical correctness of a design is dependent upon the precise timing of certain events then we cannot complete our reasoning within the untimed formalism.

If we wish to use CSP to describe real-time systems, or any system in which the precise timing of events is important, then we must employ timed models for the language. The first timed model for CSP—proposed by Jones (1982)—proved unsatisfactory for a number of technical reasons. It was suggested that a better model could be obtained by recording the events refused *during* the observation of a trace; this is a feature of the later, more successful attempt made by Reed and Roscoe.

Since Jones's attempt, a number of other timed models have been proposed for CSP-like languages, notably by Zwarico (1986) and Boucher (1987). However, the timed models proposed by Reed and Roscoe have the following advantages:

- the models are compatible with the existing untimed models of CSP;
- infinite hiding and infinite alphabet transformations are possible;
- deadlock and divergence may be distinguished;
- divergence may be distinguished from the possibility of divergence;
- the models are arranged in a hierarchy.

The last consideration is an important one. In reasoning about complex systems, we may use the simplest semantic model that is sufficient to express the current requirement, safe in the knowledge that the argument remains valid in the other models of the hierarchy.

Reed's thesis presents five timed models for CSP. In each model, a process is associated with a set of possible timed observations. A typical element of a semantic set is a tuple, the elements of which represent different aspects of a possible observation. Just as the untimed models recorded trace, refusal and stability information, the timed models record timed traces, timed refusals, and timed stabilities. The hierarchy of models is ordered by the information content of the semantic sets, and the models are linked by projection mappings: see Figure 1.2.

The untimed models of CSP occupy the lowest positions in the hierarchy, with the untimed traces model $\mathcal{M}_{UT}$ at the very bottom. The simplest of the timed models, $\mathcal{M}_{TT}$, associates a process with a set of timed traces. The timed failures model $\mathcal{M}_{TF}$, and the

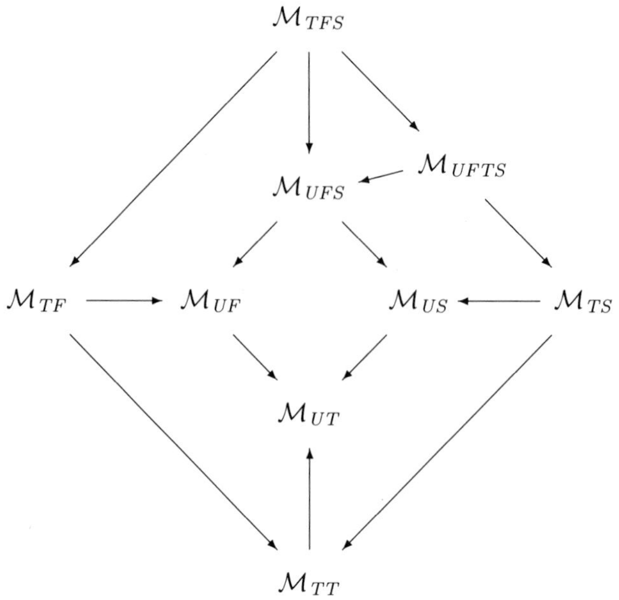

Figure 1.2 Reed's hierarchy

timed failures-stability model $\mathcal{M}_{TFS}$ record the events refused by a process during and after the observation of each timed trace.

The timed stability models $\mathcal{M}_{TS}$, $\mathcal{M}_{UFTS}$, and $\mathcal{M}_{TFS}$ include information about the presence of internal activity. The stability value of a observation is the earliest time by which all internal activity is *guaranteed* to have ceased. In the timed failures-stability model each timed failure (s, X) of a process is associated with a single stability value α between *0* and ∞, inclusive. If the process exhibits the external behaviour described by (s, X), then all internal activity must cease at or before time α.

The untimed failures-timed stability model $\mathcal{M}_{UFTS}$ records the set of events refused after a timed trace, once the process has stabilised. This model bridges the gap between the timed stability model $\mathcal{M}_{TS}$ and the timed failures-stability model $\mathcal{M}_{TFS}$. These models are used by Schneider (1989) to support a theory of timed refinement; simple processes may be refined by the introduction of timing information and results established in the lower models give rise to corresponding results in models further up the hierarchy.

In the specification of a real-time system, internal activity is usually of only secondary importance. The correctness of a design will be expressed as a set of constraints upon the occurrence and availability of observable events or external synchronisations.

This is precisely the information that may be obtained from the timed failures model $\mathcal{M}_{TF}$. Furthermore, the timed models without timed refusals are complicated by the need to record the times at which events first become available, in order to give a satisfactory semantics to the hiding operator. For these reasons, we will restrict our attention to the timed failures model of CSP.

1.3 A MODEL OF COMPUTATION

Reed's timed semantic models are compatible with the untimed models defined by Roscoe and Brookes. They share the same model of computation, in which processes communicate by *handshaking*, observable events require the cooperation of the environment, and any execution of a process appears the same to all observers. To introduce timing information into this model of computation, several assumptions are required:

Real Time. With the non-negative real numbers as our time domain, we have no lower bound on the interval between consecutive events. This allows us to model asynchronous processes in a satisfactory fashion, without artificial constraints upon the times at which independent events may be observed.

Global Clock. All observations are recorded with reference to an imaginary global clock, but this clock cannot be accessed by any part of the system being modelled. If a system clock is required, it can be modelled as a simple timed CSP process. Separate clocks may be modelled as separate processes, and need not keep the same time.

Instantaneous Events. All events have zero duration. If a system action takes a significant amount of time to perform, we use two events in our representation: one corresponding to the start of the action, another to the end. Similarly, we consider communications between processes to be instantaneous: delays in transmission, reception, and synchronisation are made explicit.

Termination. There is a single *termination* event, $\checkmark$, whose occurrence signals the successful termination of a construct. If this construct is followed immediately by a sequential composition operator, then the $\checkmark$ event is hidden from the environment, and termination occurs as soon as possible.

Finite Speed. We assume that no process can engage in infinitely many events within a finite time interval. This assumption is enforced by the axioms of our semantic model, and leads to constraints upon the application of certain operators: e.g., indexed nondeterministic choice.

Hiding and Control. Observable events cannot occur without the cooperation of the environment. Further, if a process and its environment are both prepared to engage in an event at a particular time, then it occurs at that time. Hidden events do not require the cooperation of the environment, and occur as soon as they become available.

Delay Constant. We choose a strictly positive delay constant δ as a lower bound between consecutive events in a sequential process. This ensures that cause precedes effect in any observation of a process: if the occurrence of event a makes another event b possible, then b cannot occur at the same time as a.

1.4 TIMED CSP

Reed and Roscoe suggested a basic timed syntax for the language of processes, defined by the following grammar rule:

$$\begin{aligned} P \;::=\;& \bot \mid STOP \mid SKIP \mid WAIT\ t \mid a \rightarrow P \mid P \,;\, P \mid \\ & P \Box P \mid P \sqcap P \mid P \parallel P \mid P\ {}_{A}\!\parallel_{A}\ P \mid P \mid\mid\mid P \mid \\ & P \setminus A \mid f(P) \mid f^{-1}(P) \mid \mu X \bullet F(X) \end{aligned}$$

The term $\bot$ denotes the livelock process; this is unable to engage in external communication, although internal activity may continue indefinitely. Despite the choice of symbol, this process is not a timed equivalent of the chaotic process of Hoare (1985), nor is it the bottom element of any partial order based upon nondeterminism.

The deadlock process $STOP$ is also unable to engage in any external communication; in this case, internal activity is also impossible. $SKIP$ is a process which does nothing except terminate, and is ready to terminate immediately. The new operator $WAIT$ is a delayed form of $SKIP$; it does nothing, but is ready to terminate successfully after the specified time.

The prefix operator $\rightarrow$ prefixes a term P with a single event a. A constant delay δ is associated with this operation: control is not passed to P until δ after a is observed. The sequential composition operator ; passes control from one process to another, once the first process has terminated successfully. No delay is associated with the transfer of control from one process to another.

The construct $P \Box Q$ is an external choice between processes P and Q. If the environment is prepared to cooperate with P but not Q, then the choice is resolved in favour of P, and *vice versa*. $P \sqcap Q$ is an internal choice between P and Q; the environment has no influence over the outcome of this choice. The external and internal choice operators are usually called deterministic choice and nondeterministic choice, respectively.

In the parallel combination $P\ {}_{A}\!\parallel_{B}\ Q$ process P may perform events from set A, while process Q may perform events from set B; both processes must cooperate upon events drawn from the intersection of these two sets. In the lockstep parallel combination $P \parallel Q$ both processes must cooperate upon every event. In the interleaved parallel combination $P \mid\mid\mid Q$ both processes evolve concurrently without interacting; if two interleaved processes are capable of performing the same event a, then a degree of nondeterminism may be introduced.

The relabelled processes $f(P)$ and $f^{-1}(P)$ have a similar control structure to P, but observable events are renamed according to functions f and f^{-1}, respectively. The process

$P \setminus A$ behaves as P, except that events from set A are concealed from the environment of the process. Hidden events no longer require the cooperation of the environment, and so occur as soon as P is ready to perform them.

The recursive process $\mu X \bullet F(X)$ behaves as $F(X)$, with each instance of variable X representing a recursive invocation. To facilitate a treatment of mutual recursion, we will be considering a syntax of CSP terms, rather than processes. In chapter 2, we will add a clause X to the syntax to introduce variables from a set VAR, and write recursive terms in the form $\mu X \bullet P$. A process will be a term with no free variables.

This language is identical to the untimed language employed by Brookes, but for the inclusion of the *WAIT* construct. The addition of this operator operator allows us to model most forms of timed interaction.

1.5 EXAMPLE

Consider the user interface of a simple timed vending machine VM, capable of accepting coins and dispensing drinks. Users of this machine may insert a coin and, after a short delay, press a button to release a drink. The machine then returns to its original state.

The insertion of a coin is modelled by the event *coin*, and we allow a time t_{drop} for the coin to drop, before the event *button* is made available. If the user then presses the button, the machine will offer a drink: this corresponds to the availability of the event *coke* after a short delay of time t_{coke}. Once the user has accepted the drink, the machine requires a further delay t_{reset} to prepare for another transaction.

$$
\begin{aligned}
VM \;\widehat{=}\;\; & coin \rightarrow WAIT(t_{drop} - \delta); \\
& \quad button \rightarrow WAIT(t_{coke} - \delta); \\
& \quad\quad coke \rightarrow WAIT(t_{reset} - \delta) \; ; \; VM
\end{aligned}
$$

This version of the vending machine presents the user with no choice of product, so the button is an unnecessary feature of the interface. We may use the hiding operator to conceal the event *button* from the user.

$$
\begin{aligned}
VM \setminus button \;\equiv\;\; & coin \rightarrow WAIT(t_{drop} + t_{coke} - \delta); \\
& \quad coke \rightarrow WAIT(t_{reset} - \delta) \; ; \; (VM \setminus button)
\end{aligned}
$$

Internal actions occur as soon as they are ready; if a coin is inserted, the new vending machine will be ready to dispense a drink after a delay of $t_{drop} + t_{coke}$.

The process relabelling operators may be used to rename the events of a process while retaining the control structure. If we wish to describe a machine with a similar pattern of communication, or to take a different view of an existing interface, then we have only to choose a suitable relabelling function for the events in our alphabet.

For example, we may wish to describe a simple vending machine which dispenses an entirely different product. Instead of producing a new design from scratch, we can apply a suitable relabelling function to the existing design. If f is a relabelling function such that

$$\begin{aligned} f(coin) &\mathrel{\widehat{=}} coin \\ f(coke) &\mathrel{\widehat{=}} pepsi \end{aligned}$$

then the following equivalence holds:

$$\begin{aligned} f(VM \setminus button) \equiv\ & coin \rightarrow WAIT(t_{drop} + t_{coke} - \delta); \\ & \quad pepsi \rightarrow WAIT(t_{reset} - \delta)\,;\, f(VM \setminus button) \end{aligned}$$

The pattern of control and delay is unaffected, but the relabelled machine dispenses *pepsi* whenever the original machine would dispense *coke*.

In the above example, the arguments of the delay operator *WAIT* are adjusted to take account of the constant delay of δ that is associated with the event prefix operator. A more elegant description may be obtained using the delayed form of the prefix operator, introduced in the next chapter.

2 THE TIMED FAILURES MODEL

2.1 TIMED OBSERVATIONS

In this chapter, we will present a denotational semantic model based upon timed observations. This model is an enhancement of Reed's timed failures model; each observation records a sequence of timed events performed, and a set of timed events refused. A timed event is a $(time, event)$ pair in which *time* is any non-negative real number and *event* is any element of our universal alphabet Σ. A timed trace is a finite sequence of timed events arranged in chronological order. The presence of a timed event (t, a) in a trace corresponds to the observation of event a at time t. For example,

$$s = \langle (1, a), (3, b) \rangle$$

defines a timed trace s in which event a is observed at time 1, and event b is observed at time 3. The order of events in a trace depends only on the times at which they occur. If more than one event is observed at the same time, then these events may appear in any order in the trace.

A timed refusal is a set of timed events. The presence of a timed event (t, a) in a refusal set corresponds to the refusal of a process to participate in event a at time t. One of the assumptions of our computational model, that processes can evolve only at a finite rate, allows us to place the following constraint upon the construction of timed refusals: they are formed by a finite union of product sets, called refusal tokens. A refusal token is a cross product $I \times A$, where I is a half-open finite interval within $[0, \infty)$ and A is a set of events. For example, the timed refusal defined by

$$X = [1, 2) \times \{a, b\}$$

consists of a single refusal token, and corresponds to the refusal of a process to participate in events a and b between time 1 and time 2.

A timed observation in our semantic model is a (*timed trace*, *timed refusal*) pair in which the timed trace records the sequence of timed events observed, and the refusal records the set of timed events refused. Following Reed (1988), we will refer to our observations as *timed failures*, to emphasise the connection with the established failures model of CSP.

There is no reason why the same timed event (t, a) should not appear in both components of the same timed failure. This will occur whenever a process performs as many copies of event a as it can at time t, and thus refuses to perform a further copy of a at that time. For example,

$$(\langle(1, a), (3, b)\rangle, [1, 2) \times \{a, b\})$$

is an observation in which a process engages in event a at time 1, and refuses to perform a second a from this time onwards.

When considering the interaction of a process with its environment, we may view a timed trace as a result of an experiment performed upon a process: the environment offers timed events to the process, which the process may or may not accept. The refusal set represents a *partial* record of these offers: our knowledge of the experiment. The presence of a pair (t, a) in the refusal set indicates that the environment offered more copies of the event a at time t than the process was willing to perform.

2.2 NOTATION

To give a semantics to our language, and to simplify the process of reasoning about it, we define a variety of basic sets and simple operators. We use TE to denote the set of all timed events, and TT to denote the set of all timed traces. TI denotes the set of all bounded half-open intervals within the domain of time values $TIME$, which is the non-negative real numbers. RT is the set of all possible refusal tokens, TR is the set of all timed refusals, and $\mathcal{O}_{TF}$ is the set of all timed failures:

$$\begin{aligned}
TE &= TIME \times \Sigma \\
TT &= \{s \in \text{seq}\, TE \mid (t, a) \text{ precedes } (t', a') \text{ in } s \Rightarrow t \leqslant t'\} \\
TI &= \{[b, e) \mid 0 \leqslant b < e < \infty\} \\
RT &= \{I \times A \mid I \in TI \wedge A \in \mathbb{P}\Sigma\} \\
TR &= \{\bigcup C \mid C \in \mathbb{F}\, RT\} \\
\mathcal{O}_{TF} &= TT \times TR \\
\mathcal{S}_{TF} &= \mathbb{P}\,\mathcal{O}_{TF}
\end{aligned}$$

In the timed failures model, processes are represented by elements of $\mathcal{S}_{TF}$, the space of sets of timed failures. To reason about the timed failures of a process, we will use the language of set and sequence theory. The following notation is due to Hoare (1985):

$\langle\rangle$	the empty trace	$\leqslant$	trace prefix
$\frown$	concatenation of traces	$\underline{\text{in}}$	contiguous subsequence

The predicate $s_1 \ \underline{\text{in}}\ s_2$ holds precisely when trace s_1 is a contiguous subsequence of s_2.

2.2.1 First and last

The *first* and *last* operators are defined for all timed traces, returning the first and last events in a trace, if non-empty. If the trace is empty, they return the special non-event η. All that is required of η is that $\eta \notin \Sigma$. We also define *begin* and *end* operators, which yield the times of the first and last events:

$$
\begin{array}{rcl@{\qquad}rcl}
first(\langle\rangle) & = & \eta & begin(\langle\rangle) & = & \infty \\
first(\langle(t,a)\rangle^\frown s) & = & a & begin(\langle(t,a)\rangle^\frown s) & = & t \\
last(\langle\rangle) & = & \eta & end(\langle\rangle) & = & 0 \\
last(s^\frown\langle(t,a)\rangle) & = & a & end(s^\frown\langle(t,a)\rangle) & = & t
\end{array}
$$

The values chosen for the empty trace are the most convenient for the subsequent mathematics: the possibility of a trace being empty will not require special consideration in our specifications and proofs. It proves convenient to define *head* and *foot* operators on traces such that $head(s) = (begin(s), first(s))$ and $foot(s) = (end(s), last(s))$.

2.2.2 Times

The *times* operator returns the set of time values that appear in a refusal set:

$$times(X) \mathrel{\widehat{=}} \{t \mid \exists\, a \bullet (t,a) \in X\}$$

We may use this operator to define *begin* and *end* operators on refusal sets:

$$
\begin{array}{rcl@{\qquad}l}
begin(X) & = & inf(times(X)) & \text{if } X \neq \{\} \\
begin(\{\}) & = & \infty & \\
end(X) & = & sup(times(X)) & \text{if } X \neq \{\} \\
end(\{\}) & = & 0 &
\end{array}
$$

For convenience, we extend the above definitions to timed failures:

$$
\begin{array}{rcl}
begin(s, X) & = & min\{begin(s), begin(X)\} \\
end(s, X) & = & max\{end(s), end(X)\}
\end{array}
$$

2.2.3 Restriction

We use the $\upharpoonright$ symbol to denote the restriction of a trace or refusal to a set of events A.

$$
\begin{array}{rcl@{\qquad}l}
\langle\rangle \upharpoonright A & = & \langle\rangle & \\
\langle(t,a)\rangle^\frown s \upharpoonright A & = & \langle(t,a)\rangle^\frown(s \upharpoonright A) & \text{if } a \in A \\
 & & s \upharpoonright A & \text{otherwise} \\
X \upharpoonright A & = & X \cap ([0,\infty) \times A) &
\end{array}
$$

The hiding operator on traces may be defined as a restriction:

$$s \setminus A \;=\; s \upharpoonright (\Sigma - A)$$

2.2.4 During, before and after

We define the *during* ($\uparrow$), *before* ($\upharpoonright$), and *after* ($\upharpoonleft$) operators on timed traces. The first returns the maximal subsequence of the trace with times drawn from set I. The others return the parts of the trace before and after the specified time.

$$\begin{array}{rcll} \langle\rangle \uparrow I & \mathrel{\widehat{=}} & \langle\rangle & \\ (\langle(t,a)\rangle^\frown s) \uparrow I & \mathrel{\widehat{=}} & \langle(t,a)\rangle^\frown(s \uparrow I) & \text{if } t \in I \\ & & (s \uparrow I) & \text{otherwise} \\ s \upharpoonright t & \mathrel{\widehat{=}} & s \uparrow [0,t] & \\ s \upharpoonleft t & \mathrel{\widehat{=}} & s \uparrow (t,\infty) & \end{array}$$

where I is a set of real numbers. In the case that $I = \{t\}$ for some time t, we may omit the set brackets. These operators may also be applied to timed refusals, with the following interpretations:

$$\begin{array}{rcl} X \upharpoonright t & \mathrel{\widehat{=}} & X \cap ([0,t) \times \Sigma) \\ X \upharpoonleft t & \mathrel{\widehat{=}} & X \cap ([t,\infty) \times \Sigma) \\ X \uparrow [t_1,t_2) & \mathrel{\widehat{=}} & X \cap ([t_1,t_2) \times \Sigma) \end{array}$$

Recalling that Σ denotes the set of all events, we see that these restrict a refusal set to events that may be refused before, during, and after the specified times. The definitions of *before* and *after* on refusal sets differ from those on timed traces. For traces, $s \upharpoonright t$ includes events at t; in the case of refusals, such events are excluded. The opposite is true of the *after* operator. This choice of definitions is the most convenient for timed failures specifications.

2.2.5 Subtraction

To reason about any form of sequential composition or delay, we require a subtraction operator that shifts timed traces and refusals through time:

$$\begin{array}{rcll} \langle\rangle \dot{-} t & \mathrel{\widehat{=}} & \langle\rangle & \\ (\langle(t_1,a)\rangle^\frown s) \dot{-} t & \mathrel{\widehat{=}} & \langle(t_1 - t,a)\rangle^\frown(s \dot{-} t) & \text{if } t_1 \geqslant t \\ (\langle(t_1,a)\rangle^\frown s) \dot{-} t & \mathrel{\widehat{=}} & s \dot{-} t & \text{otherwise} \\ X \dot{-} t & \mathrel{\widehat{=}} & \{(t_1 - t, a) \mid (t_1,a) \in X \wedge t_1 \geqslant t\} & \end{array}$$

It proves economical to define a subtraction operator on timed failures:

$$(s,X) - t \mathrel{\widehat{=}} (s \dot{-} t, X \dot{-} t)$$

2.2.6 Equivalence and closure

We define an equivalence relation upon the set of timed traces:

$$u \cong v \quad \Leftrightarrow \quad u \text{ is a permutation of } v$$

Note that, as timed traces are chronologically ordered sequences, equivalent traces may differ only in the order of appearance of simultaneous events. We use this equivalence to define a closure operator on sets of timed failures:

$$CL_{\cong}(S) \quad \widehat{=} \quad \{(s, X) \in \mathcal{O}_{TF} \mid \exists (w, X) \in S \bullet s \cong w\}$$

2.3 THE TIMED FAILURES MODEL

The timed failures Model $\mathcal{M}_{TF}$ is defined to be those elements S of $\mathcal{S}_{TF}$ which satisfy the following axioms:

1. $(\langle\rangle, \{\}) \in S$
2. $(s ^\frown w, X) \in S \Rightarrow (s, X \upharpoonright begin(w)) \in S$
3. $(s, X) \in S \wedge s \cong w \Rightarrow (w, X) \in S$
4. $(s, X) \in S \wedge t \geqslant 0 \Rightarrow \exists X' : TR \bullet X \subseteq X' \wedge (s, X') \in S \wedge$
   $((t' \leqslant t \wedge (t', a) \notin X') \Rightarrow (s \upharpoonright t' ^\frown \langle (t', a) \rangle, X' \upharpoonright t') \in S)$
5. $\forall t : [0, \infty) \bullet \exists n(t) : \mathbb{N} \bullet (s, X) \in S \wedge end(s) \leqslant t \Rightarrow \#(s) \leqslant n(t)$
6. $\forall X' : TR \bullet (s, X) \in S \wedge X' \subseteq X \Rightarrow (s, X') \in S$

The first axiom requires that the empty failure $(\langle\rangle, \{\})$ is a possible behaviour of any process. The second is a prefix closure condition: if a process may perform a trace $s ^\frown w$ while refusing X, then it should be able to perform the prefix s, with the refusal set truncated accordingly. The third axiom insists that the order of events in a timed trace depends only upon the times at which they are observed, no additional information about causal relationships is available.

The fourth axiom enforces our assumption that processes may undergo only a finite number of state changes in a finite time. For any failure (s, X) and time value t, there will always be a maximal refusal set X' that captures all of the refusal information for the current trace, at least until time t. Given any time $t' \leqslant t$, every timed event (t', a) not in X' is a possible extension of $s \upharpoonright t'$. As X' is a refusal set, it must be a *finite* union of refusal tokens, and hence represents only finitely many changes of state.

The fifth axiom places a similar condition upon traces. For any process S, we can exhibit a function n that places a bound upon the number of events observed before a given time. If trace s ends at or before time t, then the length of s must be no greater than $n(t)$. This bounded speed condition leads to constraints upon the application of infinitary operators such as prefix choice and indexed nondeterminism. The final axiom states that if a process may refuse the whole of X, then it may refuse any subset of X; a similar condition holds in the untimed failures model described in Brookes (1983).

We define a distance metric d on $\mathcal{S}_{TF}$ by considering the first time at which the elements of two sets may be distinguished. If (s, X) is a timed failure, we define a projection function on elements of $\mathcal{S}_{TF}$:

$$S \upharpoonright t \;\widehat{=}\; \{(s, X) \mid (s, X) \in S \wedge end(s, X) \leqslant t\}$$

If S is a element of $\mathcal{S}_{TF}$ then $S \upharpoonright t$ is the set of elements of S which do not extend beyond time t. We may now define the metric:

$$d(S, T) \;\widehat{=}\; \mathit{inf}(\{2^{-t} \mid S \upharpoonright t = T \upharpoonright t\} \cup \{1\})$$

This definition is equivalent to the one defined by Reed (1988), although the definition of $S \upharpoonright t$ differs slightly. The metric will be needed when we give a semantics to recursive process definitions.

2.4 A SEMANTIC FUNCTION

We will give a semantics to a language of timed CSP terms, defined by

$$\begin{array}{lll} P \;::=\; & \bot \mid STOP \mid SKIP \mid WAIT\,t \mid X \mid & \text{atoms} \\ & a \rightarrow P \mid a \xrightarrow{t} P \mid P\,;P \mid P \mathbin{\text{⨾}} P \mid & \text{sequential composition} \\ & P \,\square\, P \mid P \sqcap P \mid a : A \xrightarrow{ta} P_a \mid & \text{alternation} \\ & P \parallel P \mid P \;{}_A\!\!\parallel_B P \mid P \interleave P \mid P \underset{A}{\parallel} P \mid & \text{parallel composition} \\ & P \setminus A \mid f(P) \mid f^{-1}(P) \mid & \text{abstraction and renaming} \\ & P \underset{t}{\lightning} P \mid P \underset{e}{\nabla} P \mid P \overset{t}{\rhd} P \mid & \text{timing} \\ & \mu X \bullet P \mid \mu X \circ P \mid \langle X_i = P_i \rangle_j & \text{recursion} \end{array}$$

In the above syntax, clause X introduces variables from a set VAR; these are required for the treatment of mutual recursion presented in chapter 3. To give a semantics to this language, we require a formal treatment of variable bindings. We define a domain of environments, ENV, consisting of all mappings from variables VAR to the space of all sets of timed failures $\mathcal{S}_{TF}$, and thus a semantic function for terms:

$$\begin{array}{lll} ENV & \widehat{=} & VAR \rightarrow \mathcal{S}_{TF} \\ \mathcal{F}_{TF} & \in & CSP \rightarrow ENV \rightarrow \mathcal{S}_{TF} \end{array}$$

We write $\mathcal{F}_{TF}[\![P]\!]\rho$ to denote the semantics of a term P in an environment ρ. This may be evaluated by associating each free variable X with its value $\rho[\![X]\!]$ in the current environment. Syntactic substitutions give rise to simple semantic equivalences:

$$\mathcal{F}_{TF}[\![P[Q/X]]\!]\rho \equiv \mathcal{F}_{TF}[\![P]\!]\rho[\mathcal{F}_{TF}[\![Q]\!]\rho/X]$$

where $\rho[Y/X]$ is a new environment, defined as follows:

$$\begin{array}{lcll} \rho[Y/X][\![Z]\!] & \widehat{=} & Y & \text{if } Z = X \\ & & \rho[\![Z]\!] & \text{otherwise} \end{array}$$

A process will be represented by a CSP term with no free variables: its meaning will be independent of the current environment. If P is a process then we may infer that

$$\forall \rho, \rho' : ENV \bullet \mathcal{F}_{TF}[\![P]\!]\rho = \mathcal{F}_{TF}[\![P]\!]\rho'$$

In this case, we may sensibly omit the environment parameter.

2.5 SEQUENTIAL PROCESSES

2.5.1 Livelock and Deadlock

The livelock process $\perp$ can perform no observable actions, but internal activity may continue indefinitely. In the timed failures model we do not record the possibility of internal activity, and so $\perp$ is identified with the deadlock process $STOP$. The only trace of either process is $\langle\rangle$, the empty trace.

$$\begin{array}{rcl} \mathcal{F}_{TF}[\![\perp]\!]\rho & \widehat{=} & \{(\langle\rangle, X) \mid X \in TR\} \\ \mathcal{F}_{TF}[\![STOP]\!]\rho & \widehat{=} & \{(\langle\rangle, X) \mid X \in TR\} \end{array}$$

Both processes are capable of refusing any event from Σ at any time.

2.5.2 Termination and delay

The process $SKIP$ models successful termination in timed CSP. This is signalled by an occurrence of the special event $\checkmark$, the only action that this process may perform:

$$\begin{array}{rcl} \mathcal{F}_{TF}[\![SKIP]\!]\rho & \widehat{=} & \{(\langle\rangle, X) \mid \checkmark \notin \sigma(X)\} \\ & & \cup \\ & & \{(\langle(t, \checkmark)\rangle, X) \mid t \geqslant 0 \wedge \checkmark \notin \sigma(X \upharpoonright t)\} \end{array}$$

Either no events have been observed and the event $\checkmark$ is available, or $\checkmark$ has been observed at some time t and was continuously available beforehand.

The delay process $WAIT\ t$ represents delayed successful termination, with the termination event becoming available at time t. It can be used to introduce an additional delay into a sequential process, or combined with other operators to produce timeout and interrupt constructs.

$$\begin{aligned}\mathcal{F}_{TF}[\![WAIT\ t]\!]\rho \ \ \widehat{=}\ \ & \{(\langle\rangle, X) \mid \checkmark \notin \sigma(X \uparrow t)\} \\ & \cup \\ & \{(\langle(t', \checkmark)\rangle, X) \mid t' \geqslant t \wedge \checkmark \notin \sigma(X \uparrow [t, t'))\}\end{aligned}$$

If no events have been observed then ✓ must be available continuously from time t onwards. Otherwise, ✓ is observed at a time $t' \geqslant t$ and made available at all times between t and t'.

2.5.3 Prefix

The event prefix operator is used to introduce observable events into process descriptions; the expression $a \to P$ denotes a process that is prepared initially to engage only in event a, and then behave as process P. There is a non-zero delay associated with this operation, corresponding to the time taken to change from a state in which event a is available, to one in which it has been performed. The undecorated prefix operator is associated with a constant delay δ.

$$\begin{aligned}\mathcal{F}_{TF}[\![a \to P]\!]\rho \ \ \widehat{=}\ \ & \{(\langle\rangle, X) \mid a \notin \sigma(X)\} \\ & \cup \\ & \{(\langle(t, a)\rangle^\frown s, X) \mid t \geqslant 0 \wedge a \notin \sigma(X \upharpoonright t) \\ & \qquad\qquad (s, X) - (t + \delta) \in \mathcal{F}_{TF}[\![P]\!]\rho\}\end{aligned}$$

If no events have been observed in a history of $a \to P$, then event a cannot be refused. Otherwise, a is the first event to be observed and the subsequent behaviour, following a delay of δ, is due to P.

The above operator will be used only when the minimum delay following an event is unimportant. If we are interested in the delay following the observation of an event a then we decorate the prefix operator with a time value: the expression $a \xrightarrow{t} P$ denotes a process which is willing to perform an event a. If a occurs, the process will then behave as process P, once a delay of time t has elapsed. During the time delay, the process behaves as $WAIT$, refusing to participate in any external activity. This is illustrated by the equivalence:

$$a \xrightarrow{t} P \ \ \equiv\ \ a \to WAIT(t - \delta)\,;P$$

The semantics of this operator may be derived from the equations for the delay, prefix and sequential composition operators.

We retain the δ constant as a lower bound on the delay associated with the prefix operation. This is necessary if we wish to avoid the possibility of causally-related simultaneous events. To see why this is a problem, postulate the existence of an instantaneous prefix operator $\twoheadrightarrow$ with the following interpretation: the expression $a \twoheadrightarrow P$ denotes a process that is initially prepared to engage in an event a; once a is observed, the process immediately behaves as P. If P is ready to perform an event immediately, then that event may be observed at the same time as a. Consider the process $a \rightarrow b \rightarrow STOP$. This process may perform b at any time t, providing that it performs a at (or before) that time. Now consider the parallel combination

$$a \rightarrow b \rightarrow STOP \quad \| \quad b \rightarrow a \rightarrow STOP$$

We expect this combination to deadlock immediately. However, both components may perform a and b together at any time t. Simultaneous events may appear in any order in a timed trace, so the parallel combination may perform traces from the following set:

$$\{\langle\rangle\} \cup \{s \mid t \geqslant 0 \wedge s \cong \langle(t, a), (t, b)\rangle\}$$

This clashes with our intuition about processes and observable events. Events a and b are inseparable, yet they appear separately in traces of a process. As we might expect, this situation is proscribed by an axiom of the semantic model:

$$(s^\frown w, X) \in S \quad \Rightarrow \quad (s, X \upharpoonright begin(w)) \in S$$

We do not allow an effect to precede its cause in a trace.

2.5.4 Sequential composition

The expression $P\,;Q$ denotes the sequential composition of processes P and Q. No delay is associated with this operator; the last event of process P may occur at the same time as the first event from process Q. This need not conflict with our intuition about causal delay, as the initial state of Q is independent of the final state of P. A behaviour (s, X) of $P;Q$ may be either a behaviour of P which does not correspond to successful termination, or a terminating behaviour of P, followed by some behaviour of Q.

In the first case, s is a trace of P in which $\checkmark$ is not observed, and would be refused if offered; this corresponds to the first component of the semantic set. In the second case, the trace s is obtained from two traces, s_P and s_Q, performed by P and Q respectively:

$$\begin{aligned}
\mathcal{F}_{TF}[\![P\,;Q]\!]\rho \;\widehat{=}\;& \{(s, X) \mid \checkmark \notin \sigma(s) \\
& \qquad \forall I : TI \bullet (s, X \cup (I \times \{\checkmark\})) \in \mathcal{F}_{TF}[\![P]\!]\rho\} \\
& \cup \\
& CL_{\cong}\{(s_P{}^\frown s_Q, X) \mid \checkmark \notin \sigma(s_P) \wedge (s_Q, X) - t \in \mathcal{F}_{TF}[\![Q]\!]\rho \wedge \\
& \qquad (s_P{}^\frown\langle(t, \checkmark)\rangle, X \upharpoonright t \cup ([0, t) \times \{\checkmark\})) \in \mathcal{F}_{TF}[\![P]\!]\rho\}
\end{aligned}$$

If control has been transferred at time t, then the trace s_P could have been extended with a $\checkmark$ event at that time. This event is hidden from the environment by the sequential composition operator, and occurs as soon as it becomes available; it must be possible for P to refuse $\checkmark$ up until time t while performing trace s_P. The subsequent behaviour is due to process Q.

The above equation is complicated by the fact that both processes are able to perform actions at time t. Simultaneous events may appear in any order in a timed trace, so we must ensure that our semantic set is closed under trace equivalence. The resulting definition is unsuitable for some applications; in chapter 5 we will see that it fails to preserve timewise refinements. Because of this, we introduce a delayed form of the sequential composition operator:

$$P \fatsemi Q \;\widehat{=}\; P\,;\, \mathit{WAIT}\,\delta\,;\, Q$$

This defines a process that behaves as P until successful termination is signalled, then waits for an interval length δ before behaving as Q. This delay allows us to separate the events of the first process from those of the second.

2.5.5 Nondeterministic choice

The expression $P \sqcap Q$ denotes the nondeterministic choice between two processes P and Q. This operator is sometimes called *internal choice*, as there is no way for the environment to influence the flow of control at this point:

$$\mathcal{F}_{TF}[\![P \sqcap Q]\!]\rho \;\widehat{=}\; \mathcal{F}_{TF}[\![P]\!]\rho \cup \mathcal{F}_{TF}[\![Q]\!]\rho$$

We require only that every behaviour of a nondeterministic choice is a possible behaviour of at least one component.

If wish to model arbitrary nondeterministic choice, then we must verify that there is a uniform bound upon the speed of the alternatives. This will ensure that the resulting process can perform only a bounded number of events before any finite time t, in accordance with axiom 5 of section 2.3. We say that a set of processes $\{P_i \mid i \in I\}$ is *uniformly bounded* if there exists a function $n : \mathit{TIME} \to \mathbb{N}$ such that for all environments ρ

$$\forall\, i : I\,;\, t : \mathit{TIME} \;\bullet\; (s, X) \in \mathcal{F}_{TF}[\![P_i]\!]\rho \wedge \mathit{end}(s) \leqslant t \Rightarrow \#(s \upharpoonright t) \leqslant n(t)$$

This definition is due to Steve Schneider, and provides a necessary and sufficient condition for the following semantics to be well-defined:

$$\mathcal{F}_{TF}[\![\textstyle\bigsqcap_{i \in I} P_i]\!]\rho \;\widehat{=}\; \textstyle\bigcup_{i \in I} \mathcal{F}_{TF}[\![P_i]\!]\rho$$

This operator may be used to model nondeterministic delays in sequential processes. We overload the delay operator

$$\mathit{WAIT}\; T \;\widehat{=}\; \textstyle\bigsqcap_{t \in T} \mathit{WAIT}\; t$$

to define a process that is prepared to terminate after some time t, where t is drawn from the set T.

2.5.6 Deterministic choice

The expression $P \square Q$ denotes a deterministic choice between processes P and Q. This operator is sometimes called *external choice* (or general choice) as the environment may select either P or Q by offering to engage in events which are initially possible for just one of the two processes. The choice is resolved by the first observable event that occurs.

$$\begin{aligned} \mathcal{F}_{TF}[\![P \square Q]\!]\rho \;\widehat{=}\; & \{(\langle\rangle, X) \mid (\langle\rangle, X) \in \mathcal{F}_{TF}[\![P]\!]\rho \cap \mathcal{F}_{TF}[\![Q]\!]\rho\} \\ & \cup \\ & \{(s, X) \mid s \neq \langle\rangle \wedge (s, X) \in \mathcal{F}_{TF}[\![P]\!]\rho \cup \mathcal{F}_{TF}[\![Q]\!]\rho \\ & \qquad \wedge \\ & \qquad (\langle\rangle, X \restriction begin(s)) \in \mathcal{F}_{TF}[\![P]\!]\rho \cap \mathcal{F}_{TF}[\![Q]\!]\rho\} \end{aligned}$$

Any behaviour must be a behaviour of at least one component, and any event refused before the first observable event must be refused by both processes.

We know from Reed (1988) that it is not possible to define a deterministic choice operator for timed CSP which offers a choice over an infinite set of processes. However, Schneider (1989) shows that we may offer a choice over an infinite set of events. As an example, suppose that we wish to define a process that is ready to accept any natural number value on a channel c. Such a process may be modelled as an infinite prefix choice. The expression

$$c.n : c.\mathbb{N} \xrightarrow{t_n} P_n$$

denotes a process that is ready initially to engage in any event $c.n$ for $n \in \mathbb{N}$. If $c.n$ is observed, the process delays for time t_n and then behaves as P_n.

$$\begin{aligned} \mathcal{F}_{TF}[\![a : A \xrightarrow{t_a} P_a]\!]\rho \;\widehat{=}\; & \{(\langle\rangle, X) \mid A \cap \sigma(X) = \{\}\} \\ & \cup \\ & \{(\langle(t, a)\rangle^\frown s, X) \mid a \in A \wedge t \geqslant 0 \\ & \qquad\qquad begin(s) \geqslant t + t_a \\ & \qquad\qquad A \cap \sigma(X \restriction t) = \{\} \\ & \qquad\qquad (s, X) - (t + t_a) \in \mathcal{F}_{TF}[\![P_a]\!]\rho\} \end{aligned}$$

If no events have been observed then all of the events in set A are available. Otherwise some event a from A has occurred, and the subsequent behaviour is that of P_a. As in the case of indexed nondeterministic choice, this semantics is well-defined if and only if the set of alternative processes is uniformly bounded.

The standard CSP convention for channel input—the query symbol—is defined using the prefix choice operator: if channel c carries values of type T, then

$$c?x : T \rightarrow P_x \quad = \quad a : \{c.v \mid v \in T\} \rightarrow P'_a$$

where $P'_{c.v} = P_v$. The process $c?x : T \rightarrow P_x$ is prepared to accept any value v of type T on channel c, and then behave accordingly. No choice construct is required to define the convention for channel output—the exclamation mark—the data transmitted is determined by the sending process.

2.5.7 Relabelling

We use process relabelling functions to systematically rename the observable events of a process while retaining the control structure. There are two syntactic clauses for relabelling processes, allowing the use of many-to-one or one-to-many relations, providing that either the relation or its inverse is a function f on Σ. Suppose that a and b are events such that $b = f(a)$. The *inverse image* of P may perform a whenever P may perform b:

$$\mathcal{F}_{TF}[\![f^{-1}(P)]\!]\rho \;\widehat{=}\; \{(s, X) \mid (f(s), f(X)) \in \mathcal{F}_{TF}[\![P]\!]\rho\}$$

and refuse a whenever P may refuse b. The *direct image* of P may perform b whenever P may perform a. As f may be many-to-one, the refusal of an event by process P corresponds to the refusal of a set of events by the image process.

$$\mathcal{F}_{TF}[\![f(P)]\!]\rho \;\widehat{=}\; \{(f(s), X) \mid (s, f^{-1}(X)) \in \mathcal{F}_{TF}[\![P]\!]\rho\}$$

In the above equation, the expression $f^{-1}(X)$ denotes the set

$$\{(t, a) \mid (t, f(a)) \in X\}$$

This is the inverse image of refusal set X under function f.

2.5.8 Abstraction

The hiding operator allows us to conceal those events in the history of a system which do not require the cooperation of the environment. Such a structuring mechanism is necessary if we wish to produce readable descriptions of large, complex systems. The expression $P \setminus A$ denotes a process that behaves as P, except that

- events from A happen as soon as they become available
- only events outside A may appear in a trace

In our model of computation, an event occurs as soon as all of the processes involved are willing to cooperate. A hidden event does not require the cooperation of the environment and will occur as soon as it becomes available.

Events which occur as soon as they are made available may be continuously refused by the process in question: if (s, X) is a behaviour of a process P in which every instance of event a occurs as soon as possible, then

$$(s, X \cup [0, end(s, X)) \times \{a\})$$

is also a behaviour of P. This is a consequence of the fourth axiom of our semantic model, which asserts the existence of a maximal refusal set containing X:

$$\begin{aligned}(s, X) \in S \wedge t \geqslant 0 \;\Rightarrow\; & \exists X' : TR \bullet X \subseteq X' \wedge (s, X') \in S \wedge \\ & ((t' \leqslant t \wedge (t', a) \notin X') \Rightarrow (s \upharpoonright t' ^\frown \langle (t', a) \rangle, X' \upharpoonright t') \in S)\end{aligned}$$

Now suppose that there exists a time $t < end(s, X)$ such that $(t, a) \notin X'$. By our choice of X', we may infer that (t, a) is a possible extension of the trace $s \upharpoonright t$. This conflicts with our assumption that (s, X) is a behaviour in which every copy of a occurred as soon as it becomes available: $s \upharpoonright t$ already contains as many copies of a as P was able to perform up to and including that time. Hence

$$(X \cup [0, end(s, X)) \times \{a\}) \subseteq X' \quad \wedge \quad (s, X') \in \mathcal{F}_{TF}[\![P]\!]$$

The result follows by the sixth axiom of the semantic model: the refusal sets corresponding to a trace s are closed under the subset relation.

The behaviours of $P \setminus A$ may be obtained from those failures of P in which events from A are continuously refused:

$$\mathcal{F}_{TF}[\![P \setminus A]\!]\rho \;\widehat{=}\; \{(s \setminus A, X) \mid (s, X \cup ([0, end(s, X) \times A) \in \mathcal{F}_{TF}[\![P]\!]\rho\}$$

Any events from A which appear in trace s are removed by the trace concealment operator, defined in section 2.2 by

$$s \setminus A \;\widehat{=}\; s \downharpoonright (\Sigma - A)$$

where $\downharpoonright$ denotes set restriction.

2.6 PARALLEL PROCESSES

2.6.1 Alphabet parallel

In Hoare's original language, each process P is associated with a set of events αP, the process alphabet. If P appears in a synchronised parallel combination then every event from αP requires the cooperation of P. In timed CSP, the need for process alphabets is removed by the introduction of an alphabet parallel operator. This operator is parameterised by two sets of events; in the parallel combination $P \;{}_A\|_B\; Q$ process P may perform only those events in A, process Q may perform only those events in B, and the two processes must cooperate on events drawn from the intersection of A and B. Events that are in neither A nor B are proscribed.

If s is a trace of this parallel combination, the restriction of s to events from set A yields the trace of events performed by process P. Similarly, restricting s to the set B yields the trace of events performed by Q. If these traces are s_P and s_Q respectively, then s is an element of the set

$$s_P \;{}_A\|_B\; s_Q \;\widehat{=}\; \{s \in TT \mid s \downharpoonright A = s_P \wedge s \downharpoonright B = s_Q \wedge s \downharpoonright (A \cup B) = s\}$$

For an alphabet parallel combination to refuse an event, that event must be refused by one of the component processes. A typical refusal set is thus the union of refusal sets from P and Q, together with any set of events from outside $A \cup B$.

$$\begin{aligned} \mathcal{F}_{TF}[\![P \ {}_A\|_B \ Q]\!]\rho \ \ \widehat{=} \ \ \{(s, X_P \cup X_Q \cup X_R) \mid \exists\, s_P, s_Q \bullet \\ \sigma(X_P) \subseteq A \wedge \sigma(X_Q) \subseteq B \\ \sigma(X_R) \subseteq \Sigma - (A \cup B) \wedge s \in (s_P \ {}_A\|_B \ s_Q) \\ (s_P, X_P) \in \mathcal{F}_{TF}[\![P]\!]\rho \wedge (s_Q, X_Q) \in \mathcal{F}_{TF}[\![Q]\!]\rho \ \} \end{aligned}$$

2.6.2 Simple parallel

The synchronised parallel operator places two processes in *lockstep*. In the parallel combination $P \parallel Q$ processes P and Q must cooperate on every action that is performed. This operator is thus a special case of alphabet parallelism

$$P \parallel Q \ \ \equiv \ \ P \ {}_\Sigma\|_\Sigma \ Q$$

with a simple derived semantics

$$\mathcal{F}_{TF}[\![P \parallel Q]\!]\rho \ \ \widehat{=} \ \ \{(s, X_P \cup X_Q) \mid (s, X_P) \in \mathcal{F}_{TF}[\![P]\!]\rho \wedge (s, X_Q) \in \mathcal{F}_{TF}[\![Q]\!]\rho\}$$

2.6.3 Interleaving

The interleaving parallel operator allows two processes to evolve asynchronously. In the parallel combination

$$P \parallel\!| \ Q$$

the two processes are independent of each other; no cooperation is required on any action. As a result, any trace of the process $P \parallel\!| \ Q$ will be an interleaving of two traces, one from each component. The set of possible interleavings of two timed traces u and v is given by

$$u \parallel\!| \ v \ \ \widehat{=} \ \ \{s : TT \mid \forall\, t : TIME \bullet s \uparrow t \cong u \uparrow t \frown v \uparrow t\}$$

Trace s is a possible interleaving of traces u and v if, for all t, an event is in s at time t iff it is in u or v at that time. The equivalence operator $\cong$ is required, as the order of simultaneous events in s may differ from the order of the same events in u or v. Note that we cannot simply require that $s \cong u \frown v$, as $u \frown v$ need not be a valid timed trace.

$$\begin{aligned} \mathcal{F}_{TF}[\![P \parallel\!| \ Q]\!]\rho \ \ \widehat{=} \ \ \{(s, X) \mid \exists\, s_P, s_Q \bullet s \in (s_P \parallel\!| \ s_Q) \\ (s_P, X) \in \mathcal{F}_{TF}[\![P]\!]\rho \\ (s_Q, X) \in \mathcal{F}_{TF}[\![Q]\!]\rho\} \end{aligned}$$

An interleaving of two processes will refuse a timed event exactly when both components are unwilling to participate; any refusal set of the parallel combination must be common to both processes.

2.6.4 Communicating parallel

We can define a hybrid parallel operator which allows processes to interleave on all but a given set of events; in the parallel combination

$$P \underset{C}{\|} Q$$

processes P and Q must cooperate on actions from set C. Other actions may be freely performed by either component, with no need for synchronisation:

$$\begin{aligned}\mathcal{F}_{TF}[\![P \underset{C}{\|} Q]\!] \;\widehat{=}\; \{(s, X) \mid \exists\, s_P, X_P, s_Q, X_Q \bullet\ & s \in s_P \underset{C}{\|} s_Q \\ & X \downharpoonright C = (X_P \cup X_Q) \downharpoonright C \\ & X \setminus C = (X_P \cap X_Q) \setminus C \\ & (s_P, X_P) \in \mathcal{F}_{TF}[\![P]\!]\rho \\ & (s_Q, X_Q) \in \mathcal{F}_{TF}[\![Q]\!]\rho \quad \}\end{aligned}$$

Events from the interface set C must be performed by both components, while other events are interleaved:

$$u \underset{C}{\|} v \;\widehat{=}\; \{s \mid s \downharpoonright C = u \downharpoonright C = v \downharpoonright C \wedge s \setminus C \in (u \setminus C \mid\mid\mid v \setminus C)\}$$

Events from C are refused if they are refused by at least one of the components; other events must be refused by both components.

The semantic set of this operator is well-defined: it satisfies the axioms of $\mathcal{M}_{TF}$ and may be used in recursive definitions. This is a consequence of the following syntactic equivalence:

$$P \underset{C}{\|} Q \;\equiv\; c\,(l(P)\ {}_A\|_B\ r(Q))$$

where the process relabelling functions l, r, and c are

$$\begin{array}{lcll} l(a) & \widehat{=} & a & \text{if } a \in C \\ & & l.a & \text{otherwise} \\ r(a) & \widehat{=} & a & \text{if } a \in C \\ & & r.a & \text{otherwise} \end{array} \qquad \begin{array}{lcll} c(a) & \widehat{=} & a & \text{if } a \in C \\ c(l.a) & \widehat{=} & a & \text{if } a \notin C \\ c(r.a) & \widehat{=} & a & \text{if } a \notin C \end{array}$$

and the interface sets are

$$\begin{array}{lcl} A & \widehat{=} & l(\Sigma - C) \cup C \\ B & \widehat{=} & r(\Sigma - C) \cup C \end{array}$$

This equivalence may be demonstrated by reasoning about the observations present in each semantic set.

2.6.5 Indexed parallel

An indexed form of the alphabet parallel operator can be used to define networks of communicating processes:

$$
\begin{array}{lll}
(\|_{A_i} P_i) \quad i \in 1\,..\,2 & \mathrel{\widehat=} & P_1 \;{}_{A_1}\|_{A_2}\; P_2 \\
(\|_{A_i} P_i) \quad i \in 1\,..\,n & \mathrel{\widehat=} & P_n \;{}_{A_n}\|_{\bigcup_i A_i}\; (\|_{A_i} P_i) \qquad i \in 1\,..\,n-1
\end{array}
$$

Each component P_i may perform only those events which lie in the corresponding interface set A_i. If an event a is present in more than one of these sets, then every process in the set $\{P_i \mid a \in A_i\}$ must cooperate on every occurrence of a.

2.7 TIMEOUTS AND INTERRUPTS

2.7.1 Timeout

The expression $P \overset{t}{\triangleright} Q$ denotes a timeout construct, in which control is passed to process Q if P fails to perform any external actions before time t. A delay of δ is associated with the transfer of control:

$$
\begin{array}{lll}
\mathcal{F}_{TF}[\![P \overset{t}{\triangleright} Q]\!]\rho & \mathrel{\widehat=} & \{(s, X) \mid \mathit{begin}(s) \leqslant t \wedge (s, X) \in \mathcal{F}_{TF}[\![P]\!]\rho\} \\
& & \cup \\
& & \{(s, X) \mid \mathit{begin}(s) \geqslant t + \delta \wedge (\langle\rangle, X \restriction t) \in \mathcal{F}_{TF}[\![P]\!]\rho \\
& & \qquad \wedge \\
& & \qquad (s, X) - (t + \delta) \in \mathcal{F}_{TF}[\![Q]\!]\rho\,\}
\end{array}
$$

A trace s is a trace of P if an event is observed before time t, and a trace of Q otherwise. Any event refused before time t must be refused by P. The δ delay may be removed without affecting the validity of the semantic definition, although its presence gives rise to a syntactic equivalence:

$$
P \overset{t}{\triangleright} Q \;\equiv\; g\,((f(P) \,\Box\, \mathit{WAIT}\; t\,;\, e \rightarrow f(Q)) \setminus e)
$$

where the process relabelling functions f and g are defined by

$$
\begin{array}{lll}
f(a) & \mathrel{\widehat=} & f.a \\
g(f.a) & \mathrel{\widehat=} & a
\end{array}
$$

and event e is chosen such that $\forall\, a : \Sigma \bullet e \neq f.a$. As in the case of the communicating parallel operator, we may use this equivalence to show that the semantics of the timeout operator is well-defined.

2.7.2 Timed interrupt

Another useful timing construct is the timed interrupt operator. The expression

$$P \underset{t}{\lightning} Q$$

denotes a process in which control is passed from P to Q at time t, regardless of the progress made by P. A delay of δ is associated with the transfer of control.

$$\begin{aligned} \mathcal{F}_{TF}[\![P \underset{t}{\lightning} Q]\!]\rho \;\widehat{=}\; \{(s, X) \mid\ & begin(s \upharpoonleft t) \geqslant t + \delta \\ & (s \upharpoonright t, X \upharpoonright t) \in \mathcal{F}_{TF}[\![P]\!]\rho \\ & (s, X) - (t + \delta) \in \mathcal{F}_{TF}[\![Q]\!]\rho\ \} \end{aligned}$$

Any behaviour of this process may be decomposed into behaviours of P and Q by considering the parts of the behaviour that occur before and after time t.

2.7.3 Event interrupt

Although not strictly a timing construct, the event interrupt operator is easily modelled within a timed context. The expression

$$P \underset{e}{\nabla} Q$$

denotes a process that behaves as P until the first occurrence of event e. Once e is observed, control is passed to process Q, following a small delay of δ. The delay is required by our intuition concerning cause and effect; an initial event from process Q may be enabled by e, and so cannot occur at the same time.

$$\begin{aligned} \mathcal{F}_{TF}[\![P \underset{e}{\nabla} Q]\!]\rho \;\widehat{=}\; & \{(s, X) \mid e \notin \sigma(s, X) \wedge (s, X) \in \mathcal{F}_{TF}[\![P]\!]\rho\} \\ & \cup \\ & \{(s, X) \mid \exists\, t \bullet s \upharpoonright t \downharpoonleft e = \langle (t, e) \rangle \\ & \qquad e \notin \sigma(X \upharpoonright t) \\ & \qquad begin(s \upharpoonleft t) \geqslant t + \delta \\ & \qquad (s \upharpoonright t \setminus e, X \upharpoonright t) \in \mathcal{F}_{TF}[\![P]\!]\rho \\ & \qquad (s, X) - (t + \delta) \in \mathcal{F}_{TF}[\![Q]\!]\rho\ \} \end{aligned}$$

Any behaviour in which e has not been observed must be a behaviour of P; in this case, e must be available. Otherwise, e must be observed first at some time t; we may then decompose the behaviour to obtain behaviours of P and Q. A sensible requirement is that $e \notin \sigma(P)$, to avoid the possibility of P interrupting itself.

2.8 INTERACTION

2.8.1 Choice and delay

Consider the process P defined by

$$\begin{aligned} P \;\widehat{=}\;& a \rightarrow STOP \\ & \Box \\ & WAIT\ 1\ ;\ b \rightarrow SKIP \end{aligned}$$

At any time before time 1, this process is prepared to engage only in event a; the subsequent behaviour is that of the deadlocked process $STOP$. However, if one time unit has elapsed since control was passed to the process, the event b is also available. Now consider the process Q defined by

$$\begin{aligned} Q \;\widehat{=}\;& (a \rightarrow STOP \\ & \Box \\ & WAIT\ 1)\ ;\ b \rightarrow SKIP \end{aligned}$$

This process also offers event a until time 1. Unlike process P, it then withdraws the offer. At time 1, if a has not occurred, the $WAIT$ construct offers the termination event. This event is hidden from the environment by the sequential composition operator and occurs immediately, resolving the deterministic choice and passing control to the process $b \rightarrow SKIP$ If event a is offered to the process at time 1, the outcome will be nondeterministic.

In process P, the $WAIT$ operator simply delays the offer of event b, it does not affect the availability of event a; the termination event that enables event b is hidden from the choice construct. In process Q, it acts as a timeout on the offer of a; if this event does not occur at or before time 1, the choice construct terminates and the offer is withdrawn.

2.8.2 Interleaving and termination

The termination event can be used to interrupt the execution of a process. In the expression

$$(a \rightarrow b \rightarrow STOP \;|||\; WAIT\ 2)\ ;\ P$$

control is passed to process P after two seconds, regardless of the progress made by the first component of the parallel construct. Note that the subsequent behaviour is independent of the state of the interrupted process. The same is true of the interrupt constructs $P \underset{t}{\lightning} Q$ and $P \underset{e}{\nabla} Q$.

Without an explicit record of the system state, we must use some form of polling if we are to interrupt a process in a reliable way; a process must cooperate on an interrupt event. For example, in the construct below, the interrupt event *break* is disabled after process P performs a *lock* event; the *break* remains disabled until one second after the next *unlock* event.

$$
\begin{aligned}
P \;\hat{=}\;& WAIT\ 1 \;;\; lock \xrightarrow{2} unlock \xrightarrow{1} P \\
& \Box \\
& break \xrightarrow{1} SKIP
\end{aligned}
$$

The deterministic choice ensures that the environment is offered *break* for a full second before *lock* becomes available (again).

Process P permits a *break* event only when the number of *lock* events is equal to the number of *unlock* events; this condition might be a prerequisite for a safe termination of the process. The combination of deterministic choice and delay provides for a simple representation of priority choice in timed CSP.

2.8.3 Hiding and synchronisation

Consider the process P defined by

$$P \;\hat{=}\; ((WAIT1 \;;\; a \rightarrow STOP) \;{}_{\{a\}}\|_{\{a,b\}}\; (b \rightarrow SKIP \,\Box\, a \rightarrow STOP)) \setminus a$$

For the first second of its existence, P is prepared to engage in event b and terminate time δ later. Internal event a is not yet possible, as it requires the cooperation of both sides of the parallel combination. At time 1, if event b has not occurred, a becomes available on both sides of the parallel operator. As a hidden event, a occurs as soon as it becomes available, resolving the choice against b. The possible behaviours of process P are precisely those of the timeout process

$$Q \;\hat{=}\; b \rightarrow SKIP \overset{1}{\triangleright} STOP$$

If the environment offers b at time 1, the outcome is nondeterministic.

2.9 EXAMPLE

We consider the definition of a sensitive vending machine SVM which behaves as VM in section 1.5, except that it may fail to dispense a drink if kicked while the coin is dropping. As before, we use the events *coin* and *coke* to represent the insertion of a coin and the removal of a drink, respectively. Without timing information, our process description is

$$
\begin{aligned}
SVM \;\hat{=}\;& coin \rightarrow (PAID \,\Box\, reset \rightarrow SVM \\
& \qquad\qquad \sqcap \\
& \qquad\qquad PAID) \\
PAID \;\hat{=}\;& coke \rightarrow SVM
\end{aligned}
$$

The event *reset* represents the effect of a kick on the machine; although the machine may be kicked at any time, there is no effect unless a coin is dropping. Without timing information, we have no way of modelling the progress of the coin inside the machine. The event *reset* is nondeterministically available until a drink is collected.

Adding timing information to our description, we assume that the machine becomes sensitive to kicks after a delay of t_1, following the insertion of a coin. After an additional delay of time t_2, the coin has passed through the mechanism, and the machine may be kicked with impunity:

$$\begin{array}{rcl} TSVM & \widehat{=} & coin \xrightarrow{t_1} (reset \xrightarrow{t_3} TSVM \\ & & \qquad \overset{t_2}{\rhd} \\ & & \qquad PAID) \\ PAID & \widehat{=} & coke \xrightarrow{t_4} TSVM \end{array}$$

The process *TSVM* offers the event *coin* to the environment. If this event is observed at a time t, then the event *reset* is available between time $t + t_1$ and time $t + t_1 + t_2$. If this event occurs, the machine returns to its initial state after a further time t_3, without offering a drink.

If the event *reset* has not occurred by the time the coin has dropped, then the offer of *reset* is withdrawn by the timeout construct, and the machine offers the environment a drink. The addition of timing information has eliminated the nondeterminism present in the untimed description; the process *TSVM* is a timewise refinement of *SVM*, in the sense of section 5.7.

3 RECURSIVE PROCESSES

3.1 RECURSIVE DEFINITIONS

In the untimed language of Hoare (1985), processes may be defined by using the μ symbol to bind recursive variables: e.g.,

$$P \;\widehat{=}\; \mu X \bullet F(X)$$

defines a process P which behaves as $F(X)$, with variable X representing a recursive invocation of the whole process. In Reed and Roscoe's timed language, a delay of δ is associated with each recursive call. This has the advantage of making all syntactic recursions well-defined: any term of the form $\mu X \bullet F(X)$ has a valid representation in the semantic model. If we accept that some syntactic recursions will be invalid, we can dispense with this constant delay.

In this chapter, we define an immediate form of the recursion operator, and give a sufficient condition for the validity of a recursive definition. This treatment of recursion is extended to permit mutual recursion: processes may be defined by mutually recursive sets of equations. These sets may be arbitrarily large.

3.2 CONSTRUCTIVE TERMS

The semantics of a timed CSP term P is a function of the set of term variables appearing in P. For example, the term defined by

$$P \;\widehat{=}\; a \xrightarrow{1} X$$

has a semantic set that is parameterised by $\rho[\![X]\!]$, the semantics of X in the current environment. If P appears as the body of a recursive process, then that process has a well-defined semantics if and only if P corresponds to a contraction mapping in the semantic model $\mathcal{M}_{TF}$. For this to be true, it is sufficient that P is *constructive* for the variable bound by the recursion.

Definition 3.1 If P is a timed CSP term, possibly including free occurrences of term variable X, then P is *t-constructive* for X if

$$\forall\, t_0 : \mathit{TIME}\, ; \rho : \mathit{ENV} \bullet$$
$$\mathcal{F}_{TF}[\![P]\!]\rho \upharpoonright t_0 + t = \mathcal{F}_{TF}[\![P]\!]\rho[\rho[\![X]\!] \upharpoonright t_0/X] \upharpoonright t_0 + t$$

If term P is t-constructive for variable X, then the behaviour of P up until a time $t_0 + t$ is independent of the behaviour of X after time t_0. The reader should recall the over-riding notation for environments defined in section 2.4:

$$\rho[Y/X][\![Z]\!] \;\widehat{=}\; \begin{array}{ll} Y & \text{if } Z = X \\ \rho[\![Z]\!] & \text{otherwise} \end{array}$$

Definition 3.2 We say that a term P is *constructive* for X if there is a strictly positive time t such that P is t-constructive for X.

Our definition of *constructive* differs from the one used by Reed (1988), in which a term P is constructive for variable X iff

$$\forall\, t_0 : \mathit{TIME}\, ; S, T : \mathcal{M}_{TF}\, ; \rho : \mathit{ENV} \bullet$$
$$S \upharpoonright t_0 = T \upharpoonright t_0 \Rightarrow (\mathcal{F}_{TF}[\![P]\!]\rho[S/X]) \upharpoonright t_0 + t = (\mathcal{F}_{TF}[\![P]\!]\rho[T/X]) \upharpoonright t_0 + t$$

Our definition places a stronger condition upon P and X.

Lemma 3.3 If term P is t-constructive for variable X, then

$$\forall\, t_0 : \mathit{TIME}\, ; S, T : \mathcal{S}_{TF}\, ; \rho : \mathit{ENV} \bullet$$
$$S \upharpoonright t_0 = T \upharpoonright t_0 \Rightarrow (\mathcal{F}_{TF}[\![P]\!]\rho[S/X]) \upharpoonright t_0 + t = (\mathcal{F}_{TF}[\![P]\!]\rho[T/X]) \upharpoonright t_0 + t$$

From the semantic equations for the timed CSP operators we can derive a number of useful results about constructive terms.

Lemma 3.4 For any X and t,

1. STOP, SKIP, $\perp$, and $\mathit{WAIT}\ t_0$ are all t-constructive for X
2. X is *0*-constructive for X, and t-constructive for $Y \neq X$
3. $\mu X \bullet P$ is t-constructive for X

Lemma 3.5 If P is t-constructive for X,

1. $a \xrightarrow{t_0} P$ and $\mathit{WAIT}\ t_0\, ; P$ are $(t + t_0)$-constructive for X
2. $\mu Y \bullet P$, $P \setminus A$, $f(P)$, $f^{-1}(P)$ are all t-constructive for X
3. P is t'-constructive for X, for any $t' < t$

Lemma 3.6 If P is t_1-constructive for X and Q is t_2-constructive for X,

1. $P \,\Box\, Q$, $P \sqcap Q$, $P\,;\,Q$, $P \parallel\!| Q$, $P \parallel Q$, $P \;{}_A\|_B\; Q$
   are all $min\{t_1, t_2\}$-constructive for X
2. $P \overset{t}{\rhd} Q$ and $P \underset{t}{\overset{\not{}}{}} Q$ are both $min\{t_1, t_2 + t\}$-constructive for X
3. $P \,⨾\, Q$ and $P \underset{e}{\nabla} Q$ are $\min\{t_1, t_2 + \delta\}$-constructive for X

Observe that all timed CSP terms are *0*-constructive for any process variable.

3.2.1 Restrained terms

A sequential composition of terms is also constructive if the first term is constructive, and cannot terminate immediately. We say that a term P is *t-restrained* if it cannot terminate within time t:

Definition 3.7 If P is a timed CSP term, then

$$P \text{ is } t\text{-restrained} \quad \Leftrightarrow \quad (s \in traces(P) \wedge end(s) < t) \Rightarrow \checkmark \notin \sigma(s)$$

for any instantiation of free variables in P.

A timed CSP process is t-restrained if the event $\checkmark$, signalling successful termination, is not included in the set of events that may be observed before time t. A timed CSP term P is t-restrained if this condition holds whatever the values of any free variables in P. In particular, we must be able to replace these with the termination process *SKIP*. From the semantic equations of the CSP operators, we can obtain a number of simple results about restrained terms.

Lemma 3.8 For any time t,

1. *SKIP* is *0*-restrained
2. $WAIT\ t$ is t-restrained
3. $STOP$ and $\bot$ are ∞-restrained

Lemma 3.9 If term P is t-restrained,

1. $a \xrightarrow{t_0} P$ and $WAIT\ t_0\ ;\ P$ are $(t + t_0)$-restrained
2. $\mu\, Y \bullet P$, $P \setminus A$, $P\,;\,X$, $f(P)$, and $f^{-1}(P)$ are all t-restrained
3. P is t'-restrained, for any $t' < t$

Lemma 3.10 If P is t_1-restrained, and Q is t_2-restrained,

1. $P \Box Q$, $P \sqcap Q$, $P \;{}_A\|_B\; Q$, and $P \;|||\; Q$ are all $min\{t_1, t_2\}$-restrained
2. $P \,;\, Q$ is $(t_1 + t_2)$-restrained
3. $P \overset{t}{\rhd} Q$ and $P \underset{t}{\not\downarrow} Q$ are both $min\{t_1, t_2 + t\}$-restrained
4. $P \underset{e}{\nabla} Q$ is $min\{t_1, t_2 + \delta\}$-restrained
5. $P \parallel Q$ is $max\{t_1, t_2\}$-restrained
6. $\checkmark \notin A \cup B \Rightarrow P \;{}_A\|_B\; Q$ is ∞-restrained
7. $\checkmark \in A \cap B \Rightarrow P \;{}_A\|_B\; Q$ is $max\{t_1, t_2\}$-restrained

Using the notion of a restrained term, we can add a further result to our list of lemmas about constructive terms:

Lemma 3.11 If term P is t-restrained and t-constructive for X, then the term $P \,;\, Q$ is t-constructive for X, for any t and Q.

3.3 RECURSIVE PROCESSES

We extend our syntax with two single fixed point recursion operators:

$$P \quad ::= \quad \mu\, X \bullet P \;\big|\; \mu\, X \circ P$$

The first of these associates a delay of time δ with each recursive call, while the second transfers control to a recursive invocation of the process immediately upon reaching an instance of variable X. We will refer to these operators as *delayed* and *immediate* recursion, respectively.

We may regard the semantics of a term P with free variable X and environment ρ as a function defined upon $\mathcal{S}_{TF}$. This function maps a set of failures S to the semantics of P evaluated in an environment $(\rho[S/X])$ obtained by associating variable X with the set S.

Definition 3.12 If P is a timed CSP term, and X and Y are variables such that Y does not occur free in P, then

$$M(X, P)\rho \;\widehat{=}\; \lambda\, Y \bullet \mathcal{F}_{TF}[\![P]\!]\rho[Y/X]$$

To give a semantics to the delayed recursion operator, we consider the composition of this mapping with the function W_δ.

Definition 3.13 If P is a timed CSP term, and X and Y are variables such that Y does not occur free in P, then

$$M_\delta(X, P)\rho \;\widehat{=}\; W_\delta \cdot \lambda\, Y \bullet \mathcal{F}_{TF}[\![P]\!]\rho[Y/X]$$

where W_δ is the mapping defined by

$$W_\delta \ \widehat{=}\ \lambda\, Y \bullet \mathcal{F}_{TF}[\![\, WAIT\delta\, ;\, X]\!]\rho[Y/X]$$

The environment parameter provides a binding for any free variables remaining in term P, and the definition of W_δ reflects the delay associated with this form of recursion—observe that W_δ does not depend upon the choice of environment ρ. We may now give the semantics of the recursion operators.

$$\mathcal{F}_{TF}[\![\, \mu\, X \circ P]\!]\rho \ \widehat{=}\ \text{the unique fixed point of the mapping } M(X, P)\rho$$

$$\mathcal{F}_{TF}[\![\, \mu\, X \bullet P]\!]\rho \ \widehat{=}\ \text{the unique fixed point of the mapping } M_\delta(X, P)\rho$$

Reed (1988) shows that the mapping $M_\delta(X, P)\rho$ will always have a unique fixed point in $\mathcal{M}_{TF}$, and hence that the semantics of delayed recursion is always well-defined. This result does not hold for the immediate recursion operator. We will show that the semantics of immediate recursion is well-defined if term P is constructive for variable X.

Lemma 3.14 If term P is constructive for process variable X then the mapping $M(X, P)\rho$ is a contraction mapping on the space of sets of failures $\mathcal{S}_{TF}$.

Proof A mapping F in $\mathcal{S}_{TF}$ is a contraction mapping if and only if

$$\exists\, r < 1 \ \bullet\ \forall\, S, T : \mathcal{S}_{TF} \bullet d(F(S), F(T)) \leqslant r.d(S, T)$$

where d is the metric defined by

$$d(S, T) \ \widehat{=}\ \mathit{inf}(\{2^{-k} \mid S \restriction k = T \restriction k\} \cup \{1\})$$

Now take any two processes S and T in $\mathcal{S}_{TF}$. If $S = T$ then $F(S) = F(T)$ and both sides of the above inequality are zero. Else, let

$$d(S, T) \ = \ 2^{-k}$$

If we take F to be the mapping $M(X, P)\rho$, then

$$\forall\, R : \mathcal{S}_{TF} \ \bullet\ F(R) = \mathcal{F}_{TF}[\![P]\!]\rho[R/X]$$

From the definition of constructive and lemma 3.3, we know that there is a strictly positive time t such that

$$S \restriction k = T \restriction k \ \Rightarrow\ F(S) \restriction k + t = F(T) \restriction k + t$$

for any S and T in $\mathcal{S}_{TF}$. From this, we obtain

$$d(F(S), F(T)) \ \leqslant\ 2^{-(k+t)} \ = \ 2^{-t}.d(S, T)$$

We note that $2^{-t} < 1$ as t is strictly positive, and conclude that F is a contraction mapping in $\mathcal{S}_{TF}$. □

We have established that the mapping corresponding to a constructive term is a contraction mapping on $\mathcal{S}_{TF}$. To establish that such a mapping has a unique fixed point, we require the following result from Sutherland (1985):

The Banach Fixed Point Theorem If (M, d) is a complete metric space and $F : M \rightarrow M$ is a contraction mapping, then F has a unique fixed point $\mathit{fix}(F)$. Furthermore, for all S in M, $\mathit{fix}(F) = \lim_{n \rightarrow \infty} F^n(S)$.

The semantic model $\mathcal{M}_{TF}$ is a subset of $\mathcal{S}_{TF}$, and both are complete metric spaces under the metric d defined in section 2.3. A contraction mapping on $\mathcal{S}_{TF}$ is therefore a contraction mapping on the complete subspace $\mathcal{M}_{TF}$, hence

Lemma 3.15 If $F : \mathcal{S}_{TF} \rightarrow \mathcal{S}_{TF}$ is a contraction mapping which maps $\mathcal{M}_{TF}$ into $\mathcal{M}_{TF}$, then F has a unique fixed point $\mathit{fix}(F)$ in $\mathcal{M}_{TF}$.

Any function derived from the semantics of a timed CSP term will preserve the axioms of the semantic model, mapping $\mathcal{M}_{TF}$ into $\mathcal{M}_{TF}$. We may combine lemmas 3.14 and 3.15 to obtain the required result:

Theorem 3.16 If term P is constructive for variable X, then the semantics

$$\mathcal{F}_{TF}[\![\, \mu X \circ P]\!] \rho$$

is well-defined for all environments ρ.

The semantics of immediate recursion gives rise to the familiar equivalence

Theorem 3.17

$$\mu X \circ F(X) \quad \equiv \quad F(\mu X \circ F(X))$$

This result justifies the use of recursive equations as process definitions. For example, a process that is willing to perform the event a at one second intervals may be defined by the equation

$$P \quad = \quad a \xrightarrow{1} P$$

This equational definition is equivalent to the following definition of P using the immediate recursion operator:

$$P \quad \widehat{=} \quad \mu X \circ a \xrightarrow{1} X$$

In fact, we can easily prove that

Corollary 3.18 If $\mu X \circ F(X)$ is well-defined, then

$$P \quad = \quad F(P) \quad \text{if and only if} \quad P \quad = \quad \mu X \circ F(X)$$

The equational style is more concise, especially in the case of mutual recursion. Indeed, we cannot reasonably write an infinite mutual recursion using μ-notation.

It should be remembered that this result (theorem 3.17) does not hold for the delayed recursion operator; we have instead that

$$\mu X \bullet F(X) \quad \equiv \quad F(\mathit{WAIT}\,\delta\,;(\mu X \bullet F(X)))$$

which is inconsistent with the use of equations to define recursive processes: e.g., there is no delayed recursive process which will satisfy the recursive equation $P = a \rightarrow P$.

3.4 MUTUAL RECURSION

We will now consider processes defined by sets of mutually recursive equations. The definition of *constructive* in section 3.2 extends in a natural way to vectors of terms and variables, and we are able to exhibit a sufficient condition for a syntactic mutual recursion to have a well-defined semantics.

3.4.1 Syntax

A timed CSP term P may be defined by a vector of mutually recursive equations

$$P \quad \widehat{=} \quad \langle X_i = P_i \rangle_j \qquad i \in I$$

with an initial index j to indicate the starting point of the recursion. We will employ a simple vector notation for terms:

$$\underline{P} \quad = \quad \langle P_1, P_2, \,..\, P_n, \,..\,\rangle$$

The sets used to index these vectors need not be finite. Using this notation, we can write our equation vectors in the form $(\mu\,\underline{X} \circ \underline{P})$.

As an example, consider the process algebra representation of a device that has two states: *ON* and *OFF*. This device may produce a *beep* as often as once a second when *ON*. The two states correspond to the two mutually recursive equations below.

$$\begin{aligned} \mathit{ON} &= (\mathit{beep} \xrightarrow{1} \mathit{ON}) \,\Box\, (\mathit{off} \xrightarrow{1} \mathit{OFF}) \\ \mathit{OFF} &= \mathit{on} \xrightarrow{3} \mathit{ON} \end{aligned}$$

This may be considered as a single recursive equation, on a vector of process variables $\langle \mathit{ON}, \mathit{OFF} \rangle$. The device is then modelled by the component of the vector corresponding to the initial state *OFF*. Alternatively, we may represent the device as a single recursive process:

$$\mathit{OFF} \quad \widehat{=} \quad \mu X \circ \mathit{on} \xrightarrow{3} (\mu Y \circ (\mathit{beep} \xrightarrow{1} Y) \,\Box\, (\mathit{off} \xrightarrow{1} X))$$

This nested recursion defines the same process as the first component of the mutual recursion above, and falls within the basic syntax for timed CSP used by Reed (1988). In practice, it will be more convenient to represent mutually recursive processes using equation sets, particularly when the set of named states is infinite. For example, consider the case of an integer store STO. Initially, the store is willing to input an integer value:

$$STO \;\widehat{=}\; in?x \xrightarrow{1} STO_x$$

Thereafter, it is prepared to accept another input, or output the current value stored, as often as once a second:

$$\begin{aligned} STO_x \;\widehat{=}\; & in?y \xrightarrow{1} STO_y \\ & \Box \\ & out!x \xrightarrow{1} STO_x \end{aligned}$$

This is an infinite set of mutually recursive equations, where STO_x models the state of the store containing x.

With the delayed form of recursion, mutually recursive definitions should not be written with an equality symbol, as the left- and right-hand sides do not represent equivalent processes. For example, we might use a symbol such as $\mapsto$ to indicate that a constant delay is associated with any recursive invocations on the right-hand side of an equation. In this case, the integer store example would look like this:

$$STO \;\widehat{=}\; in?x \xrightarrow{1} STO_x$$

$$\begin{aligned} STO_x \;\mapsto\; & in?y \xrightarrow{1-\delta} STO_y \\ & \Box \\ & out!x \xrightarrow{1-\delta} STO_x \end{aligned}$$

This form of recursion is always valid in the semantic model. However, the immediate recursion operator makes recursive definitions easier to understand, and allows the user to choose the point and duration of any delay.

3.4.2 Semantics

Consider an equation set $\langle X_i = P_i \rangle_j$, where the indices i and j are drawn from set I. The semantic domain required to model a solution is $\mathcal{S}_{TF}^I$; this is a product space with one copy of the model $\mathcal{S}_{TF}$ for each $i \in I$. For any I, this domain is a complete metric space, with the following distance metric on vectors.

$$\underline{d}(\underline{V}, \underline{W}) \;\widehat{=}\; sup\{d(V_i, W_i) \mid i \in I\}$$

To construct a semantic function for vectors of terms, we extend the use of environments to include mappings from vectors of variables to vectors of processes.

$$\rho[\![\underline{X}]\!] \;\widehat{=}\; \langle \rho[\![X_i]\!] \mid i \in I \rangle$$

where I is the indexing set of vector $\underline{X}$. We overload the mapping notation defined in section 3.3 with

Definition 3.19 If $\underline{P}$ a vector of timed CSP terms, and $\underline{X}$ and $\underline{Y}$ are vectors of variables, all indexed by set I, and no component of $\underline{Y}$ occurs free in $\underline{P}$, then

$$M(\underline{X}, \underline{P})\rho \;\widehat{=}\; \lambda\, \underline{Y} \bullet \mathcal{F}_{TF}[\![\underline{P}]\!]\rho[\underline{Y}/\underline{X}]$$

is the mapping on $\mathcal{S}_{TF}^{I}$ corresponding to $\underline{X}$ and $\underline{P}$.

Definition 3.20 If $\underline{P}$ is a vector of timed CSP terms, then

$$\mathcal{F}_{TF}[\![\langle X_i = P_i \rangle_j]\!]\rho \;\widehat{=}\; S_j \text{ where } \underline{S} \text{ is a fixed point of } M(\underline{X}, \underline{P})\rho$$

This semantics is well-defined when all fixed points of the mapping $M(\underline{X}, \underline{P})\rho$ agree on the j component. Clearly, it is enough that this mapping has a unique fixed point. For this to be true, it is sufficient that the vector of terms $\underline{P}$ is *constructive* for the vector of variables.

3.5 CONSTRUCTIVE VECTORS

A partial ordering $\preceq$ on a set S is a well-ordering if and only if there are no infinite descending sequences $\langle s_i \mid i : \mathbb{N} \rangle$ such that $\forall\, i : \mathbb{N} \bullet s_{i+1} \preceq s_i$. We define the initial segment of an element of i in the usual way.

Definition 3.21 If $\preceq$ is a partial ordering on I, and i is an element of I, then the initial segment of i in $(I, \preceq)$ is defined by

$$\text{seg}(i) \;\widehat{=}\; \{j : I \mid j \preceq i\}$$

For the mapping $M(\underline{X}, \underline{P})\rho$ to have a unique fixed point, it is sufficient that the vector of terms $\underline{P}$ is *constructive* for the vector of variables $\underline{X}$.

Definition 3.22 A vector of terms $\underline{P}$ is t-constructive for a vector of process variables $\underline{X}$ if there is a well-ordering $\preceq$ of the indexing set I such that

$$\forall\, j, i : I \bullet j \notin \text{seg}(i) \Rightarrow P_i \text{ is } t\text{-constructive for } X_j$$

Definition 3.23 A vector of terms $\underline{P}$ is *constructive* for a vector of process variables $\underline{X}$ if there is a strictly positive time t such that $\underline{P}$ is t-constructive for $\underline{X}$.

If this condition is met then the only possible unguarded recursive calls in term P_i correspond to variables X_j where $j \preceq i$. Thus any sequence of unguarded recursive calls is indexed by a descending sequence from the set I, and must therefore be finite. Any particular behaviour of the process is generated by a finite number of recursive calls, and an infinite number of recursive calls in a finite time is impossible.

In many applications, it is not necessary to identify a well-ordering of the index set I. If all recursive calls are guarded by a single positive time t, then any well-ordering of I will be enough to show that the vector of terms is constructive for the vector of variables. In this case, we say that the vector of terms is *uniformly constructive*. Formally,

Definition 3.24 A vector of terms $\underline{P}$ is uniformly t-constructive for a vector of variables $\underline{X}$ if P_i is t-constructive for all X_j.

Definition 3.25 A vector of terms $\underline{P}$ is uniformly constructive for a vector of variables $\underline{X}$ if there exists a positive time t such that $\underline{P}$ is uniformly t-constructive for $\underline{X}$.

Observe that any uniformly constructive vector of terms is constructive. In this case $M(\underline{X}, \underline{P})\rho$ will be a contraction mapping in the semantic model $\mathcal{S}^I_{TF}$.

We have defined *constructive* for vectors in a component-wise fashion. That a vector of terms is constructive for a vector of variables can be established by a case analysis on pairs (X_i, P_j) in our equation set, a relatively simple procedure. We will show that this is a sufficient condition for the semantics of a mutual recursion to be well-defined. First, we must demonstrate that our pointwise definitions are enough to establish the corresponding vector results.

Theorem 3.26 (Finite Dependency Theorem) If P is a timed CSP term, possibly containing free occurrences of process variables drawn from the set $\{X_i \mid i \in I\}$, and ρ is an environment, then

$$\begin{aligned}(s, X) \in \mathcal{F}_{TF}[\![P]\!]\rho \;\Rightarrow\; & \exists\, N : \mathbb{F}\, I \bullet \forall\, \rho' : ENV \bullet \\ & (\forall\, i : N \bullet \rho[\![X_i]\!] = \rho'[\![X_i]\!]) \Rightarrow (s, X) \in \mathcal{F}_{TF}[\![P]\!]\rho'\end{aligned}$$

The presence of a given behaviour (s, X) in the semantic set of a term P depends only upon the values of a finite set of variables N, even if the term is an infinite mutual recursion. We may change the environment of the term without removing the behaviour, providing that we preserve the values of the variables in N.

Proof To establish the Finite Dependency Theorem, we will establish a stronger result by structural induction on the syntax of timed CSP.

Lemma 3.27 If (s_0, X_0) is an element of $\mathcal{F}_{TF}[\![P]\!]\rho$, then

$$\exists\, M \in \mathbb{F}(VAR \times TF) \;\bullet\; PROP(M, s_0, X_0, P, \rho)$$

where

$$\begin{aligned}PROP(M, s_0, X_0, P, \rho) \;\widehat{=}\; & (\forall (X, (s, X)) \in M \bullet (s, X) \in \rho[\![X]\!]) \\ & \wedge \\ & \forall\, \rho' \in ENV \bullet (\forall (X, (s, X)) \in M \bullet (s, X) \in \rho'[\![X]\!]) \\ & \qquad \Rightarrow (s_0, X_0) \in \mathcal{F}_{TF}[\![P]\!]\rho'\end{aligned}$$

That is, we may find a *finite* set M of (*variable*, *behaviour*) pairs such that the behaviour (s_0, X_0) depends only upon the elements of M. In the proof of this result, the following result will be useful. It states that if we can find a finite set M such that *PROP* holds for M, then we can obtain a second set M' in which all of the behaviours corresponding to variables for which term P is t-constructive end at least t before (s_0, X_0). We establish this secondary result by showing that *PROP* holds of the subset of M obtained by discarding those behaviours which do not meet this condition.

Lemma 3.28 If *PROP* is as defined in lemma 3.27, then

$$PROP(M, s_0, X_0, P, \rho) \;\Rightarrow\; \exists\, M' \bullet PROP(M', s_0, X_0, P, \rho)$$

$$\forall (X, (s, X)) \in M' \bullet (P\ t_X\text{-constructive for } X \Rightarrow end(s, X) + t_X \leqslant end(s_0, X_0))$$

To see that this is true, define

$$M' \;\widehat{=}\; \{(X, (s, X)) \in M \mid P\ t_X\text{-constructive for } X \Rightarrow end(s, X) + t \leqslant end(s_0, X_0)\ \}$$

and observe that $PROP(M', s_0, X_0, P, \rho)$ holds. The first conjunct is immediate, as $M' \subseteq M$. To establish the second, let ρ' be such that

$$\forall (X, (s, X)) \in M' \bullet (s, X) \in \rho'[\![X]\!]$$

Then define ρ'' by

$$\rho''[\![X]\!] \;\widehat{=}\; \rho'[\![X]\!] \cup \{(s, X) \mid (X, (s, X)) \in M\}$$

In this case,

$$\forall (X, (s, X)) \in M \;\bullet\; (s, X) \in \rho''[\![X]\!]$$

and hence

$$(s_0, X_0) \;\in\; \mathcal{F}_{TF}[\![P]\!]\rho''$$

If we choose $t_0 = end(s_0, X_0)$, we obtain

$$(s_0, X_0) \;\in\; \mathcal{F}_{TF}[\![P]\!]\rho'' \restriction t_0$$

From this we may obtain

$$\begin{aligned}(s_0, X_0) \in \mathcal{F}_{TF}[\![P]\!]\rho''[\rho''[\![X]\!] \restriction t_0 - t_X / X] \\ \Rightarrow\; (s_0, X_0) \in \mathcal{F}_{TF}[\![P]\!]\rho'[\rho'[\![X]\!] \restriction t_0 - t_X / X] \\ \Rightarrow\; (s_0, X_0) \in \mathcal{F}_{TF}[\![P]\!]\rho'\end{aligned}$$

The final implication above follows from the definition of t-constructive. We may now proceed to establish lemma 3.27.

Proof of lemma 3.27 We proceed by structural induction upon the syntax of timed CSP terms, observing that the result is trivially true for all closed terms or processes—these have the same semantics in every environment, and the empty set is a suitable choice for set M. The remaining base case for our induction is the variable clause:

case X Suppose that (s_0, X_0) is an element of $\rho[\![X]\!]$, and choose M to be the singleton set $\{(X, (s_0, X_0))\}$. The result follows immediately.

The inductive step is straightforward in every case except that of mutual recursion; a typical example is the case of the parallel operator.

case $P \parallel Q$ Suppose that (s_0, X_0) is an element of $\mathcal{F}_{TF}[\![P \parallel Q]\!]\rho$. From the semantics of the parallel operator we obtain that

$$\begin{aligned} \exists X_P, X_Q \quad \bullet \quad & X_0 = X_P \cup X_Q \\ & \wedge (s_0, X_P) \in \mathcal{F}_{TF}[\![P]\!]\rho \\ & \wedge (s_0, X_Q) \in \mathcal{F}_{TF}[\![Q]\!]\rho \end{aligned}$$

By our inductive hypothesis, there exist sets M_P and M_Q corresponding to (s_0, X_P) and (s_0, X_Q) to satisfy the proposition. If we take M to be the union of these sets, then we have that

$$\begin{aligned} (X, (s, X)) \in M \quad & \Rightarrow \quad (X, (s, X)) \in M_P \vee (X, (s, X)) \in M_Q \\ & \Rightarrow \quad (s, X) \in \rho[\![X]\!] \vee (s, X) \in \rho[\![X]\!] \end{aligned}$$

which establishes that M satisfies the first requirement. Now suppose that ρ' is such that

$$\forall (X, (s, X)) : M \quad \bullet \quad (s, X) \in \rho'[\![X]\!]$$

then, as $M_P \subseteq M$,

$$\forall (X, (s, X)) : M_P \quad \bullet \quad (s, X) \in \rho'[\![X]\!]$$

we apply the inductive hypothesis and deduce that $(s_0, X_P) \in \mathcal{F}_{TF}[\![P]\!]\rho'$. Similarly, we may deduce that $(s_0, X_Q) \in \mathcal{F}_{TF}[\![Q]\!]\rho'$. From the semantics of the parallel operator, we have that $(s_0, X_P \cup X_Q)$ in $\mathcal{F}_{TF}[\![P \parallel Q]\!]\rho'$, which establishes the case.

case $\langle X_i = P_i \rangle_j$ Consider (s_0, X_0) in $\mathcal{F}_{TF}[\![\langle X_i = P_i \rangle_j]\!]\rho$, where the recursive equations are indexed by set I. Unfolding the recursion, we see that

$$(s_0, X_0) \quad \in \quad \mathcal{F}_{TF}[\![P_j]\!]\rho_1$$

where

$$\rho_1 \quad = \quad \rho[\mathcal{F}_{TF}[\![\langle X_i = P_i \rangle_k]\!]\rho / X_k \mid k \in I]$$

Applying the inductive hypothesis to every term P_l, we know that for any (s_1, X_1) in $\mathcal{F}_{TF}[\![P_l]\!]\rho$ there is a corresponding set $M(s_1, X_1, l)$ such that

$$\begin{array}{ll} (i) & \forall (X,(s,X)) : M(s_1,X_1,l) \bullet (s,X) \in \rho[X] \\ (ii) & \forall \rho' : ENV \bullet (\forall (X,(s,X)) : M(s_1,X_1,l) \bullet (s,X) \in \rho'[\![X]\!]) \\ & \qquad \Rightarrow (s_1,X_1) \in \mathcal{F}_{TF}[\![P_l]\!]\rho' \end{array}$$

Applying lemma 3.28, we obtain that there exists $M'(s_1, X_1, l)$, a subset of $M(s_1, X_1, l)$, satisfying (i) and (ii) above, such that

$$\begin{array}{ll} (iii) & \forall (X,(s,X)) \in M' \bullet P \; t_X\text{-constructive for } X \Rightarrow \\ & \qquad\qquad\qquad end(s,X) + t_X \leqslant end(s_0,X_0) \end{array}$$

We define a function $m : (VAR \times TF) \to \mathbb{P}(VAR \times TF)$ as follows:

$$m(X,(s,X)) \;\widehat{=}\; \begin{array}{ll} \{\} & \text{if } X \notin \{X_i \mid i \in I\} \\ M'(s,X,l) & \text{if } X = X_l \wedge l \in I \end{array}$$

In the second case, if the variable X appears in the variable vector $\underline{X}$, we let $m(X,(s,X))$ be the set whose existence is guaranteed by the inductive hypothesis applied to the corresponding term. We define a relation R on $VAR \times TF$ by

$$(X_1,(s_1,X_1)) \; R \; (X_2,(s_2,X_2)) \;\; \Leftrightarrow \;\; (X_1,(s_1,X_1)) \in m(X_2,(s_2,X_2))$$

This is a well-founded finite-to-one relation. That is:

1. there are no infinite chains $\{C_n\}$ such that $\forall n \bullet C_{n+1} \; R \; C_n$
2. for any C, the set $\{C' \mid C' \; R \; C\}$ is finite

The second of these requirements follows immediately from the definition of m, and the first is established as follows:

Suppose that $\{(X_n,(s_n,X_n)) \mid n : \mathbb{N}\}$ is such a infinite chain, then each X_n must be an X_i for some $i \in I$, for otherwise X_{n+1} cannot exist (by the definitions of R and m). For each index n, let i_n be the vector index such that $X_n = X_{i_n}$. Construct an infinite chain of natural numbers N_p by

$$\begin{array}{lcl} N_0 & \widehat{=} & 0 \\ N_{p+1} & \widehat{=} & min\{n : \mathbb{N} \mid n > N_p \wedge i_n \not\preceq i_{n-1}\} \end{array}$$

that is, the successor N_{p+1} is defined to be the least number n greater than N_p for which the vector index i_n is not beneath i_{n-1} in the well-ordering of the vector indexing set I. This is a good definition: if the defining set is empty for N_{p+1} then the infinite sequence $\{i_k \mid k > N_p\}$ will be strictly decreasing with respect to the well-order $\preceq$, forcing a contradiction. If we define

$$t_k \;\widehat{=}\; end(s_k, X_k)$$

then recalling that property (*iii*) holds of M', which defines m, we have

$$\begin{array}{lcl} \forall p & \bullet & t_{p+1} \leqslant t_p \\ \forall p & \bullet & t_{N_{p+1}} + t \leqslant t_{N_{p+1}-1} \end{array}$$

hence

$$\forall p \bullet t_{N_{p+1}} + t \leqslant t_{N_p}$$

and thus t_{N_p} is a sequence tending to $-\infty$, contradicting the fact that each t_k is non-negative. Hence there can be no infinite chain C_n, and the relation R is indeed well-founded. We appeal to the following result from Enderton (1977):

König's Lemma If R is a well-founded relation such that, for all y, the set $\{x \mid xRy\}$ is finite, then

$$\forall y \bullet \{x \mid x\ R^t\ y\} \text{ is finite}$$

Applying this, the set $M = \{C \mid C\ R^t\ (X_j, (s_0, X_0))\}$ is a finite set. We claim that

$$PROP(M, s_0, X_0, \langle X_i = P_i \rangle_j, \rho)$$

Recall that

$$\begin{array}{rcl} PROP(M, s_0, X_0, P, \rho) & \widehat{=} & (\forall (X, (s, X)) \in M \bullet (s, X) \in \rho[\![X]\!]) \\ & & \wedge \\ & & \forall \rho' \in ENV \bullet (\forall (X, (s, X)) \in M \bullet (s, X) \in \rho'[\![X]\!]) \\ & & \qquad \Rightarrow (s_0, X_0) \in \mathcal{F}_{TF}[\![P]\!]\rho' \end{array}$$

and observe that

$$\begin{array}{rcl} (X, (s, X)) \in M & \Rightarrow & \exists X', s', X' \bullet (X, (s, X)) \in m(X', (s', X')) \\ & \Rightarrow & \exists l, s', X' \bullet (X, (s, X)) \in M(s', X', l) \end{array}$$

The first conjunct of $PROP(M, s_0, X_0, \langle X_i = P_i \rangle_j, \rho)$ follows immediately from the corresponding result for $PROP(M(s', X', l), s', X', P_l, \rho)$. To see that the second conjunct is true, it is enough to show that, given any $(X, (s, X))$ in M,

$$(\forall (X', (s', X')) \in m(X, (s, X)) \bullet HYP(X', (s', X'))) \Rightarrow HYP(X, (s, X))$$

where

$$HYP(X, (s, X)) \ \widehat{=}\ (s, X) \in \rho'[\mathcal{F}_{TF}[\![\langle X_i = P_i \rangle_k]\!]\rho' / X_k][\![X]\!]$$

We establish this as follows: assume the left-hand side of the above implication, and consider the identity of variable X. If X is an element of $\{X_i \mid i \in I\}$ then

$$\rho'[\mathcal{F}_{TF}[\![\langle X_i = P_i \rangle_k]\!]\rho' / X_k][\![X]\!] = \rho'[\![X]\!]$$

which contains (s, X), by the antecedent to the second conjunct of *PROP*. Otherwise, let $X = X_l$ for $l \in I$. In this case,

$$m(X, (s, X)) \quad = \quad M(s, X, l)$$

and for each $(X', (s', X'))$ in $M(s, X, l)$, we have that

$$\begin{array}{ll} & (s', X') \in \rho'[\mathcal{F}_{TF}[\![\langle X_i = P_i \rangle_k]\!]\rho'/X_k][\![X']\!] \\ \Rightarrow & (s, X) \in \mathcal{F}_{TF}[\![P_l]\!]\rho'[\mathcal{F}_{TF}[\![\langle X_i = P_i \rangle_k]\!]\rho'/X_k] \\ \Rightarrow & (s, X) \in \mathcal{F}_{TF}[\![\langle X_i = P_i \rangle_l]\!]\rho' \end{array}$$

which establishes $HYP(X, (s, X))$, but then the result holds for all elements of M, in particular we have that

$$HYP(X_j, (s_0, X_0))$$

which says that

$$(s_0, X_0) \quad \in \quad \rho'[\mathcal{F}_{TF}[\![\langle X_i = P_i \rangle_k]\!]\rho'/X_k][\![X_j]\!]$$

finally yielding

$$(s_0, X_0) \quad \in \quad \mathcal{F}_{TF}[\![\langle X_i = P_i \rangle_j]\!]\rho'$$

the consequent of the second conjunct of *PROP*, which establishes the case.

This completes the proof of lemma 3.27. □

The Finite Dependency Theorem follows immediately. □

We may restate the Finite Dependency Theorem in a more applicable form, using the over-riding notation for environments:

Corollary 3.29 If P is a timed CSP term, possibly containing free occurrences of process variables drawn from the set $\{X_i \mid i \in I\}$, and ρ and ρ' are environments, then

$$(s, X) \in \mathcal{F}_{TF}[\![P]\!]\rho \;\Rightarrow\; \exists\, N : \mathbb{F}\, I \bullet \forall\, \rho' \bullet (s, X) \in \mathcal{F}_{TF}[\![P]\!]\rho'[\rho[\![X_i]\!]/X_i \mid i \in N]$$

We say that a term P is t-constructive for a vector of variables $\underline{X}$ if the semantics of P up until a time t_0 is independent of the behaviour of every component of $\underline{X}$ after time t_0. This is a simple extension of definition 3.1.

Definition 3.30 If P is a timed CSP term, then P is *t-constructive* for a vector of variables $\underline{X}$, indexed by set I, iff

$$\begin{array}{l} \forall\, t_0 : \mathit{TIME}\,;\, \rho : \mathit{ENV} \bullet \\ \quad \mathcal{F}_{TF}[\![P]\!]\rho \upharpoonright t_0 + t = \mathcal{F}_{TF}[\![P]\!]\rho[\rho[\![X_i]\!] \upharpoonright t_0/X_i \mid i \in I] \upharpoonright t_0 + t \end{array}$$

With this definition, a simple induction upon the length of finite vector $\underline{X}$ is enough to establish the following lemma:

Lemma 3.31 If P is t-constructive for each of $\{X_i \mid i \in N\}$, and N is a finite set, then P is t-constructive for the vector $\underline{X}$ indexed by N.

We may combine this result with the Finite Dependency Theorem to obtain the theorem below, which will allow us to obtain vector results from our pointwise definitions.

Theorem 3.32 If P is t-constructive for each of $\{X_i \mid i \in I\}$ then P is t-constructive for the vector $\underline{X}$ indexed by I.

Proof To show that P is t-constructive for vector $\underline{X}$, we must show that for any time t_0 and environment ρ,

$$\mathcal{F}_{TF}[\![P]\!]\rho \upharpoonright t_0 + t \quad = \quad \mathcal{F}_{TF}[\![P]\!]\rho[\rho[\![X_i]\!] \upharpoonright t_0 / X_i \mid i \in I] \upharpoonright t_0 + t$$

If we take (s, X) to be an element of the left-hand side, we may apply the corollary to the Finite Dependency Theorem, yielding

$$\exists N : \mathbb{F}\, I \bullet \forall \rho' \;\bullet\; (s, X) \in \mathcal{F}_{TF}[\![P]\!]\rho'[\rho[\![X_i]\!] / X_i \mid i \in N] \upharpoonright t_0 + t$$

We take ρ' to be the environment

$$\rho[(\rho[\![X_i]\!] \upharpoonright t_0)/X_i \mid i \in I \wedge i \notin N]$$

and appeal to lemma 3.31. We have assumed that P is t-constructive for each X_i, so it must be t-constructive for the finite vector $\langle X_i \mid i \in N \rangle$. Expanding definition 3.30, we discover that

$$\begin{aligned}\mathcal{F}_{TF}[\![P]\!]\rho'[\rho[\![X_i]\!]/X_i \mid i \in N] \upharpoonright t_0 + t &= \mathcal{F}_{TF}[\![P]\!]\rho'[\rho[\![X_i]\!] \upharpoonright t_0/X_i \mid i \in N] \upharpoonright t_0 + t \\ &= \mathcal{F}_{TF}[\![P]\!]\rho[\rho[\![X_i]\!] \upharpoonright t_0/X_i \mid i \in I] \upharpoonright t_0 + t\end{aligned}$$

and hence that (s, X) is an element of the right-hand side. A symmetric argument will establish the converse, completing the proof of the theorem. □

We may use this theorem to show that any mutual recursion in which the vector of terms is constructive for the vector of variables has a well-defined semantics.

Theorem 3.33 (Unique Fixed Point Theorem) If vector of terms $\underline{P}$ is constructive for vector of variables $\underline{X}$, then the mapping $M(\underline{X}, \underline{P})\rho$ has a unique fixed point in $\mathcal{S}_{TF}^{I}$.

Although the proof is quite involved, it is both important and instructive.

Proof We begin by defining a secondary vector of terms $\underline{Q}$ by transfinite recursion. We show that the mapping $M(\underline{X}, \underline{Q})\rho$ has a unique fixed point, and that this is also a fixed point of the mapping $M(\underline{X}, \underline{P})\rho$. We complete the proof by demonstrating that this fixed point is unique.

The vector of timed CSP terms $\underline{Q}$ is defined by

$$Q_i \;\widehat{=}\; P_i[Q_j/X_j \mid j \in \mathrm{seg}(i)]$$

The i component of $\underline{Q}$ is that of $\underline{P}$, with the following modification: we replace every variable with an index lower than i with the corresponding component of $\underline{Q}$.

Lemma A The vector $\underline{Q}$ is well-defined. This is an instance of the following theorem schema, established in Enderton (1977):

Transfinite Recursion Theorem If $\preceq$ is a well-ordering on I, and for any function f there is a unique y such that $\varphi(f, y)$ is true, then there exists a unique function F such that

$$\forall\, i : I \bullet \varphi(F \downharpoonright \mathrm{seg}(i), F(i))$$

and the domain of F is the whole of I.

We use this theorem to construct a function F of type $I \to (I \to \mathit{CSP})$. That is, a function from indices to vectors of timed CSP terms. We choose the formula φ carefully:

$$\varphi(f, y) \;\widehat{=}\; y = \underline{P}[f(j)_j/X_j \mid j \in \mathrm{dom}(f)]$$

This formula holds of (f, y) exactly when y is the vector obtained from $\underline{P}$ by replacing every occurrence of variable X_j, for every j in the domain of function f. Each term X_j is replaced with the j component of the vector $f(j)$. It is clear that this defines a unique y for every function f. If F is the φ-constructed function, then we define

$$Q_i \;\widehat{=}\; F(i)_i$$

yielding the required vector $\underline{Q}$

$$\begin{array}{rrcl} & F(i)_i & = & (\underline{P}[(F \downharpoonright \mathrm{seg}(i))(j)_j/X_j \mid j \in \mathrm{dom}(F \downharpoonright \mathrm{seg}(i))])_i \\ \Rightarrow & F(i)_i & = & (\underline{P}[Q_j/X_j \mid j \in \mathrm{seg}(i)])_i \\ \Rightarrow & Q_i & = & P_i[Q_j/X_j \mid j \in \mathrm{seg}(i)] \end{array}$$

Lemma B The mapping $M(\underline{X}, \underline{Q})\rho$ is a contraction mapping in $\mathcal{S}^I_{TF}$, and hence has a unique fixed point. By analogy with theorem 3.16, it is enough to show that there exists a strictly positive time t such that

$$\begin{array}{l} \forall\, \underline{S}, \underline{T} : \mathcal{S}^I_{TF} \;;\; t_0 : \mathit{TIME} \bullet \\ \qquad \underline{S} \upharpoonright t_0 = \underline{T} \upharpoonright t_0 \Rightarrow (M(\underline{X}, \underline{Q})\rho\; \underline{S}) \upharpoonright t_0 + t = (M(\underline{X}, \underline{Q})\rho\; \underline{T}) \upharpoonright t_0 + t \end{array}$$

To prove this, we will assume that $\underline{S} \upharpoonright t_0 = \underline{T} \upharpoonright t_0$ and deduce the consequent above, which is equivalent to

$$\mathcal{F}_{TF}[\![\underline{Q}]\!]\rho[\underline{S}/\underline{X}] \upharpoonright t_0 + t \quad = \quad \mathcal{F}_{TF}[\![\underline{Q}]\!]\rho[\underline{T}/\underline{X}] \upharpoonright t_0 + t$$

We will employ the following result:

Transfinite Induction Principle If $\preceq$ is a well-ordering on set I, and J is a subset of I with the property

$$\forall i : I \bullet \text{seg}(i) \subseteq J \Rightarrow i \in J$$

then J coincides with I.

We define J to be the set

$$J \;\widehat{=}\; \{i : I \mid \mathcal{F}_{TF}[\![Q_i]\!]\rho[\underline{S}/\underline{X}] \upharpoonright t_0 + t = \mathcal{F}_{TF}[\![Q_i]\!]\rho[\underline{T}/\underline{X}] \upharpoonright t_0 + t\}$$

and assume that $\text{seg}(i) \subseteq J$. To use the induction principle, we must show that $i \in J$: i.e.,

$$\mathcal{F}_{TF}[\![Q_i]\!]\rho_S \upharpoonright t_0 + t \quad = \quad \mathcal{F}_{TF}[\![Q_i]\!]\rho_T \upharpoonright t_0 + t$$

where

$$\begin{aligned} \rho_S &\;\widehat{=}\; \rho[\underline{S}/\underline{X}] \\ \rho_T &\;\widehat{=}\; \rho[\underline{T}/\underline{X}] \end{aligned}$$

From the definition of vector $\underline{Q}$, we obtain

$$\begin{aligned} \mathcal{F}_{TF}[\![Q_i]\!]\rho_S &= \mathcal{F}_{TF}[\![P_i[Q_j/X_j \mid j \in \text{seg}(i)]\!]\rho_S \\ &= \mathcal{F}_{TF}[\![P_i]\!]\rho_S[\mathcal{F}_{TF}[\![Q_j]\!]\rho_S/X_j \mid j \in \text{seg}(i)] \end{aligned}$$

A similar argument applies for ρ_T, and if we let

$$\begin{aligned} \rho'_S &\;\widehat{=}\; \rho_S[\mathcal{F}_{TF}[\![Q_j]\!]\rho_S/X_j \mid j \in \text{seg}(i)] \\ \rho'_T &\;\widehat{=}\; \rho_T[\mathcal{F}_{TF}[\![Q_j]\!]\rho_T/X_j \mid j \in \text{seg}(i)] \end{aligned}$$

we reduce our proof obligation to

$$\mathcal{F}_{TF}[\![P_i]\!]\rho'_S \upharpoonright t_0 + t \quad = \quad \mathcal{F}_{TF}[\![P_i]\!]\rho'_T \upharpoonright t_0 + t$$

We assume that (s, X) is an element of the left-hand side, and apply the first corollary to the Finite Dependency Theorem, corollary 3.29. In this case, there must exist a finite set N such that

$$(s, X) \;\in\; \mathcal{F}_{TF}[\![P_i]\!]\rho'_T[\rho'_S[\![X_k]\!]/X_k \mid k \in N]$$

We partition the set N into two sets, and give names to two useful vectors

$$\begin{array}{lcl} A & \widehat{=} & N \cap \mathrm{seg}(i) \\ B & \widehat{=} & N - \mathrm{seg}(i) \\ Y & \widehat{=} & \langle \mathcal{F}_{TF}[\![Q_j]\!]\rho_S \mid j \in I\rangle \\ Z & \widehat{=} & \langle \mathcal{F}_{TF}[\![Q_j]\!]\rho_T \mid j \in I\rangle \end{array}$$

and define, for each vector $\underline{V}$ in $\{\underline{X}, \underline{Y}, \underline{Z}\}$

$$\begin{array}{lcl} V_A & \widehat{=} & \langle V_i \mid i \in A\rangle \\ V_B & \widehat{=} & \langle V_i \mid i \in B\rangle \end{array}$$

Our inductive hypothesis can then be re-written as

$$\forall\, k : \mathrm{seg}(i) \;\bullet\; Y_k \upharpoonright t_0 + t = Z_k \upharpoonright t_0 + t$$

which implies that

$$Y_A \upharpoonright t_0 + t \;=\; Z_A \upharpoonright t_0 + t$$

All timed CSP terms are *0*-constructive for any variable, so by Theorem 3.32 all timed CSP terms are *0*-constructive for any vector. Applying this result to the terms Q_j, given that the vectors $\underline{S}$ and $\underline{T}$ agree up until time t_0, we obtain

$$Y_B \upharpoonright t_0 = Z_B \upharpoonright t_0$$

We recall our assumption about behaviour (s, X):

$$\begin{array}{lcl} (s, X) & \in & \mathcal{F}_{TF}[\![P_i]\!]\rho'_T[\rho'_S[\![X_k]\!]/X_k \mid k \in A][\rho'_S[\![X_k]\!]/X_k \mid k \in B] \\ & = & \mathcal{F}_{TF}[\![P_i]\!]\rho'_T[\mathcal{F}_{TF}[\![Q_k]\!]\rho_S/X_k \mid k \in A][\mathcal{F}_{TF}[\![Q_k]\!]\rho_S/X_k \mid k \in B] \\ & = & \mathcal{F}_{TF}[\![P_i]\!]\rho'_T[Y_A/X_A][Y_B/X_B] \end{array}$$

Again, any timed CSP term is *0*-constructive for any vector, so P_i is *0*-constructive for X_A. Hence

$$\mathcal{F}_{TF}[\![P_i]\!]\rho'_T[Y_A/X_A][Y_B/X_B] \upharpoonright t_0 + t \;=\; \mathcal{F}_{TF}[\![P_i]\!]\rho'_T[Z_A/X_A][Y_B/X_B] \upharpoonright t_0 + t$$

Further, vector $\underline{P}$ is t-constructive, so term P_i is t-constructive for any X_j with $j \notin \mathrm{seg}(i)$. By Theorem 3.32, P_i is t-constructive for vector X_B. Hence

$$\begin{array}{lcl} \mathcal{F}_{TF}[\![P_i]\!]\rho'_T[Z_A/X_A][Y_B/X_B] \upharpoonright t_0 + t & = & \mathcal{F}_{TF}[\![P_i]\!]\rho'_T[Z_A/X_A][Z_B/X_B] \upharpoonright t_0 + t \\ & = & \mathcal{F}_{TF}[\![P_i]\!]\rho'_T \upharpoonright t_0 + t \end{array}$$

Remembering that $\mathit{end}(s, X) < t_0 + t$, we have established that

$$(s, X) \;\in\; \mathcal{F}_{TF}[\![P_i]\!]\rho'_T \upharpoonright t_0 + t$$

The argument is symmetrical in S and T, and hence

$$\begin{array}{rcl} \mathcal{F}_{TF}[\![P_i]\!]\rho'_S \upharpoonright t_0 + t & = & \mathcal{F}_{TF}[\![P_i]\!]\rho'_T \upharpoonright t_0 + t \\ (\Rightarrow \ \mathcal{F}_{TF}[\![Q_i]\!]\rho_S \upharpoonright t_0 + t & = & \mathcal{F}_{TF}[\![Q_i]\!]\rho_T \upharpoonright t_0 + t\ ) \end{array}$$

and we see that $i \in J$. By transfinite induction

$$\mathcal{F}_{TF}[\![\underline{Q}]\!]\rho[\underline{S}/\underline{X}] \upharpoonright t_0 + t \quad = \quad \mathcal{F}_{TF}[\![\underline{Q}]\!]\rho[\underline{T}/\underline{X}] \upharpoonright t_0 + t$$

We conclude that $M(\underline{X}, \underline{Q})\rho$ is a contraction mapping, with a unique fixed point.

Lemma C The unique fixed point of $M(\underline{X}, \underline{Q})\rho$ is a fixed point of $M(\underline{X}, \underline{P})\rho$. To see this, let $\underline{S}$ be the unique fixed point of $M(\underline{X}, \underline{Q})\rho$, and observe that

$$\begin{array}{rl} & (M(\underline{X}, \underline{P})\rho\ (\underline{S}))_i \\ = & (\mathcal{F}_{TF}[\![\underline{P}]\!]\rho[\underline{S}/\underline{X}])_i \\ = & (\mathcal{F}_{TF}[\![\underline{P}]\!]\rho[(M(\underline{X}, \underline{Q})\rho\ (\underline{S}))_j/X_j \mid j \in \mathrm{seg}(i)][S_j/X_j \mid j \notin \mathrm{seg}(i)])_i \\ = & \mathcal{F}_{TF}[\![P_i]\!]\rho[(M(\underline{X}, \underline{Q})\rho\ (\underline{S}))_j/X_j \mid j \in \mathrm{seg}(i)][S_j/X_j \mid j \notin \mathrm{seg}(i)] \\ = & \mathcal{F}_{TF}[\![P_i]\!]\rho[\mathcal{F}_{TF}[\![Q_j]\!]\rho[\underline{S}/\underline{X}]/X_j \mid j \in \mathrm{seg}(i)][S_j/X_j \mid j \notin \mathrm{seg}(i)] \\ = & \mathcal{F}_{TF}[\![P_i[Q_j/X_j \mid j \in \mathrm{seg}(i)]]\!]\rho[\underline{S}/\underline{X}] \\ = & \mathcal{F}_{TF}[\![Q_i]\!]\rho[\underline{S}/\underline{X}] \\ = & (M(\underline{X}, \underline{Q})\rho\ (\underline{S}))_i \\ = & S_i \end{array}$$

Hence, as this holds for every $i \in I$, we have that

$$M(\underline{X}, \underline{P})\rho\ (\underline{S}) \quad = \quad \underline{S}$$

establishing that $\underline{S}$ is a fixed point of $M(\underline{X}, \underline{P})\rho$.

Lemma D The above fixed point ($\underline{S}$) is the only fixed point of $M(\underline{X}, \underline{P})\rho$. We know that there is a positive time t such that $\underline{P}$ is t-constructive for $\underline{X}$. Let $\underline{T}$ be an arbitrary fixed point of $M(\underline{X}, \underline{P})\rho$, and define a counterexample set C

$$\begin{array}{rcl} C & \widehat{=} & \{k : I \mid \exists\, t_0 \bullet j \in \mathrm{seg}(k) \Rightarrow T_j \upharpoonright (t_0 + t) = S_j \upharpoonright (t_0 + t) \\ & & \qquad\qquad \wedge \\ & & \qquad\qquad T_k \upharpoonright (t_0 + t) \neq S_k \upharpoonright (t_0 + t) \\ & & \qquad\qquad \wedge \\ & & \qquad\qquad j \notin \mathrm{seg}(k) \Rightarrow T_j \upharpoonright t_0 = S_j \upharpoonright t_0 \end{array}$$

Then C is the set of indices k such that the two vectors $\underline{S}$ and $\underline{T}$ first become different at component k between times t_0 and $t_0 + t$, agree on all components indexed from $\mathrm{seg}(k)$ up until time $t_0 + t$, and agree on all other components up until time t_0. We claim that

$$C = \{\} \quad \Rightarrow \quad \underline{S} = \underline{T}$$

To show this, we establish the contrapositive of the result, by assuming that $\underline{S} \neq \underline{T}$. Define a sequence of indices i_n from I and a sequence of times t_n such that

$$\begin{array}{rcl} i_0 & \in & \{i : I \mid S_i \neq T_i \wedge j \in \text{seg}(i) \Rightarrow S_j = T_j\} \\ t_0 & = & t + sup\{t' \mid S_{i_0} \upharpoonright t' = T_{i_0} \upharpoonright t'\} \\ i_{n+1} & \in & \{i : I \mid S_i \upharpoonright t_n \neq T_i \upharpoonright t_n \wedge j \in \text{seg}(i) \Rightarrow S_j \upharpoonright t_n = T_j \upharpoonright t_n\} \\ t_{n+1} & = & t_n - t \end{array}$$

Observe that i_0 exists, and that t_0 is therefore finite. We are assuming that $\underline{S}$ differs at some point from $\underline{T}$, and hence (as the index set I is well-ordered) there will be a least index i_0 where the two vectors differ. Either i_n exists for all $n : \mathbb{N}$, in which case

$$\forall n : \mathbb{N} \bullet t_0 - nt > 0$$

which contradicts the fact that t_0 is finite, or there is a n such that i_n exists but i_{n+1} does not. In this case, $i_n \in C$ and so C is not empty, as required. This establishes our claim.

We have now to prove that the set C is empty. To do this, we assume for a contradiction that $k \in C$, then we know that

$$\begin{array}{rl} \exists\, t_0 \bullet & T_k \upharpoonright t_0 + t \neq S_k \upharpoonright t_0 + t \\ & \wedge\, j \in \text{seg}(k) \Rightarrow T_j \upharpoonright t_0 + t = S_j \upharpoonright t_0 + t \\ & \wedge\, j \notin \text{seg}(k) \Rightarrow T_j \upharpoonright t_0 = S_j \upharpoonright t_0 \end{array}$$

The vector $\underline{P}$ is t-constructive for $\underline{X}$, hence

$$j \notin \text{seg}(k) \Rightarrow P_k \text{ is } t\text{-constructive for } X_j$$

Applying lemma 3.3 we have that, for $j \notin \text{seg}(k)$,

$$S_j \upharpoonright t_0 = T_j \upharpoonright t_0 \quad \Rightarrow \quad \mathcal{F}_{TF}[\![P_k]\!]\rho[S_j/X_j] \upharpoonright t_0 + t = \mathcal{F}_{TF}[\![P_k]\!]\rho[T_j/X_j] \upharpoonright t_0 + t$$

and recalling that P_k must be 0-constructive for all X_j, we obtain

$$\forall j : I \bullet \mathcal{F}_{TF}[\![P_k]\!]\rho[S_j/X_j] \upharpoonright t_0 + t = \mathcal{F}_{TF}[\![P_k]\!]\rho[T_j/X_j] \upharpoonright t_0 + t$$

We may now apply Theorem 3.32. This gives us that

$$\mathcal{F}_{TF}[\![P_k]\!]\rho[\underline{S}/\underline{X}] \upharpoonright t_0 + t \quad = \quad \mathcal{F}_{TF}[\![P_k]\!]\rho[\underline{T}/\underline{X}] \upharpoonright t_0 + t$$

We have also that $\underline{S}$ is a fixed point of $M(\underline{X}, \underline{P})\rho$. In this case

$$\begin{array}{rrcl} & M(\underline{X}, \underline{P})\rho\ \underline{S} & = & \underline{S} \\ \Rightarrow & \lambda\, \underline{Y} \bullet \mathcal{F}_{TF}[\![\underline{P}]\!]\rho[\underline{Y}/\underline{X}]\ \underline{S} & = & \underline{S} \\ \Rightarrow & \mathcal{F}_{TF}[\![\underline{P}]\!]\rho[\underline{S}/\underline{X}] & = & \underline{S} \\ \Rightarrow & \mathcal{F}_{TF}[\![P_k]\!]\rho[\underline{S}/\underline{X}] & = & S_k \end{array}$$

and a similar result holds for the other fixed point, $\underline{T}$. Hence

$$S_k \upharpoonright t_0 = T_k \upharpoonright t_0 \quad \Rightarrow \quad S_k \upharpoonright t_0 + t = T_k \upharpoonright t_0 + t$$

which contradicts our choice of $k \in C$. Hence the set C is empty. By our earlier claim, this means that the two vectors $\underline{S}$ and $\underline{T}$ are identical. Hence $\underline{S}$ is the only fixed point of $M(\underline{X}, \underline{P})\rho$.

To summarise: the secondary vector $\underline{Q}$ is well-defined, and corresponds to a contraction mapping in the semantic model; the unique fixed point of this mapping is a fixed point of $M(\underline{X}, \underline{P})\rho$, the mapping corresponding to $\underline{P}$ and $\underline{X}$; further, it is the *only* fixed point of this mapping. We may conclude that, although the mapping corresponding to $\underline{P}$ need not be contraction mapping, it has a unique fixed point in $\mathcal{S}^I_{TF}$. □

From this result, we may deduce the welcome corollary:

Corollary 3.34 If vector of terms $\underline{P}$ is constructive for vector of variables $\underline{X}$, then the recursion $\mu\,\underline{X} \circ \underline{P}$ is well-defined.

This justifies our definition of *constructive*, and lays the foundation for the theory of recursion induction presented in chapter 5.

3.6 EQUATION SETS

Consider the following mutual recursion:

$$\begin{aligned} P &= a \xrightarrow{1} Q \\ Q &= b \xrightarrow{1} P \end{aligned}$$

It should be obvious that

$$P \;=\; a \xrightarrow{1} b \xrightarrow{1} P$$

We can derive rules that allow us to make such transformations while preserving the semantics of the term defined by the equation set. For example, we may wish to replace all free occurrences of a recursive variable.

Rule 3.35 (Substitution) If the equation $X_k = P_k$ has a unique solution in $\mathcal{S}_{TF}$, and appears in $\langle X_i = P_i \rangle$, then we may substitute $\mu\, X_k \circ P_k$ for all free occurrences of X_k in all equations of the equation set. Formally,

$$\langle X_i = P_i \rangle_j \;\equiv\; \langle X_i = P_i[\mu\, X_k \circ P_k / X_k] \rangle_j$$

Proof If $X_k = P_k$ has a unique solution in $\mathcal{M}_{TF}$, and $\underline{S}$ is a fixed point of $M(\underline{X}, \underline{P})$, then we know that

$$\mathcal{F}_{TF}[\![P_k]\!]\rho[\underline{S}/\underline{X}][\mathcal{F}_{TF}[\![\,\mu\, X_k \circ P_k]\!]\rho[\underline{S}/\underline{X}]/X_k] \quad = \quad S_k$$

To see this, observe that

$$\begin{aligned} S_k &= (M(\underline{X}, \underline{P})\rho\ \underline{S})_k \\ &= \mathcal{F}_{TF}[\![P_k]\!]\rho[\underline{S}/\underline{X}] \\ &= \mathcal{F}_{TF}[\![P_k]\!]\rho[\underline{S}/\underline{X}][S_k/X_k] \end{aligned}$$

Hence S_k is the fixed point of the function $M(X_k, P_k)\rho[\underline{S}/\underline{X}]$, and is therefore equal to

$$\mathcal{F}_{TF}[\![\,\mu\, X_k \circ P_k]\!]\rho[\underline{S}/\underline{X}] \quad = \quad \mathcal{F}_{TF}[\![P_k]\!]\rho[\underline{S}/\underline{X}][\mathcal{F}_{TF}[\![\,\mu\, X_k \circ P_k]\!]\rho[\underline{S}/\underline{X}]$$

Assuming that $\underline{S}$ is a fixed point of $M(\underline{X}, \underline{P})\rho$, we define $\underline{Q}$ to be the vector obtained by substituting $\mu\, X_k \circ P_k$ for all free occurrences of X_k in the vector $\underline{P}$.

$$\begin{aligned} (M(\underline{X}, \underline{Q})\rho\ \underline{S})_j &= \mathcal{F}_{TF}[\![P_j[\mu\, X_k \circ P_k/X_k]]\!]\rho[\underline{S}/\underline{X}] \\ &= \mathcal{F}_{TF}[\![P_j]\!]\rho[\underline{S}/\underline{X}][\mathcal{F}_{TF}[\![\,\mu\, X_k \circ P_k]\!]\rho[\underline{S}/\underline{X}]/X_k] \\ &= \mathcal{F}_{TF}[\![P_j]\!]\rho[\underline{S}/\underline{X}][S_k/X_k] \\ &= S_j \end{aligned}$$

Conversely, if $\underline{T}$ is a fixed point of the function $M(\underline{X}, \underline{Q})\rho$, then

$$\mathcal{F}_{TF}[\![\,\mu\, X_k \circ P_k]\!]\rho[\underline{T}/\underline{X}] \quad = \quad T_k$$

To see this, observe that

$$\begin{aligned} T_k &= (M(\underline{X}, \underline{Q})\rho\ \underline{T})_k \\ &= \mathcal{F}_{TF}[\![Q_k]\!]\rho[\underline{T}/\underline{X}] \\ &= \mathcal{F}_{TF}[\![P_k[\mu\, X_k \circ P_k/X_k]]\!]\rho[\underline{T}/\underline{X}] \\ &= \mathcal{F}_{TF}[\![\,\mu\, X_k \circ P_k]\!]\rho[\underline{T}/\underline{X}] \end{aligned}$$

Assuming that $\underline{T}$ is a fixed point of $M(\underline{X}, \underline{Q})\rho$, we have that

$$\begin{aligned} (M(\underline{X}, \underline{P})\rho\ \underline{T})_j &= \mathcal{F}_{TF}[\![P_j]\!]\rho[\underline{T}/\underline{X}] \\ &= \mathcal{F}_{TF}[\![P_j]\!]\rho[\underline{T}/\underline{X}][T_k/X_k] \\ &= \mathcal{F}_{TF}[\![P_j]\!]\rho[\underline{T}/\underline{X}][\mathcal{F}_{TF}[\![\,\mu\, X_k \circ P_k]\!]\rho[\underline{T}/\underline{X}]/X_k] \\ &= \mathcal{F}_{TF}[\![P_j[\mu\, X_k \circ P_k/X_k]]\!]\rho[\underline{T}/\underline{X}] \\ &= \mathcal{F}_{TF}[\![Q_j]\!]\rho[\underline{T}/\underline{X}] \\ &= T_j \end{aligned}$$

We have demonstrated that a vector U is a fixed point of $M(\underline{X}, \underline{P})\rho$ if and only if it is a fixed point of $M(\underline{X}, \underline{Q})\rho$. The soundness of the rewrite rule follows immediately. □

The presence of *0*-constructive terms in an equation set may mean that there is more than one solution to the equations. In this case, the semantics of the recursion is not well-defined. However, if the offending terms do not affect the semantics of the selected component, we can rewrite the equation set to eliminate them. For example, in the equation set

$$\begin{aligned} P &= a \xrightarrow{1} P \\ Q &= P \sqcap Q \end{aligned}$$

recursive variable Q does not appear free in the term part of the first equation. We may remove the second equation from the equation set without affecting the P component of the solution. In this way, we may delete unnecessary or undesirable equations from our equation set. We capture this result as a proof rule:

Rule 3.36 (Elimination)

$$\frac{\forall j : J \bullet \forall i : (I - J) \bullet X_i \text{ is not free in } P_j}{\langle X_i = P_i \mid i \in I \rangle_k \equiv \langle X_i = P_i \mid i \in J \rangle_k} \quad [\, k \in J \wedge J \subseteq I \,]$$

In a set of equations indexed by I, we may eliminate those equations

$$X_i = P_i$$

for which X_i does not occur free in any of the terms $P_j \mid j \in J$, where J indexes the set of remaining equations. This is enough to ensure that the semantics of the remaining components is preserved: that

$$\langle X_i = P_i \mid i \in I \rangle_k = \langle X_i = P_i \mid i \in J \rangle_k$$

whenever $k \in J$.

Proof Suppose that $\underline{S}$ is a fixed point of the function $M(\underline{X}, \underline{P})\rho$, where $\underline{P}$ and $\underline{X}$ are indexed by I. Let $\underline{X}'$, $\underline{P}'$ and $\underline{S}'$ be the corresponding vectors indexed by set J.

$$\begin{aligned} S'_j &= S_j \\ &= \mathcal{F}_{TF}[\![P_j]\!]\rho[\underline{S}/\underline{X}] \\ &= \mathcal{F}_{TF}[\![P_j]\!]\rho[\underline{S}'/\underline{X}'] \\ &= (M(\underline{X}', \underline{P}')\rho\, S')_j \end{aligned}$$

Hence, any solution to the equation set $\langle X_i = P_i \rangle$ gives rise to a solution of the set $\langle X'_i = P'_i \rangle$. This is enough to establish the soundness of the rule. □

Returning to the example at the beginning of this section, we may now establish that the two definitions of P given below are equivalent:

$$\begin{aligned} P &\mathrel{\widehat{=}} a \xrightarrow{1} Q \\ Q &\mathrel{\widehat{=}} b \xrightarrow{1} P \end{aligned} \qquad\qquad P \mathrel{\widehat{=}} a \xrightarrow{1} b \xrightarrow{1} P$$

We begin by writing the left-hand definition in vector form:

$$P \mathrel{\hat{=}} \left\langle \begin{array}{lcl} X_1 & = & a \xrightarrow{1} X_2 \\ X_2 & = & b \xrightarrow{1} X_1 \end{array} \right\rangle_1$$

From lemma 3.5, we know that $b \xrightarrow{1} X_1$ is constructive for X_2, hence the second equation has a unique solution in $\mathcal{S}_{TF}$. Applying the rule 3.35, we obtain

$$P = \left\langle \begin{array}{lcl} X_1 & = & a \xrightarrow{1} (\mu\, X_2 \circ b \xrightarrow{1} X_1) \\ X_2 & = & b \xrightarrow{1} X_1 \end{array} \right\rangle_1$$

and X_2 is not free in any of the right-hand terms, rule 3.36 gives us that

$$\begin{array}{lcl} P & = & \left\langle X_1 = a \xrightarrow{1} (\mu\, X_2 \circ b \xrightarrow{1} X_1) \right\rangle_1 \\ & = & \left\langle X_1 = a \xrightarrow{1} b \xrightarrow{1} X_1 \right\rangle_1 \\ & = & (\mu \langle X_1 \rangle \circ \langle a \xrightarrow{1} b \xrightarrow{1} X_1 \rangle)_1 \\ & = & \mu\, X_1 \circ a \xrightarrow{1} b \xrightarrow{1} X_1 \end{array}$$

We may then apply corollary 3.18, yielding

$$P = a \xrightarrow{1} b \xrightarrow{1} P$$

as required. From this example, it is clear that the following derived rule will be useful:

Rule 3.37 Given the equation set $\langle X_i = P_i \rangle_j$, where X_k does not occur free in P_k, we may substitute P_k for all free occurrences of X_k in the remaining equations of the equation set, and remove $X_k = P_k$ from the equation set. Formally,

$$\langle X_i = P_i \rangle_j = \langle X_i = P_i[P_k / X_k \mid i \neq k] \rangle_j$$

providing that $j \neq k$.

Proof This rule follows easily from rules 3.35 and 3.36. □

3.7 EXAMPLES

Consider the timed sensitive vending machine of section 2.9:

$$\begin{array}{lcl} TSVM & \mathrel{\hat{=}} & coin \xrightarrow{t_1} (reset \xrightarrow{t_3} TSVM \\ & & \qquad \overset{t_2}{\rhd} \\ & & \quad PAID) \\ PAID & \mathrel{\hat{=}} & coke \xrightarrow{t_4} TVSM \end{array}$$

This process is defined by a set of mutually recursive equations, in which the vector of terms is uniformly constructive for the vector of variables. To see this, observe that the terms

$$coin \xrightarrow{t_1} (reset \xrightarrow{t_3} TSVM \overset{t_2}{\rhd} PAID) \qquad \text{and} \qquad coke \xrightarrow{t_4} TVSM$$

are both $min\{t_1, t_4\}$-constructive for any variable, by lemma 3.5. We may conclude that this mutual recursion has a well-defined semantics.

We may apply rule 3.37 to eliminate the second equation

$$TSVM \;\widehat{=}\; coin \xrightarrow{t_1} (reset \xrightarrow{t_3} TSVM \overset{t_2}{\rhd} coke \xrightarrow{t_4} TSVM)$$

and rewrite the process definition as a single recursion.

As an example of a mutual recursion in which the term vector is constructive but not uniformly constructive, consider the process *POINTER* defined by

$$POINTER \;\widehat{=}\; POINTER_0$$

$$POINTER_0 \;\widehat{=}\; incr \xrightarrow{1} POINTER_1$$

$$POINTER_{n+1} \;\widehat{=}\; incr \xrightarrow{1} POINTER_{n+2} \;\sqcap\; POINTER_n$$

where index n is drawn from the set of natural numbers $\mathbb{N}$. The form of the equations prevents the application of rules 3.35 and 3.36; an infinite number of substitutions would be required.

However, the term corresponding to $POINTER_{n+1}$ is 1-constructive for any instance of $POINTER_{n+m}$, whenever $m \geqslant 1$. With the usual ordering on the natural numbers, we may establish that the vector of terms is constructive for the vector of variables. If X_n denotes the nth element of the variable vector, and P_n denotes the nth element of the term vector, then

$$\forall\, i, j : \mathbb{N} \;\bullet\; j \geqslant i \Rightarrow P_i \text{ is constructive for } X_j$$

This is precisely the condition for $\underline{P}$ to be constructive for $\underline{X}$. We conclude that this mutual recursion has a well-defined semantics.

4 SPECIFICATION

4.1 BEHAVIOURAL SPECIFICATIONS

A *specification* of a system is a formal description of its intended behaviour. In our denotational models, the semantics of a process is the set of all possible behaviours of that process; we may write specifications as predicates upon these semantic sets. In the timed failures model, each behaviour is recorded as a timed failure: a trace of events performed, and a set of events refused. Reed (1988) defines a specification A as a mapping from the model $\mathcal{M}_{TF}$ to $\{true, false\}$: the space of truth values. The specification A holds for a process P if and only if

$$A(\mathcal{F}_{TF}[\![P]\!]\rho) \quad = \quad true$$

We choose instead to define predicates upon a typical element of the semantic set of a process: these are *behavioural specifications*.

In the timed failures model, a behavioural specification is a predicate $S(s, X)$, with free variables s and X representing the two components of a possible behaviour. We say that a term P satisfies a behavioural specification $S(s, X)$ in environment ρ if predicate S holds of every behaviour of P. Formally,

Definition 4.1

$$P \ \mathbf{sat}_\rho \ S(s, X) \quad \widehat{=} \quad \forall s, X \bullet (s, X) \in \mathcal{F}_{TF}[\![P]\!]\rho \Rightarrow S(s, X)$$

If P is a process, then we may omit the environment parameter to obtain the familiar satisfaction notation of Hoare (1985):

Definition 4.2

$$P \ \mathbf{sat} \ S(s, X) \quad \widehat{=} \quad \forall \rho, s, X \bullet (s, X) \in \mathcal{F}_{TF}[\![P]\!]\rho \Rightarrow S(s, X)$$

Reed's approach is more powerful: for every statement of the form $P\ \mathbf{sat}_\rho\ S(s, X)$ there is a mapping A_S from $\mathcal{M}_{TF}$ to $\{true, false\}$ given by

$$A_S(Y) \ \widehat{=}\ \forall s, X \bullet (s, X) \in Y \bullet S(s, X)$$

such that the following equivalence holds

$$P\ \mathbf{sat}_\rho\ S(s, X) \ \equiv\ A_S(\mathcal{F}_{TF}[\![P]\!]\rho)$$

and some of Reed's statements cannot be expressed with the satisfaction notation. For example, consider the predicate A given by:

$$A(Y) \ \widehat{=}\ \exists s, X \bullet (s, X) \in Y \wedge a \in \sigma(s)$$

This requires that event a is a possible observation of any process represented by set Y in $\mathcal{M}_{TF}$. There is no behavioural specification S such that

$$P\ \mathbf{sat}_\rho\ S(s, X) \ \equiv\ A(\mathcal{F}_{TF}[\![P]\!]\rho)$$

Reed's approach permits a more detailed analysis of the process semantics; ours is more suitable for the capture of process requirements. A behavioural specification is satisfied only when every behaviour of a term is acceptable. A statement of the form $P\ \mathbf{sat}\ S(s, X)$ is a guarantee of satisfactory behaviour.

4.1.1 Example

As an example of a behavioural specification, consider the following requirement upon a cash dispenser *CASH*: that it should not allow a user to make more than one withdrawal in any twenty-four hour period. We choose the event $u.cash$ to represent a withdrawal by user u, where u is drawn from a set of all possible users, *USER*. We capture this requirement as follows:

$$CASH\ \ \mathbf{sat}\ \ \forall u : USER\ ; I : TI \bullet \\ length(I) > 24 \Rightarrow \#(s \uparrow I \restriction u.cash) \leqslant 1$$

Given any user u, if we consider the events observed during any interval of time longer than twenty-four hours, then there should be no more than one occurrence of the event $u.cash$; the length of the trace s during interval I restricted to this event should be no greater than 1.

The number of occurrences of a given event is a useful quantity. To simplify future specifications, we define a counting operator

$$s \downarrow A \ \widehat{=}\ \#(s \restriction A)$$

to yield the number of occurrences of events from set A in trace s. As usual, if A is a singleton set, we will omit the set braces.

4.1.2 Satisfiable specifications

We say that a behavioural specification is *satisfiable* if there exists a timed CSP process that satisfies it.

Definition 4.3 If $S(s, X)$ is a behavioural specification, then S is satisfiable in the model $\mathcal{M}_{TF}$ if and only if

$$\exists\, Y : \mathcal{S}_{TF} \;\bullet\; Y \in \mathcal{M}_{TF} \;\wedge\; \forall\, s, X \bullet (s, X) \in Y \Rightarrow S(s, X)$$

As we shall see in chapter 9, the existing syntax of timed CSP is not enough to implement all of the processes in $\mathcal{M}_{TF}$. Our definition of *satisfiable* allows for further additions to the syntax, or a strengthening of the axiom set. We may demonstrate that a specification is satisfiable by exhibiting a suitable piece of syntax:

Lemma 4.4 If $S(s, X)$ is a behavioural specification such that

$$\exists\, P : CSP \;\bullet\; P \textbf{ sat } S(s, X)$$

then $S(s, X)$ is satisfiable.

This result will be useful in chapter 5, when we consider the theory of recursion induction. To show that a recursive process meets a satisfiable behavioural specification S, we have only to show that S is preserved by each recursive call.

In applying timed CSP to the specification and development of a real-time system, we would prefer to identify specifications that are not satisfiable before suggesting an implementation. The axioms of the semantic model give rise to necessary conditions for a specification to be satisfiable. For example,

Lemma 4.5 If $S(s, X)$ is satisfiable, then $S(\langle\rangle, \{\})$.

Proof From definition 4.3:

$$\exists\, Y : \mathcal{S}_{TF} \;\bullet\; Y \in \mathcal{M}_{TF} \wedge \forall (s, X) \bullet (s, X) \in Y \Rightarrow S(s, X)$$

From the first axiom of the semantic model given in 2.3, we have that:

$$\exists\, Y : \mathcal{S}_{TF} \;\bullet\; (\langle\rangle, \{\}) \in Y \wedge \forall (s, X) \bullet (s, X) \in Y \Rightarrow S(s, X)$$

The result follows immediately. □

Any satisfiable behavioural specification must be true of the empty behaviour, which is a possible behaviour of every process. As a result, such specifications may not insist that a certain timed event appears in a trace or refusal, without a qualifying assumption. A more surprising result is:

Lemma 4.6 If $S(s, X)$ is a behavioural specification such that

$$\exists\, e : TE \;\bullet\; S(s, X) \Rightarrow e \notin X$$

then $S(s, X)$ is not satisfiable.

Proof Suppose for a contradiction that $S(s, X)$ is satisfiable, and that there exists a timed event e for which

$$S(s, X) \;\Rightarrow\; e \notin X$$

Let Y be a process satisfying $S(s, X)$, and choose t and a such that $e = (t, a)$.

$$\begin{aligned}(s, X) \in Y \;&\Rightarrow\; S(s, X)\\ &\Rightarrow\; (t, a) \notin X\end{aligned}$$

From the fourth axiom of the semantic model, given in section 2.3, we obtain

$$\begin{aligned}(s, X) \in Y \;\Rightarrow\; &\exists\, X' : TR \bullet X \subseteq X' \wedge (s, X') \in Y \wedge\\ &((t, a) \notin X' \Rightarrow (s \upharpoonright t ^\frown \langle (t, a) \rangle, X' \upharpoonright t) \in Y)\end{aligned}$$

If an event a is excluded from all refusal sets at time t, then it must be possible for a to occur at that time. We know that (t, a) is excluded from all refusal sets of process Y, hence we have that

$$\begin{aligned}(s, X) \in Y \;\Rightarrow\; &\exists\, X' : TR \bullet X \subseteq X' \wedge (s, X') \in Y \wedge\\ &(s \upharpoonright t ^\frown \langle (t, a) \rangle, X' \upharpoonright t) \in Y\end{aligned}$$

From the first axiom of $\mathcal{M}_{TF}$ we know that the empty behaviour $(\langle\rangle, \{\})$ is present in Y. With this choice for (s, X), the above implication yields that

$$\exists\, X : TR \;\bullet\; (\langle\rangle, X) \in Y \wedge (\langle (t, a) \rangle, X \upharpoonright t) \in Y$$

A simple induction will establish that, for any natural number n, the trace in which n copies of event a occur at time t is a possible trace of Y.

$$\exists\, X' : TR \;\bullet\; (\langle (t, a) \rangle^n, X' \upharpoonright t) \in Y$$

However, the bounded speed axiom of the semantic model places a natural number bound $n(t)$ on the number of events that may appear in any trace of Y before time t.

$$\forall\, t : [0, \infty) \;\bullet\; \exists\, n(t) : \mathbb{N} \bullet (s, X) \in S \wedge end(s) \leqslant t \Rightarrow \#(s) \leqslant n(t)$$

This forces a contradiction, and establishes the required result. □

It is always possible that a process will perform each observable event as soon as it becomes available. If process P makes n copies of event a available at time t, and it is offered $n + 1$ copies of a, then (t, a) will appear in the refusal set. Hence a satisfiable behavioural specification may not insist that a timed event is absent from the refusal set.

The first lemma shows that we cannot insist that an observable event occurs without making a qualifying assumption. This will be an assumption about the environment of the process; we will discuss such assumptions in section 4.3. Together, these lemmas dictate the form of safety and liveness specifications in the timed failures model.

4.2 SAFETY AND LIVENESS

We will follow the informal classification of safety and liveness properties suggested by Lamport (1977): a *safety property* is a requirement that 'nothing bad happens', while a *liveness property* insists that 'some good thing will occur'. In either case, we must exclude undesirable behaviours from the semantic set of the process in question. In our computational model, a safety property corresponds to the requirement that a given event may not occur except under certain conditions: e.g.

- event a does not occur within time t of event b;
- if event a occurs, it must do so within time t of event b;
- event a may occur only at specified times.

Some safety specifications require timed refusal information—we may insist that a given event is not performed unless another has been offered—but most can be captured as predicates on traces.

The lemmas of the previous section lead to the following restriction upon liveness specifications in timed CSP: we may insist only that certain timed events either occur or are made available. For example, the following constraints may be expressed as satisfiable liveness specifications:

- event a is possible at time 1;
- if the last event observed is b at time 1, then event a is available at all times after $1 + t$;
- if a has not occurred, then it is available.

Liveness properties are expressed as predicates on failures.

4.2.1 Safety specifications

Any safety specification on process Y may be written in the form

$$\forall\, s, X \;\bullet\; (s, X) \in Y \Rightarrow s \notin U$$

where U is some set of undesirable traces. If this specification is to be satisfiable, then the empty trace must be an acceptable behaviour. As a result, the deadlock process $STOP$ will satisfy any satisfiable safety specification.

We can use the operators defined in section 2.2 to construct simple safety specifications. For example, we may wish to specify that the events *tick* and *tock* occur alternately in any trace of $CLOCK$:

$$CLOCK \quad \textbf{sat} \quad (s \downarrow tick = s \downarrow tock) \vee (s \downarrow tick = s \downarrow tock + 1)$$

Recalling that $s \downarrow a$ denotes the number of occurrences of event a in trace s, we see that the process $CLOCK$ must perform a *tick* before every *tock*.

An event precondition for event a is a predicate that describes the process state necessary for a to occur. In timed CSP, any state information must be deduced from observable behaviours; we write event preconditions as predicates upon timed failures. As an example, consider the behavioural specification S defined by

$$S(s, X) \;\widehat{=}\; \langle(t, a)\rangle \;\underline{\text{in}}\; s \Rightarrow b \in \sigma(s \upharpoonright t - 1) \wedge a \notin \sigma(X \upharpoonright t)$$

This places the following precondition upon event a: if this event is observed at time t, then event b must be seen more than one time unit before t, and event a must be available up until time t. Event preconditions correspond closely to the notion of firing conditions in sequential state-based languages such as the Z notation.

Any event precondition upon event a can be written as a constraint upon the behaviour of the process up until the time at which a is observed:

$$\langle(t, a)\rangle \;\underline{\text{in}}\; s \quad \Rightarrow \quad C((s, X) \uparrow [0, t))$$

The prefix closure property of process behaviours allows us to simplify such specifications. From the second axiom of the semantic model, we know that if a appears in a trace s of process P, then there is another behaviour of P in which a is the last event observed.

Lemma 4.7 If P represents a process, then

$$P \quad \textbf{sat} \quad \langle(t, a)\rangle \;\underline{\text{in}}\; s \Rightarrow C((s, X) \uparrow [0, t))$$

if and only if

$$P \quad \textbf{sat} \quad foot(s) = (t, a) \Rightarrow C((s, X) \uparrow [0, t))$$

Proof The proof of *only if* is trivial. Conversely, assume that

$$P \quad \textbf{sat} \quad foot(s) = (t, a) \Rightarrow C((s, X) \uparrow [0, t))$$

and that

$$(s, X) \in \mathcal{F}_{TF}[\![P]\!] \quad \wedge \quad \langle(t, a)\rangle \;\underline{\text{in}}\; s$$

Choose trace w such that

$$s \uparrow [0,t) = w \uparrow [0,t) \;\wedge\; s \uparrow [t,\infty) \cong w \uparrow [t,\infty) \;\wedge\; foot(w \restriction t) = (t,a)$$

The third axiom of the semantic model (section 2.3) states that every process is closed under trace equivalence, so (w,X) is also present in the semantic set of P. From the second axiom of the semantic model we obtain:

$$((w \restriction t)^\frown(w \upharpoonright t), X) \in \mathcal{F}_{TF}[\![P]\!] \;\Rightarrow\; (w \restriction t, X \restriction begin(w \upharpoonright t)) \in \mathcal{F}_{TF}[\![P]\!]$$

Applying the first of our assumptions to the failure $(w \restriction t, X \restriction begin(w \upharpoonright t))$, we may conclude that

$$C((w \restriction t, X \restriction (begin(w \upharpoonright t))) \uparrow [0,t))$$

By our choice of w, and the properties of before, after and during:

$$\begin{aligned}(w \restriction t, X \restriction (begin(w \upharpoonright t))) \uparrow [0,t) &= (w,X) \uparrow [0,t)\\ &= (s,X) \uparrow [0,t)\end{aligned}$$

hence we have established that

$$C((s,X) \uparrow [0,t))$$

We may conclude that the two specifications are equivalent. □

A behavioural specification must be satisfied by every behaviour of a process, so it is sufficient to consider the case in which a is the last event observed. The exclusion of trace information at time t is important; our intuition concerning cause and effect excludes information about events at time t from a precondition for the timed event (t,a).

4.2.2 Liveness specifications

In our model of computation, a process and its environment cooperate on all observable actions. The visible events of a timed CSP process represent an interface with the environment. Without some knowledge of the environment, we may not insist that a process performs an event at a particular time. We express liveness conditions as requirements on the availability of events, ensuring that the process will perform an event if the environment should agree.

In section 4.1, we saw that we cannot require that an event a is available at a particular time t without considering trace information. If an event occurs as soon as it becomes available, its availability may not be recorded. As a result, liveness conditions may take the form

$$a \notin \sigma(X \uparrow I) \;\vee\; a \in \sigma(s \uparrow J)$$

The event a is made available throughout some interval I unless it occurs during some interval J.

Lemma 4.8 If the behavioural specification $S(s, X)$ defined by

$$S(s, X) \;\widehat{=}\; a \notin \sigma(X \uparrow I) \;\vee\; a \in \sigma(s \uparrow J)$$

is satisfiable, then $I \subseteq J$.

Proof Suppose for a contradiction that S is satisfied by a process Y, and that there exists a time $t \in I - J$. We observe that

$$S(s, X) \;\Rightarrow\; a \notin \sigma(X \uparrow t) \;\vee\; a \in \sigma(s \uparrow J)$$

From our assumption that Y satisfies $S(s, X)$, we may conclude that

$$(s, X) \in Y \wedge a \notin \sigma(s \uparrow J) \;\Rightarrow\; a \notin \sigma(X \uparrow t)$$

The fourth axiom of the semantic model states that

$$\begin{aligned}(s, X) \in Y \;\Rightarrow\; & \exists X' : TR \bullet X \subseteq X' \wedge (s, X') \in Y \wedge \\ & ((t, a) \notin X' \Rightarrow (s \upharpoonright t \frown \langle (t, a) \rangle, X' \upharpoonright t) \in Y)\end{aligned}$$

Combining these properties, we obtain

$$(s, X) \in Y \wedge a \notin \sigma(s \uparrow J) \;\Rightarrow\; \exists X' : TR \bullet (s \upharpoonright t \frown \langle (t, a) \rangle, X' \upharpoonright t) \in Y$$

From the first axiom of $\mathcal{M}_{TF}$ we know that the empty behaviour $(\langle\rangle, \{\})$ is present in Y. With this choice for (s, X), the above implication yields that

$$\exists X : TR \;\bullet\; (\langle\rangle, X) \in Y \wedge (\langle (t, a) \rangle, X \upharpoonright t) \in Y$$

As in the proof of lemma 4.6, a simple induction will establish that for any natural number n:

$$\exists X' : TR \;\bullet\; (\langle (t, a) \rangle^n, X' \upharpoonright t) \in Y$$

The bounded speed axiom of the semantic model places a natural number bound $n(t)$ on the number of events that may appear in any trace of Y before time t.

$$\forall t : [0, \infty) \;\bullet\; \exists n(t) : \mathbb{N} \bullet (s, X) \in S \wedge end(s) \leqslant t \Rightarrow \#(s) \leqslant n(t)$$

Again, this forces a contradiction, and establishes the required result. □

As an example of a liveness specification, consider the case of an electronic lock $LOCK$. If a key is inserted, then the lock must permit the door to be opened after five seconds. If *open* represents the act of opening the door, and *key* represents a key insertion, then this requirement may be written as follows:

$$\begin{aligned} LOCK \;\; \textbf{sat} \;\; \langle (t, key) \rangle \; \underline{\text{in}} \; s \Rightarrow \; & open \notin \sigma(X \uparrow t + 5) \\ & \vee \\ & open \in \sigma(s \uparrow t) \end{aligned}$$

For simplicity, we have assumed that the door is opened only once.

An event postcondition for a is a predicate that places a constraint upon the possible behaviours of a process following the observation of a. Any event postcondition may be written in the form:

$$\langle (t, a) \rangle \ \underline{\text{in}} \ s \quad \Rightarrow \quad C((s, X) \uparrow (t, \infty))$$

When placing an event precondition on an event a, it is sufficient to consider the case in which a is the last event observed. This result does not hold for event postconditions, even if we restrict our attention to the last occurrence of a:

$$\mathit{foot}(s \downharpoonright a) = (t, a) \quad \Rightarrow \quad C((s, X) \uparrow (t, \infty))$$

Although a useful form of specification, this is not equivalent to the event postcondition given above; the requirement that

$$a \rightarrow a \rightarrow \mathit{STOP} \quad \textbf{sat} \quad \mathit{foot}(s \downharpoonright a) = (t, a) \Rightarrow a \notin \sigma(s \upharpoonright t)$$

is easy to establish, while the following requirement is impossible:

$$a \rightarrow a \rightarrow \mathit{STOP} \quad \textbf{sat} \quad \langle (t, a) \rangle \ \underline{\text{in}} \ s \Rightarrow a \notin \sigma(s \upharpoonright t)$$

4.3 ENVIRONMENTAL CONDITIONS

We may use the notation of timed failures to analyse the behaviour of a process under a certain set of environmental conditions. in our computational model, we assume maximal progress: if a process and its environment are both prepared to engage in a particular timed event, then that event will occur. This postulate allows us to include assumptions about the offers made by the environment as preconditions in a behavioural specification.

These preconditions may be used to reason about non-robust interfaces, where correct behaviour is dependent upon the cooperation of the environment. When specifying the behaviour of a system component, we may assume that certain patterns of external communication will never be encountered.

4.3.1 Assumptions

To include an assumption about the environment in a specification of a process, we write the specification in the form

$$P \quad \textbf{sat} \quad E(s, X) \Rightarrow F(s, X)$$

where E is a predicate that corresponds to our assumption, and F characterises our requirements. This implication is vacuously true for any behaviour that does not meet the environmental condition; in this case, no requirement is placed upon the process.

However, we must ensure that predicate F is true of any behaviour of P that meets condition E.

It is instructive to consider the extreme assumptions *true* and *false*. In the first case, we are placing no constraint upon the environment; the following equivalence will hold:

$$P \ \mathbf{sat} \ (\mathit{true} \Rightarrow F(s, X)) \quad \equiv \quad P \ \mathbf{sat} \ F(s, X)$$

To show that a process P meets requirement F in any environment, we must show that F holds of all the behaviours of P. If our environmental assumption is *false* then we are assuming a miraculous environment, in which any process meets every requirement:

$$P \ \mathbf{sat} \ (\mathit{false} \Rightarrow F(s, X)) \quad \equiv \quad \mathit{true}$$

In practice, our environmental assumptions will be more reasonable.

4.3.2 Trace conditions

A timed trace is a record of observable events performed by the process; each of these events requires the cooperation of the environment. If the environment never offers a timed event (t, a), then this event will never be observed. To examine the resulting behaviour of the process, we restrict our attention to those failures which exclude this event from the trace. This may be extended to disqualify whole sequences of possible events.

For example, we may wish to specify that a personal computer PC will behave according to specification $SPEC(s, X)$, providing that it is switched on before a disk is inserted. If we use *on* to represent the activation of the machine, and *insert* to represent a disk insertion, then we may capture this requirement as follows:

$$PC \quad \mathbf{sat} \quad (\mathit{begin}(s \downharpoonleft \mathit{on}) < \mathit{begin}(s \downharpoonleft \mathit{insert})) \Rightarrow SPEC(s, X)$$

We are assuming that the machine is activated only once. The addition of an *off* event to our description would permit a more realistic treatment.

An assumption about possible traces corresponds to a safety specification upon the environment of a process. If we require that

$$P \quad \mathbf{sat} \quad s \notin U \Rightarrow SPEC(s, X)$$

where U denotes a set of disqualified traces, then we are assuming that the environment will not offer these sequences of timed events. If the environment of P is another process Q such that

$$Q \quad \mathbf{sat} \quad s \notin U$$

then the behaviours of P should meet specification $SPEC$.

4.3.3 Failure conditions

A timed refusal is a partial record of offers made by the environment of a process. If an event e is present in the refusal set, then we may infer that the environment offers more copies of e than the process is able to perform. By considering only those failures which include e in the refusal set, we may examine the result of placing a process in an environment which is willing to perform as many copies of e as necessary.

For example, we may require that a process P meets a specification F, providing that the environment is willing to accept at least one output every five time units:

$$P \quad \textbf{sat} \quad E(s, X) \Rightarrow F(s, X)$$

where E is an environmental condition defined by

$$\begin{aligned} E(s, X) \quad \widehat{=} \quad & \forall I : TI \bullet \\ & \quad \mathit{length}(I) \geqslant 5 \Rightarrow \mathit{output} \in \sigma(s \uparrow I) \vee \mathit{output} \in \sigma(X \uparrow I) \end{aligned}$$

If I is an interval of time longer than five time units, then there must be some time during that interval at which the environment offers to participate in *output*. This corresponds to the inclusion of the event (t, output) in the trace or refusal, depending on whether or not the offer was accepted.

A failure condition corresponds to a liveness specification upon the environment of a process. For example, if we wish process Q to model that part of the environment that accepts output from P, we should ensure that

$$\begin{aligned} Q \quad \textbf{sat} \quad & \forall I : TI \bullet \\ & \quad \mathit{length}(I) \geqslant 5 \Rightarrow \mathit{output} \in \sigma(s \uparrow I) \vee (I \times \{\mathit{output}\}) \not\subseteq X \end{aligned}$$

Our choice of Q means that the event *output* is concealed from the rest of the environment. Assuming that P and Q have no other events in common, we may combine them as follows:

$$(P \underset{\mathit{output}}{\|} Q) \setminus \mathit{output}$$

As we shall see, the concealment of an event corresponds to the assumption that all external offers are refused. The parallel combination of P and Q can refuse *output* when either process refuses. For any interval I longer than five time units, either P refuses *output* at some time during I or Q refuses output throughout I, in which case *output* must occur. In either case, the E condition is satisfied and specification F must hold.

The above example illustrates the dual relationship between liveness conditions and readiness assumptions:

$$\begin{array}{lcl} a \in \sigma(s \uparrow I) & & a \in \sigma(s \uparrow I) \\ \vee & \sim & \vee \\ J \times \{a\} \not\subseteq X & & a \in \sigma(X \uparrow J) \end{array}$$

If a process Q satisfies the liveness condition (on the left), then it will serve as a suitable environment for any process requiring the readiness assumption.

4.4 EXAMPLE

We consider a specification of the timed sensitive vending machine defined in section 2.9. This machine was intended to dispense a drink for every coin inserted; we use the events *coin* and *coke* to represent the insertion of a coin and the removal of a drink, respectively. The company that operates the machine requires that every drink is paid for in advance, so we must place the following safety specification upon *TSVM*:

$$SAFE(s) \;\hat{=}\; s \downarrow coke \leqslant s \downarrow coin$$

The number of drinks dispensed is no greater than the number of coins accepted.

For profitability, the company requires that the machine is ready to accept another coin within time t_4 of a drink being dispensed. We place the following liveness specification upon the implementation:

$$\begin{aligned} NEXT(s, X) \;\hat{=}\; \langle(t, coke)\rangle \;\underline{\text{in}}\; s \Rightarrow\; & coin \notin \sigma(X \upharpoonright t + t_4) \\ & \vee \\ & coin \in \sigma(s \upharpoonright t) \end{aligned}$$

If a drink is removed at time t, then the event *coin* must become available no later than time $t + t_4$. This offer is represented by the absence of the event from the refusal set, or the presence of the event in the trace.

If the machine is kicked within time t_1 of a coin being inserted, a *reset* event will occur, and the coin will be lost. Rather than design a more robust mechanism, the manufacturers construct the machine to the following specification:

$$OKAY(s, X) \;\hat{=}\; E(s, X) \Rightarrow F(s, X)$$

where $F(s, X)$ requires that a drink is made available time t_5 after a coin is inserted:

$$\begin{aligned} F(s, X) \;\hat{=}\; \langle(t, coin)\rangle \;\underline{\text{in}}\; s \Rightarrow\; & coke \notin \sigma(X \upharpoonright t + t_5) \\ & \vee \\ & coke \in \sigma(s \upharpoonright t) \end{aligned}$$

and $E(s, X)$ is an environmental condition corresponding to the assumption that the machine is treated gently for at least t_1 after each coin is inserted:

$$E(s, X) \;\hat{=}\; \langle(t, coin)\rangle \;\underline{\text{in}}\; s \Rightarrow reset \notin \sigma(s \uparrow [t, t + 1])$$

If this environmental condition is met, then the machine guarantees to offer a drink at the appropriate time.

5 PROOF

5.1 A PROOF SYSTEM

A complete proof system for the language of untimed processes has already been presented: see Brookes (1983). This system was based upon a set of semantics-preserving algebraic laws; with the addition of timing information, many of these laws must be repealed. For example, it is no longer the case that

$$(a \rightarrow P) \mathbin{|||} (b \rightarrow Q) \;\; \not\equiv \;\; \begin{array}{l} a \rightarrow (P \mathbin{|||} (b \rightarrow Q)) \\ \Box \\ b \rightarrow ((a \rightarrow P) \mathbin{|||} Q) \end{array}$$

The left-hand process may engage in the two events a and b simultaneously; the right-hand side describes a process which is initially sequential: after performing the first event, a strictly positive time δ must elapse before it can perform another. We cannot change the degree of parallelism in a real-time system without considering the behaviours of the processes involved; there is no rule for the elimination of interleaving parallel operator.

Similar problems arise when we consider the properties of the hiding operator. When we conceal a set of events from the environment of a process, we do more than simply remove them from the trace: we determine the times at which they are scheduled to occur. Although many of Brookes' equivalences are preserved, they serve only to illustrate desirable properties of our semantic model. They do not comprise a *complete* set of laws; there are other equivalences that we are unable to demonstrate without recourse to the semantic equations. This precludes the algebraic method of proof pioneered by Milner (1980), in which similar laws are used to establish that a suggested implementation is equivalent to a process already known to have the required properties.

This is no cause for alarm. We are able to produce a complete proof system for *proofs of satisfaction* in the model $\mathcal{M}_{TF}$. Whenever a process P meets a behaviour specification $S(s, X)$, it will be possible to establish that P satisfies $S(s, X)$ using only the inference rules presented in this chapter.

We will present an inference rule for each clause in the syntax of timed CSP, expressing the behavioural properties of a process in terms of component specifications. These rules will take the following form:

$$\frac{\begin{array}{c} \textit{antecedent} \\ \vdots \\ \textit{antecedent} \end{array}}{\textit{consequent}} \quad [\ \textit{side condition}\ ]$$

If we establish the truth of each *antecedent*, then we can be assured of the truth of the *consequent*, providing that the *side condition* holds.

For compound processes, the antecedent part of the rule will consist of behavioural specifications for the syntactic subcomponents. For atomic processes, the rules will be without antecedents. We do not require a proof rule for term variables. Timed CSP processes will contain no free occurrences of any variable; whenever we come to establish a result about a term P with a free variable X, we will be within the scope of an assumption $X\ \mathbf{sat}_\rho\ S(s, X)$ for some behavioural specification S.

We may use the definition of the satisfaction relation, given in the previous chapter, to establish the following logical rules:

$$\frac{}{P\ \mathbf{sat}_\rho\ \mathit{true}} \qquad \frac{\begin{array}{l} P\ \mathbf{sat}_\rho\ S(s, X) \\ P\ \mathbf{sat}_\rho\ T(s, X) \end{array}}{P\ \mathbf{sat}_\rho\ S(s, X) \wedge T(s, X)} \qquad \frac{\begin{array}{l} P\ \mathbf{sat}_\rho\ S(s, X) \\ S(s, X) \Rightarrow T(s, X) \end{array}}{P\ \mathbf{sat}_\rho\ T(s, X)}$$

The null specification is true of any process, each goal may be addressed separately, and we may weaken any specification already established.

5.2 SEQUENTIAL PROCESSES

5.2.1 Livelock and Deadlock

The livelock process $\perp$ and the deadlock process $STOP$ are both unable to participate in any external activity. The inference rules for these processes are:

$$\frac{}{\perp\ \mathbf{sat}_\rho\ s = \langle\rangle} \qquad \frac{}{STOP\ \mathbf{sat}_\rho\ s = \langle\rangle}$$

Any trace of either process must be equal to the empty trace, but we can infer nothing about a typical refusal set: X may be any element of TR.

5.2.2 Termination and delay

The process *SKIP* is initially prepared to perform the termination event $\checkmark$, the only action that this process may perform:

$$\frac{}{\begin{array}{l} \mathit{SKIP}\ \mathbf{sat}_\rho\ (s = \langle\rangle \wedge \checkmark \notin \sigma(X)) \\ \qquad\qquad \vee \\ \qquad\qquad (s = \langle(t, \checkmark)\rangle \wedge \checkmark \notin \sigma(X \upharpoonright t) \wedge t \geqslant 0) \end{array}}$$

Either no events have been observed and the event $\checkmark$ is available, or $\checkmark$ has been observed (at some time t) and was continuously available beforehand. A similar rule pertains to the delay process *WAIT* t, in which the termination event becomes available at time t:

$$\frac{}{\begin{array}{l} \mathit{WAIT}\ t\ \mathbf{sat}_\rho\ s = \langle\rangle \wedge \checkmark \notin \sigma(X \uparrow t) \\ \qquad\qquad \vee \\ \qquad\qquad s = \langle(t', \checkmark)\rangle \wedge \checkmark \notin \sigma(X \uparrow [t, t')) \wedge t' \geqslant t \end{array}}$$

If no events have been observed then $\checkmark$ must be available continuously from time t onwards. Otherwise, $\checkmark$ is observed at a time $t' \geqslant t$ and made available at all times between t and t'.

5.2.3 Prefix

The undecorated prefix operator is associated with a constant delay of δ. From the semantic equation given in chapter 2, we may derive the inference rule below:

$$\frac{P\ \mathbf{sat}_\rho\ S(s, X)}{\begin{array}{l} a \rightarrow P\ \mathbf{sat}_\rho\ s = \langle\rangle \wedge a \notin \sigma(X) \\ \qquad\qquad \vee \\ \qquad\qquad s = \langle(t, a)\rangle^\frown s' \wedge a \notin \sigma(X \upharpoonright t) \wedge\ \mathit{begin}(s') \geqslant (t + \delta) \\ \qquad\qquad\qquad\qquad\qquad\qquad\qquad \wedge\ S((s', X) - (t + \delta)) \end{array}}$$

If we assume that process P meets the behavioural specification $S(s, X)$ in the current environment ρ then we may infer the following statements about a typical behaviour of the term $a \rightarrow P$:

- if s is empty, then the event a may not be refused, and is therefore absent from the refusal set X

- if s is non-empty, then the first event must be a. If a occurs at time t, we know that a is not refused before this time. Further, if a occurs at time t, then the subsequent behaviour is that of P, following a delay of δ. This subsequent behaviour must satisfy the predicate S.

The inference rule for delayed prefix is a simple generalisation:

$$\frac{P\ \mathbf{sat}_\rho\ S(s,X)}{\begin{array}{ll} a \xrightarrow{t} P\ \mathbf{sat}_\rho & s = \langle\rangle \wedge a \notin \sigma(X) \\ & \vee \\ & s = \langle(t',a)\rangle^\frown s' \wedge a \notin \sigma(X \upharpoonright t') \wedge begin(s') \geqslant (t'+t) \\ & \qquad \wedge\ S((s',X)-(t'+t)) \end{array}}$$

In this case, if event a is observed at time t', the subsequent behaviour is that of P starting at time $t'+t$.

5.2.4 Sequential composition

The inference rule for the sequential composition $P\ ;\ Q$ is complicated by the fact that both terms are able to perform actions at the time of transfer of control. If control has not been transferred, then any trace of the composite term is a trace of P during which $\checkmark$ is not observed, and would be refused if offered. Otherwise, we may infer only that the trace is a permutation of traces s_P and s_Q, performed by P and Q respectively:

$$\frac{\begin{array}{l} P\ \mathbf{sat}_\rho\ S(s,X) \\ Q\ \mathbf{sat}_\rho\ T(s,X) \end{array}}{\begin{array}{ll} P\ ;\ Q\ \mathbf{sat}_\rho & \checkmark \notin \sigma(s) \wedge \forall I \in TI \bullet S(s, X \cup (I \times \{\checkmark\})) \\ & \vee \\ & \exists\, s_P, s_Q \bullet s \cong s_P{}^\frown s_Q \wedge \checkmark \notin \sigma(s_P) \wedge begin(s_Q) \geqslant t \\ & \qquad \wedge\ S(s_P{}^\frown\langle(t,\checkmark)\rangle, X \upharpoonright t \cup [0,t) \times \{\checkmark\}) \\ & \qquad \wedge\ T((s_Q,X)-t) \end{array}}$$

The trace s_P may be extended with a $\checkmark$ event at some time t (this event is hidden by the sequential composition operator). In the presence of the sequential composition operator, the event $\checkmark$ occurs as soon as it becomes available, so we know that it is refused at any time before t. Hence the failure

$$(s_P{}^\frown\langle(t,\checkmark)\rangle, X \upharpoonright t \cup [0,t) \times \{\checkmark\})$$

must be a behaviour of P, which meets specification S. The second part of the trace, together with the refusals after t, forms a behaviour of Q.

To simplify reasoning about sequential composition, we exhibit derived inference rules for the cases in which either P or Q is a delay process. The term $WAIT\ t; P$ behaves as P, after an initial delay of time t:

$$\frac{P \ \mathbf{sat}_\rho \ S(s, X)}{WAIT\ t\ ;\ P\ \mathbf{sat}_\rho \ begin(s) \geqslant t \wedge S((s, X) - t)}$$

The term $P\ ;\ WAIT\ t\ ;\ Q$ behaves as the sequential composition of P and Q, except that a delay of time t is associated with the transfer of control:

$$\frac{\begin{array}{l} P \ \mathbf{sat}_\rho \ S(s, X) \\ Q \ \mathbf{sat}_\rho \ T(s, X) \end{array}}{\begin{array}{l} P\ ;\ WAIT\ t\ ;\ Q\ \mathbf{sat}_\rho \ \checkmark \notin \sigma(s) \wedge \forall I \in TI \bullet S(s, X \cup I \times \{\checkmark\}) \\ \qquad\qquad\qquad\qquad \vee \\ \qquad\qquad\qquad\qquad S(s \upharpoonright t' ^\frown \langle (t', \checkmark) \rangle, X \upharpoonright t' \cup [0, t') \times \{\checkmark\}) \\ \qquad\qquad\qquad\qquad\qquad \wedge\ s \uparrow (t', t' + t) = \langle\rangle \\ \qquad\qquad\qquad\qquad\qquad \wedge\ T((s, X) - (t + t')) \end{array}}$$

The delayed sequential composition operator $\fatsemi$ is a special case of this construct.

5.2.5 Nondeterministic choice

Any behaviour of the nondeterministic choice $P \sqcap Q$ must arise from either P or Q. This gives rise to the obvious inference rule:

$$\frac{\begin{array}{l} P \ \mathbf{sat}_\rho \ S(s, X) \\ Q \ \mathbf{sat}_\rho \ T(s, X) \end{array}}{P \sqcap Q \ \mathbf{sat}_\rho \ S(s, X) \vee T(s, X)}$$

The indexed form of this operator is not well-defined unless the set of alternatives is uniformly bounded. This requirement appears as a side-condition below:

$$\frac{\forall i : I \bullet P_i \ \mathbf{sat}_\rho \ S(s, X)}{\sqcap_{i \in I} P_i \ \mathbf{sat}_\rho \ S(s, X)} \quad [\ \{P_i \mid i \in I\} \text{ is uniformly bounded }]$$

This condition is trivially true for a choice of delay processes:

$$\frac{P \ \mathbf{sat}_\rho \ S(s, X)}{WAIT\ T\ ;\ P\ \mathbf{sat}_\rho \ \exists t : T \bullet begin(s) \geqslant t \wedge S((s, X) - t)}$$

Control is passed to P at some time t, drawn from set T.

5.2.6 Deterministic choice

As in the case of nondeterministic choice, we may infer that the combination $P \Box Q$ behaves as either P or Q. We may also infer that any event refused before the first observable event occurs must be refused by both processes: any behaviour with an empty trace must be common to both alternatives.

$$\frac{P \ \mathbf{sat}_\rho \ S(s,X) \quad Q \ \mathbf{sat}_\rho \ T(s,X)}{P \Box Q \ \mathbf{sat}_\rho \ S(s,X) \lor T(s,X) \ \land \ S(\langle\rangle, X \upharpoonright begin(s)) \land T(\langle\rangle, X \upharpoonright begin(s))}$$

The inference rule for prefix choice requires a side-condition:

$$\frac{\forall a : A \bullet P_a \ \mathbf{sat}_\rho \ S_a(s,X)}{\begin{array}{l} a : A \xrightarrow{t_a} P_a \\ \quad \mathbf{sat}_\rho \\ \quad\quad s = \langle\rangle \land A \cap \sigma(X) = \{\} \\ \quad\quad \lor \\ \quad\quad a \in A \land s = \langle(t,a)\rangle ^\frown s' \\ \quad\quad\quad \land A \cap \sigma(X \upharpoonright t) = \{\} \\ \quad\quad\quad \land begin(s') \geqslant t + t_a \\ \quad\quad\quad \land S_a((s',X) - (t + t_a)) \end{array}} \quad [\,\{P_a \mid a \in A\} \text{ uniformly bounded}\,]$$

If no events have been observed, then all of the events in set A should be available; the intersection of A with the event set of the refusal X must be empty. Otherwise, if a is the first event observed, we know that $a \in A$, and the subsequent behaviour is that of process P_a. A delay of t_a is associated with the transfer of control to the process.

5.2.7 Relabelling

The inverse image of P may engage in an event a whenever P may engage in $f(a)$.

$$\frac{P \ \mathbf{sat}_\rho \ S(s,X)}{f^{-1}(P) \ \mathbf{sat}_\rho \ S(f(s), f(X))}$$

The direct image of P may engage in an event $f(a)$ whenever P can engage in a:

$$\frac{P \ \mathbf{sat}_\rho \ S(s,X)}{f(P) \ \mathbf{sat}_\rho \ \exists s' \bullet s = f(s') \land S(s', f^{-1}(X))}$$

In the second inference rule above, the expression $f^{-1}(X)$ denotes the set

$$\{(t, a) \mid (t, f(a)) \in X\}$$

This is the inverse image of refusal set X under function f.

5.2.8 Abstraction

To reason about a term of the form $P \setminus A$, we identify the behaviours of P in which events from A occur as soon as possible. In section 2.5, we saw that these are the failures of P in which events from A may be continuously refused:

$$\frac{P \ \mathbf{sat}_\rho \ S(s, X)}{P \setminus A \ \mathbf{sat}_\rho \ \exists s' \bullet s = s' \setminus A \wedge S(s', X \cup ([0, end(s', X)) \times A))}$$

If (s, X) is a behaviour of $P \setminus A$, then there is a trace s' of term P which matches s if we ignore the events from A. This trace, together with the refusal set X, must be a behaviour of P. Further, we may add events from A to the refusal set. We infer that the failure

$$(s', X \cup [0, end(s', X)) \times A)$$

is a behaviour of P, and hence satisfies specification S.

5.3 PARALLEL PROCESSES

5.3.1 Alphabet parallel

If s is a trace of the alphabet parallel combination $P \ {}_A\|_B \ Q$, then we know that the restriction of s to set A must be the trace of events performed by process P. Similarly, the restriction of s to set B is the trace of events performed by Q. We may also infer that s contains only events drawn from the union of these two sets. To summarise, the predicate

$$\exists s_P, s_Q \bullet s \downharpoonright A = s_P \wedge s \downharpoonright B = s_Q \wedge s \downharpoonright (A \cup B) = s$$

must hold for s, where s_P and s_Q are traces of P and Q.

Suppose that (s, X) is a behaviour of this parallel combination, and that it corresponds to behaviours (s_P, X_P) and (s_Q, X_Q) of components P and Q. From the semantic equation for this operator, we know that we can choose these component behaviours such that

$$\sigma(X_P) \subseteq A \wedge \sigma(X_Q) \subseteq B$$

Any event from set A will require the cooperation of component P, and any event from set B will require the cooperation of component Q, so we may infer that

$$X_P \subseteq X \downharpoonright A \quad \wedge \quad X_Q \subseteq X \downharpoonright B$$

Finally, an event from $A \cup B$ may be refused by the parallel combination only if it occurs in at least one of these refusal sets.

$$\frac{\begin{array}{l} P \ \mathbf{sat}_\rho \ S(s, X) \\ Q \ \mathbf{sat}_\rho \ T(s, X) \end{array}}{\begin{array}{ll} P \ {}_A\|_B \ Q \ \mathbf{sat}_\rho \ \exists s_P, X_P, s_Q, X_Q \bullet & S(s_P, X_P) \wedge T(s_Q, X_Q) \\ & \wedge \\ & s_P = s \downharpoonright A \wedge s_Q = s \downharpoonright B \\ & \wedge \\ & s \downharpoonright (A \cup B) = s \\ & \wedge \\ & X_P \subseteq X \downharpoonright A \wedge X_Q \subseteq X \downharpoonright B \\ & \wedge \\ & X \downharpoonright (A \cup B) = X_P \cup X_Q \end{array}}$$

5.3.2 Simple parallel

In the parallel combination $P \parallel Q$ processes P and Q must cooperate on every action that is performed. The relative simplicity of its semantics is reflected in the following inference rule:

$$\frac{\begin{array}{l} P \ \mathbf{sat}_\rho \ S(s, X) \\ Q \ \mathbf{sat}_\rho \ T(s, X) \end{array}}{P \parallel Q \ \mathbf{sat}_\rho \ \exists X_P, X_Q \bullet X = X_P \cup X_Q \wedge S(s, X_P) \wedge T(s, X_Q)}$$

5.3.3 Interleaving

The interleaved parallel combination $P \mid\mid\mid Q$ may engage in an event a when either P or Q is prepared to engage in a:

$$\frac{\begin{array}{l} P \ \mathbf{sat}_\rho \ S(s, X) \\ Q \ \mathbf{sat}_\rho \ T(s, X) \end{array}}{P \mid\mid\mid Q \ \mathbf{sat}_\rho \ \exists s_P, s_Q \bullet s \in s_P \mid\mid\mid s_Q \wedge S(s_P, X) \wedge T(s_Q, X)}$$

Recall that $s_P \mid\mid\mid s_Q$ denotes the set of possible interleavings of s_P and s_Q.

5.3.4 Communicating parallel

In the communicating parallel combination

$$P \underset{C}{\|} Q$$

processes P and Q are required to cooperate on events from set C. If s is a trace of this process, then there must exist traces s_P and s_Q such that

$$(s \upharpoonright C = s_P \upharpoonright C = s_Q \upharpoonright C) \quad \wedge \quad s \setminus C \in (s_P \setminus C \;|||\; s_Q \setminus C)$$

Trace s restricted to events outside set C must be an interleaving of s_P and s_Q, similarly restricted, and all three traces must agree on events from set C. We abbreviate this requirement to $s \in s_P \underset{C}{\|} s_Q$.

$$\frac{\begin{array}{l} P \ \mathbf{sat}_\rho \ S(s, X) \\ Q \ \mathbf{sat}_\rho \ T(s, X) \end{array}}{\begin{array}{ll} P \underset{C}{\|} Q \ \mathbf{sat}_\rho \ \exists s_P, s_Q, X_P, X_Q \bullet & s \in s_P \underset{C}{\|} s_Q \\ & \wedge \\ & X \upharpoonright C = (X_P \cup X_Q) \upharpoonright C \\ & \wedge \\ & X \setminus C = (X_P \cap X_Q) \setminus C \\ & \wedge \\ & S(s_P, X_P) \\ & \wedge \\ & T(s_Q, X_Q) \end{array}}$$

A timed event (t, a) may be refused if a is in C and either process refuses to cooperate, or a is not in C and both processes refuse to cooperate. If C is the intersection of the process alphabets, we may simplify the consequent:

$$\frac{\begin{array}{l} P \ \mathbf{sat}_\rho \ S(s, X) \\ Q \ \mathbf{sat}_\rho \ T(s, X) \end{array}}{\begin{array}{ll} P \underset{C}{\|} Q \ \mathbf{sat}_\rho \ \exists X_P, X_Q \bullet & X \upharpoonright C = (X_P \cup X_Q) \upharpoonright C \\ & \wedge \\ & X \setminus C = (X_P \cap X_Q) \setminus C \\ & \wedge \\ & S(s \upharpoonright \sigma(P), X_P) \\ & \wedge \\ & T(s \upharpoonright \sigma(Q), X_Q) \end{array}} \quad [\, \sigma(P) \cap \sigma(Q) = C \,]$$

This form of the rule will be sufficient for most applications.

5.4 TIMEOUTS AND INTERRUPTS

5.4.1 Timeout

In the timeout construct $P \overset{t}{\triangleright} Q$, control is transferred to Q unless P performs an external action before time t.

$$\frac{\begin{array}{l} P \ \mathbf{sat}_\rho \ S(s,X) \\ Q \ \mathbf{sat}_\rho \ T(s,X) \end{array}}{\begin{array}{ll} P \overset{t}{\triangleright} Q \ \mathbf{sat}_\rho & \mathit{begin}(s) \leqslant t \wedge S(s,X) \\ & \quad \vee \\ & \mathit{begin}(s) \geqslant (t+\delta) \wedge S(\langle\rangle, X \upharpoonright t) \\ & \qquad\qquad \wedge\ T((s,X) - (t+\delta)) \end{array}}$$

The δ delay allows us to determine which of the two components has given rise to the current behaviour of

$$P \overset{t}{\triangleright} Q$$

it is a behaviour of P if it starts at or before time t, and a behaviour of Q otherwise.

5.4.2 Timed interrupt

In the timed interrupt construct

$$P \underset{t}{\lightning} Q$$

control is passed from P to Q at time t, regardless of the progress made by P. Once again, a small delay of δ is associated with the transfer of control.

$$\frac{\begin{array}{l} P \ \mathbf{sat}_\rho \ S(s,X) \\ Q \ \mathbf{sat}_\rho \ T(s,X) \end{array}}{\begin{array}{ll} P \underset{t}{\lightning} Q \ \mathbf{sat}_\rho & \mathit{begin}(s \upharpoonleft t) \geqslant t+\delta \wedge S(s \upharpoonright t, X \upharpoonright t) \\ & \qquad\qquad \wedge\ T((s,X) - (t+\delta)) \end{array}}$$

No external activity is possible during transfer of control from P to Q, so

$$\mathit{begin}(s \upharpoonleft t) \geqslant t+\delta$$

Any activity before time t must be a possible behaviour of P; any activity after time $t+\delta$ must be a possible behaviour of Q.

5.4.3 Event interrupt

If (s, X) is a behaviour of the construct

$$P \underset{e}{\nabla} Q$$

in which the interrupt event e has not been observed, then e must be available. If e occurs at time t, then any behaviour up until time t must be a behaviour of P. The subsequent behaviour is due to Q.

$$\frac{\begin{array}{l} P \ \mathbf{sat}_\rho \ S(s, X) \\ Q \ \mathbf{sat}_\rho \ T(s, X) \end{array}}{\begin{array}{l} P \underset{e}{\nabla} Q \ \mathbf{sat}_\rho \ e \notin \sigma(s, X) \wedge S(s, X) \\ \qquad\qquad \vee \\ \qquad\qquad \exists\, t : \mathit{TIME} \bullet s \upharpoonright t \downharpoonleft e = \langle (t, e) \rangle \\ \qquad\qquad\qquad\qquad e \notin \sigma(X \upharpoonright t) \\ \qquad\qquad\qquad\qquad \mathit{begin}(s \upharpoonleft t) \geqslant t + \delta \\ \qquad\qquad\qquad\qquad S(s \upharpoonright t \setminus e, X \upharpoonright t) \\ \qquad\qquad\qquad\qquad T((s, X) - (t + \delta)) \end{array}} \quad [\, e \notin \sigma(P) \,]$$

The assumption that P may not interrupt itself appears as a side condition.

5.5 RECURSIVE PROCESSES

In chapter 3, we showed how the theory of metric spaces may be used to give a semantics to recursively defined processes. To reason about the properties of these processes, we give a simple topology to the space $\mathcal{M}_{TF}$ and establish a theory of recursion induction, in the style of Roscoe (1982).

5.5.1 Recursion induction

We will require the following definitions, taken from Sutherland (1975):

Definition 5.1 A topological space $T = (A, \mathcal{T})$ consists of a non-empty set A together with a fixed collection $\mathcal{T}$ of subsets of A satisfying

1. $A, \{\} \in \mathcal{T}$
2. the intersection of any two sets in $\mathcal{T}$ is again in $\mathcal{T}$
3. the union of any collection of sets in $\mathcal{T}$ is again in $\mathcal{T}$

We refer to the elements of $\mathcal{T}$ as the *open sets* of T. The *closed sets* of T are given by $\{A - U \mid U \in \mathcal{T}\}$. A mapping between topological spaces is *continuous* if inverse images of open sets are themselves open:

Definition 5.2 If $T_1 = (A_1, \mathcal{T}_1)$ and $T_2 = (A_2, \mathcal{T}_2)$ are topological spaces, then a mapping $f : A_1 \to A_2$ is continuous with respect to topologies $\mathcal{T}_1$ and $\mathcal{T}_2$ if

$$U \in \mathcal{T}_2 \quad \Rightarrow \quad f^{-1}(U) \in \mathcal{T}_1$$

We may give a topology to the metric space (A, d) by defining $\mathcal{T}$ to be the set of d-*open* subsets of A. If we define

Definition 5.3 If $M = (A, d)$ is a metric space and ϵ is a strictly positive real number, then the *open* ϵ*-ball neighbourhood of a in* M is the set

$$B_\epsilon(d\,;a) \quad \widehat{=} \quad \{x : A \mid d(x, a) < \epsilon\}$$

then we may characterise the d-open sets as unions of open balls. This is a consequence of the following definition:

Definition 5.4 A subset U of a metric space $M = (A, d)$ is d*-open in* M if given any $a \in U$ there exists $\epsilon_a > 0$ such that $B_{\epsilon_a}(d\,;a) \subset U$.

The following theorems are due to Roscoe (1982) and Reed (1988):

Theorem 5.5 Let $M = (A, d)$ be a complete metric space, and let TV be the topological space $(\{\mathit{true}, \mathit{false}\}, \mathcal{T})$ where

$$\mathcal{T} \quad \widehat{=} \quad \{\{\}, \{\mathit{false}\}, \{\mathit{true}, \mathit{false}\}\}$$

If $F : M \to T$ is continuous with respect to the d-open topology and $\mathcal{T}$, and the set $\{a \in A \mid F(a) = \mathit{true}\}$ is nonempty, then

$$(\forall\, x : A \bullet F(x) = \mathit{true} \Rightarrow F(C(x)) = \mathit{true}) \quad \Rightarrow \quad F(\mathit{fix}(C)) = \mathit{true}$$

for any contraction mapping $C : M \to M$.

Theorem 5.6 If F is a mapping from the complete metric space $(\mathcal{S}_{TF}, d)$ to TV such that for any Y in $\mathcal{S}_{TF}$

$$F(Y) = \mathit{false} \quad \Rightarrow \quad \exists\, t : \mathit{TIME} \bullet \forall\, Y' : \mathcal{S}_{TF} \bullet Y \upharpoonright t = Y \upharpoonright t' \Rightarrow F(Y') = \mathit{false}$$

then F is continuous.

Recall that the metric d upon $\mathcal{S}_{TF}$ was defined using the *before* operator on sets of failures. $Y \upharpoonright t = Y' \upharpoonright t$ if failure sets Y and Y' agree up until time t; these Y' form an open ball around Y in the metric space. If F is such that whenever $F(Y) = \mathit{false}$ there is an open ball around Y whose image is $\{\mathit{false}\}$, then F is continuous. We identify predicates on timed failure sets with mappings from $\mathcal{S}_{TF}$ to the space of truth values TV.

Definition 5.7 A predicate R on elements of $\mathcal{S}_{TF}$ is a mapping from the space of timed failure sets $\mathcal{S}_{TF}$ to the space of truth values TV,

$$(\{true, false\}, \{\{\}, \{false\}, \{true, false\}\})$$

We say that R is a *continuous* predicate if it is a continuous mapping in the sense of definition 5.2.

Definition 5.8 A predicate R is *plausible* if R is continuous and

$$\exists\, Y : \mathcal{S}_{TF} \;\bullet\; R(Y) = true$$

5.5.2 Immediate recursion

To establish that a *plausible* predicate correctly describes a well-defined recursive process $\mu\, X \circ P$, it is sufficient to show that R is preserved by the mapping corresponding to X and P. If P is *constructive* for X then the following inference rule is valid:

Rule 5.9

$$\frac{\forall\, Y : \mathcal{S}_{TF} \bullet R(Y) \Rightarrow R(\mathcal{F}_{TF}[\![P]\!]\rho[Y/X])}{R(\mathcal{F}_{TF}[\![\mu\, X \circ P]\!]\rho)} \quad [\ R \text{ plausible}\ ]$$

Proof If P is constructive for X, then the mapping $\lambda\, Y \bullet \mathcal{F}_{TF}[\![P]\!]\rho[Y/X]$ is a contraction mapping on $\mathcal{S}_{TF}$, by lemma 3.14. If R is plausible, then it is a continuous mapping from $\mathcal{S}_{TF}$ to TV such that the set $\{Y : \mathcal{S}_{TF} \mid R(Y) = true\}$ is nonempty, and we have assumed that

$$\forall\, Y : \mathcal{S}_{TF} \;\bullet\; R(Y) \Rightarrow R(\mathcal{F}_{TF}[\![P]\!]\rho[Y/X])$$

We may apply theorem 5.5 and deduce that the rule is sound. □

In our proof system, we wish to establish that a predicate holds not of a process, but of a typical behaviour of that process: we wish to show that a process satisfies a behavioural specification. In this case, our proof obligation can be simplified. We need only show that the specification is preserved by each recursive call:

Rule 5.10

$$\frac{X \ \mathbf{sat}_\rho\ S(s, X) \Rightarrow P \ \mathbf{sat}_\rho\ S(s, X)}{\mu\, X \circ P \ \mathbf{sat}_\rho\ S(s, X)}$$

Proof We recall the definition of the $\mathbf{sat}_\rho$ operator

$$P \;\mathbf{sat}_\rho\; S(s,X) \;\;\widehat{=}\;\; \forall s,X \bullet (s,X) \in \mathcal{F}_{TF}[\![P]\!] \bullet S(s,X)$$

We claim that any predicate of the form

$$R(Y) \;\;\widehat{=}\;\; \forall s,X \bullet (s,X) \in Y \Rightarrow S(s,X)$$

is plausible in $\mathcal{S}_{TF}$. Suppose that $Y \in \mathcal{S}_{TF}$ and $R(Y) = \mathit{false}$, then

$$\exists s,X \bullet (s,X) \in Y \wedge \neg S(s,X)$$

There must be a behaviour (s,X) in Y which does not meet S. If we choose a time $t > \mathit{end}(s,X)$ then

$$Y' \upharpoonright t = Y \upharpoonright t \;\;\Rightarrow\;\; (s,X) \in Y' \wedge \neg S(s,X)$$

and $R(Y') = \mathit{false}$ for all Y' in an open ball of radius 2^{-t} around Y. By theorem 5.6, R is a continuous predicate. We know that $\{\} \in \mathcal{S}_{TF}$, and it is easy to see that

$$R(\{\}) \;\;=\;\; \mathit{true}$$

Hence predicate R is plausible. The result follows by rule 5.9. □

This gives a sufficient condition for the recursive process $\mu X \circ P$ to satisfy the specification $S(s,X)$ on timed failures.

5.5.3 Delayed recursion

The delayed recursion operator associates a delay of δ with each recursive call; the mapping on $\mathcal{S}_{TF}$ corresponding to a recursion $\mu X \bullet P$ is given by

$$M_\delta(X,P)\rho \;\;\widehat{=}\;\; W_\delta \cdot \lambda Y \bullet \mathcal{F}_{TF}[\![P]\!]\rho[Y/X]$$

where the following equivalence holds for W_δ:

$$W_\delta \;\;\equiv\;\; \lambda Y \bullet \{(s,X) \mid \mathit{begin}(s) \geqslant \delta \wedge ((s,X) - \delta) \in Y\}$$

This mapping is a contraction mapping on $\mathcal{S}_{TF}$ for any choice of X, P; there is no need to establish that term P is constructive for the recursive variable. With an argument similar to that presented for rule 5.9, we may establish an inference rule for this operator:

Rule 5.11

$$\frac{\forall Y : \mathcal{S}_{TF} \bullet R(Y) \Rightarrow R(\mathcal{F}_{TF}[\![P]\!]\rho[W_\delta(Y)/X])}{R(\mathcal{F}_{TF}[\![\mu X \bullet P]\!]\rho)} \quad [\, R \text{ plausible} \,]$$

From the proof of rule 5.10, we see that any such specification corresponds to a plausible predicate on elements of $\mathcal{S}_{TF}$. If we choose R such that

$$R(Y) \mathrel{\widehat{=}} \forall s, X \bullet (s, X) \in Y \Rightarrow S(s, X)$$

then we may derive an inference rule for behavioural specifications:

Rule 5.12

$$\frac{\forall X : \mathcal{S}_{TF} \bullet X \ \mathbf{sat}_\rho \ (S((s, X) - \delta) \wedge \mathit{begin}(s) \geqslant \delta) \Rightarrow P \ \mathbf{sat}_\rho \ S(s, X)}{\mu X \bullet P \ \mathbf{sat}_\rho \ S(s, X)}$$

Proof Similar to the proof of rule 5.10. □

5.5.4 Mutual recursion

We restrict our attention to those recursive equation sets in which the vector of terms is constructive for the vector of variables. We wish to establish results about processes of the form $\langle X_i = P_i \rangle_j$: the j component of the process vector defined by equation set $\{X_i = P_i\}$. To do this, we will need to establish similar results about each component of the vector $\underline{P}$. To establish that a vector of predicates $\underline{R}$ correctly describes the fixed point of $M(\underline{X}, \underline{P})$, it is sufficient to show that $\underline{R}$ is preserved by $M(\underline{X}, \underline{P})$, and that each R_i is a plausible predicate.

Rule 5.13

$$\frac{(\forall i \bullet R_i(Y_i)) \Rightarrow \forall j \bullet R_j(\mathcal{F}_{TF}[\![P_j]\!]\rho[\underline{Y}/\underline{X}])}{\underline{R}(\mathcal{F}_{TF}[\![\mu \underline{X} \circ \underline{P}]\!]\rho)} \quad [\ R_i \text{ plausible, for all } i\ ]$$

Proof Assume that each R_i is plausible, and that

$$(\forall i : I \bullet R_i(Y_i)) \quad \Rightarrow \quad \forall j : I \bullet R_j(\mathcal{F}_{TF}[\![P_j]\!]\rho[\underline{Y}/\underline{X}])$$

We claim that

$$(\forall i : I \bullet R_i(Y_i)) \quad \Rightarrow \quad \forall j : I \bullet R_j(\mathcal{F}_{TF}[\![Q_j]\!]\rho[\underline{Y}/\underline{X}])$$

where vector $\underline{Q}$ is as defined in the proof of the Unique Fixed Point Theorem:

$$Q_i \mathrel{\widehat{=}} P_i[Q_j/X_j \mid j \in \mathrm{seg}(i)]$$

To establish this result, we proceed by transfinite induction, with inductive set J:

$$J \mathrel{\widehat{=}} \{k : I \bullet (\forall i : I \bullet R_i(Y_i)) \Rightarrow R_k(\mathcal{F}_{TF}[\![Q_k]\!]\rho[\underline{Y}/\underline{X}])\}$$

We assume that $\text{seg}(k) \subseteq J$, and observe that

$$\begin{aligned} \mathcal{F}_{TF}[\![Q_k]\!]\rho[\underline{Y}/\underline{X}] &= \mathcal{F}_{TF}[\![P_k[Q_l/X_l \mid l \in \text{seg}(k)]]\!]\rho[\underline{Y}/\underline{X}] \\ &= \mathcal{F}_{TF}[\![P_k]\!]\rho[\underline{Y}/\underline{X}][\mathcal{F}_{TF}[\![Q_l]\!]\rho[\underline{Y}/\underline{X}]/X_l \mid l \in \text{seg}(k)] \end{aligned}$$

Define a secondary vector $\underline{Z}$ by

$$Z_l \mathrel{\widehat{=}} \begin{array}{ll} Y_l & (l \notin \text{seg}(k)) \\ \mathcal{F}_{TF}[\![Q_l]\!]\rho[\underline{Y}/\underline{X}] & (l \in \text{seg}(k)) \end{array}$$

By our inductive hypothesis,

$$\forall\, i : I \bullet R_i(Y_i) \;\Rightarrow\; \forall\, i : I \bullet R_i(Z_i)$$

Whence our original assumption about $\underline{P}$ yields

$$\begin{aligned} (\forall\, i : I \bullet R_i(Y_i)) &\Rightarrow R_k(\mathcal{F}_{TF}[\![P_k]\!]\rho[\underline{Z}/\underline{X}]) \\ &\Rightarrow R_k(\mathcal{F}_{TF}[\![Q_k]\!]\rho[\underline{Y}/\underline{X}]) \end{aligned}$$

hence $k \in J$, and the claim follows by transfinite induction. From the definition of the metric $\underline{d}$ upon the product space $\mathcal{S}^I_{TF}$, we may establish that

$$(\forall\, i : I \bullet R_i \text{ plausible}) \;\Rightarrow\; \underline{R} \text{ plausible}$$

We have established that $M(\underline{X}, \underline{Q})\rho$ preserves $\underline{R}$, hence $\underline{R}$ must hold of the fixed point of this mapping, by theorem 5.5. But from the proof of the Unique Fixed Point Theorem we learn that

$$\mathit{fix}(M(\underline{X}, \underline{Q})\rho) \;=\; \mathit{fix}(M(\underline{X}, \underline{P})\rho)$$

We may conclude that the rule is sound. □

We may derive a rule for behavioural specifications by making a suitable choice for predicate $\underline{R}$:

Rule 5.14

$$\frac{(\forall\, i : I \bullet X_i \;\mathbf{sat}_\rho\; S_i(s, X)) \Rightarrow \forall\, i : I \bullet P_i \;\mathbf{sat}_\rho\; S_i(s, X)}{\langle X_i = P_i \rangle_j \;\mathbf{sat}_\rho\; S_j(s, X)}$$

The proof that this rule is sound, as an instance of the previous rule, is entirely similar to the derivation of rule 5.10 from rule 5.9.

5.6 SOUNDNESS AND COMPLETENESS

Our proof system has two desirable properties:

Theorem 5.15 The set of inference rules presented in this chapter is sound with respect to the semantic equations of chapter 2. The truth of each rule may be established from the equation for the corresponding operator, without recourse to the axioms of $\mathcal{M}_{TF}$.

Theorem 5.16 The set of inference rules presented in this chapter is complete with respect to the semantic equations of chapter 2. Any property that is true of every behaviour of a process P may be established using these rules.

5.6.1 Soundness

The presentation of the proof system has been chosen to emphasise the correspondence between inference rules and semantic equations. To see that each rule is sound, we have only to examine the defining equation for the operator in question. As an example, consider the rule for simple parallel combination:

$$\frac{\begin{array}{l} P\ \mathbf{sat}_\rho\ S(s,X) \\ Q\ \mathbf{sat}_\rho\ T(s,X) \end{array}}{P \parallel Q\ \mathbf{sat}_\rho\ \exists\, X_P, X_Q \bullet X = X_P \cup X_Q \wedge S(s,X_P) \wedge T(s,X_Q)}$$

This operator was given the following semantics:

$$\mathcal{F}_{TF}[\![P \parallel Q]\!]\rho \;\;\widehat{=}\;\; \{(s, X_P \cup X_Q) \mid (s,X_P) \in \mathcal{F}_{TF}[\![P]\!]\rho \wedge (s,X_Q) \in \mathcal{F}_{TF}[\![Q]\!]\rho\}$$

A simple logical deduction will suffice the establish the validity of the inference rule. Assume the two antecedents of the rule and suppose that (s,X) is a behaviour of $P \parallel Q$ in environment ρ. By the semantic equation,

$$\exists\, X_P, X_Q \;\;\bullet\;\; (s,X_P) \in \mathcal{F}_{TF}[\![P]\!]\rho \wedge (s,X_Q) \in \mathcal{F}_{TF}[\![Q]\!]\rho \wedge X = X_P \cup X_Q$$

From the antecedents, we obtain

$$\exists\, X_P, X_Q \;\;\bullet\;\; S(s,X_P) \wedge T(s,X_Q) \wedge X = X_P \cup X_Q$$

We conclude that the rule is sound.

Similar arguments may be presented for the other inference rules, with the exception of the recursion induction rules; soundness proofs for these rules were presented in section 5.5.

5.6.2 Completeness

We claim that, if every behaviour of a process P meets predicate $S(s, X)$, then the inference rules given in this chapter are sufficient to prove that P **sat** $S(s, X)$.

Lemma 5.17 If $P \in CSP$ meets the requirement that each recursion is constructive, then we may use the inference rules to establish that

$$P \quad \mathbf{sat}_\rho \quad (s, X) \in \mathcal{F}_{TF}[\![P]\!]\rho$$

for any environment ρ.

Proof We proceed by structural induction upon the syntax of timed CSP. The result is easy to establish for basic processes. As an example, consider the case of the deadlock process. The semantic equation for this operator yields that

$$(s, X) \in \mathcal{F}_{TF}[\![STOP]\!]\rho \quad \Leftrightarrow \quad s = \langle\rangle$$

The inference rules

$$\frac{}{STOP\ \mathbf{sat}_\rho\ s = \langle\rangle} \qquad \frac{\begin{array}{l} P\ \mathbf{sat}_\rho\ S(s, X) \\ S(s, X) \Rightarrow T(s, X) \end{array}}{P\ \mathbf{sat}_\rho\ T(s, X)}$$

are enough to establish that $STOP\ \mathbf{sat}_\rho\ (s, X) \in \mathcal{F}_{TF}[\![STOP]\!]\rho$.

For compound processes, we assume that the result holds for each component, and apply the appropriate inference rule. Consider the case of the simple parallel operator, which is associated with the following inference rule:

$$\frac{\begin{array}{l} P\ \mathbf{sat}_\rho\ S(s, X) \\ Q\ \mathbf{sat}_\rho\ T(s, X) \end{array}}{P \parallel Q\ \mathbf{sat}_\rho\ \exists X_P, X_Q \bullet X = X_P \cup X_Q \wedge S(s, X_P) \wedge T(s, X_Q)}$$

By our inductive hypothesis, the inference rules are enough to establish that

$$\begin{array}{lll} P & \mathbf{sat}_\rho & (s, X) \in \mathcal{F}_{TF}[\![P]\!]\rho \\ Q & \mathbf{sat}_\rho & (s, X) \in \mathcal{F}_{TF}[\![Q]\!]\rho \end{array}$$

With these instantiations, we obtain the following consequent

$$\begin{array}{lll} P \parallel Q & \mathbf{sat}_\rho & \exists X_P, X_Q \bullet X = X_P \cup X_Q \wedge (s, X_P) \in \mathcal{F}_{TF}[\![P]\!]\rho \\ & & \qquad \wedge (s, X_Q) \in \mathcal{F}_{TF}[\![Q]\!]\rho \end{array}$$

From the semantic equation for this operator,

$$\begin{array}{rl} (s, X) \in \mathcal{F}_{TF}[\![P \parallel Q]\!]\rho \quad \Leftrightarrow & \exists X_P, X_Q \bullet X = X_P \cup X_Q \wedge (s, X_P) \in \mathcal{F}_{TF}[\![P]\!]\rho \\ & \qquad (s, X_Q) \in \mathcal{F}_{TF}[\![Q]\!]\rho \end{array}$$

We conclude that

$$P \parallel Q \quad \mathbf{sat}_\rho \quad (s, X) \in \mathcal{F}_{TF}[\![P \parallel Q]\!]\rho$$

may be established using the inference rules of the $\mathcal{M}_{TF}$ proof system.

To see that the result is true for recursive processes, recall that the semantics of a recursive process is the unique fixed point of the corresponding mapping in the model $\mathcal{M}_{TF}$. For example, the semantics of the instant recursion $\mu X \circ P$ is defined to be the unique fixed point of the mapping $M(X, P)\rho$, where

$$M(X, P)\rho \ \widehat{=} \ \lambda Y \bullet \mathcal{F}_{TF}[\![P]\!]\rho[Y/X].$$

The following inference rule may be applied if P is constructive for X:

$$\frac{X \ \mathbf{sat}_\rho \ S(s, X) \Rightarrow P \ \mathbf{sat}_\rho \ S(s, X)}{\mu X \circ P \ \mathbf{sat}_\rho \ S(s, X)}$$

We instantiate S with the specification $(s, X) \in \mathcal{F}_{TF}[\![\mu X \circ P]\!]\rho$ and claim that the antecedent holds. Observe that

$$X \ \mathbf{sat}_\rho \ (s, X) \in \mathcal{F}_{TF}[\![\mu X \circ P]\!]\rho \quad \Rightarrow \quad \rho[\![X]\!] \subseteq \mathcal{F}_{TF}[\![\mu X \circ P]\!]\rho$$

The semantics of each operator is defined *pointwise* upon sets of timed failures. As a result, the mapping on $\mathcal{M}_{TF}$ corresponding to any timed CSP term must be monotonic with respect to the subset ordering. Hence

$$M(X, P)\rho \ (\rho[\![X]\!]) \ \subseteq \ M(X, P)\rho \ (\mathcal{F}_{TF}[\![\mu X \circ P]\!]\rho)$$

Expanding the definition of $M(X, P)\rho$, we obtain

$$\begin{array}{lrcl} & \mathcal{F}_{TF}[\![P]\!]\rho[\rho[\![X]\!]/X] & \subseteq & M(X, P)\rho \ \mathcal{F}_{TF}[\![\mu X \circ P]\!]\rho \\ \Rightarrow & \mathcal{F}_{TF}[\![P]\!]\rho & \subseteq & M(X, P)\rho \ \mathcal{F}_{TF}[\![\mu X \circ P]\!]\rho \\ \Rightarrow & \mathcal{F}_{TF}[\![P]\!]\rho & \subseteq & \mathcal{F}_{TF}[\![\mu X \circ P]\!]\rho \\ \Rightarrow & P & \mathbf{sat}_\rho & (s, X) \in \mathcal{F}_{TF}[\![\mu X \circ P]\!]\rho \end{array}$$

Hence the antecedent of the rule holds for this specification; we may infer that

$$\mu X \circ P \quad \mathbf{sat}_\rho \quad (s, X) \in \mathcal{F}_{TF}[\![\mu X \circ P]\!]\rho$$

The result follows by structural induction. □

We have shown that the inference rules of our proof system are enough to establish

$$P \quad \mathbf{sat}_\rho \quad (s, X) \in \mathcal{F}_{TF}[\![P]\!]\rho$$

for any timed CSP term P, providing that the body of any recursive term is constructive for the corresponding term variable. If a behavioural specification S holds of the timed failures semantics of P, then

$$(s, X) \in \mathcal{F}_{TF}[\![P]\!]\rho \quad \Rightarrow \quad S(s, X)$$

The logical rule for weakening specifications (used in the proof of the previous lemma) enables us to complete the proof of

$$P \quad \mathbf{sat}_\rho \quad S(s, X)$$

using only the inference rules of our proof system. We conclude that the proof system for $\mathcal{M}_{TF}$ presented in this chapter is complete for constructive recursive processes, with respect to the semantic function $\mathcal{F}_{TF}$.

5.7 TIMEWISE REFINEMENT

A formal specification of a complex system will consist of several behavioural specifications, each of which may be established separately. If we wish to prove that

$$P \quad \mathbf{sat} \quad S(s, X) \wedge T(s, X)$$

then it will suffice to show

$$P \ \mathbf{sat} \ S(s, X) \quad \wedge \quad P \ \mathbf{sat} \ T(s, X)$$

Some of these specifications may not require the full expressive power of timed failures model. If this is the case, then we may use the hierarchy of models beneath $\mathcal{M}_{TF}$ to simplify our proof obligations: see Figure 5.1.

If a predicate upon timed traces can be established without refusal information, then we may construct a proof in the timed traces model $\mathcal{M}_{TT}$. The nature of the projection mappings ensures that this proof will be valid in $\mathcal{M}_{TF}$. Similarly, if a property may be established without timing information, we may choose to construct a proof in the untimed failures model $\mathcal{M}_{UF}$, or the untimed traces model $\mathcal{M}_{UT}$. Of these models, $\mathcal{M}_{UT}$ is the most useful for simplifying timed failures specifications; $\mathcal{M}_{UF}$ is often inappropriate, and timed trace requirements may be established using a simplified version of the $\mathcal{M}_{TF}$ proof system.

To see how untimed failures specifications may be inappropriate or inadequate, recall that in an untimed failure (tr, X) the refusal set X is a set of events that may be refused following the observation of trace tr. In a timed context, X corresponds to the set of events that may be refused after all internal activity has ceased. Without a stability value, we have no record of internal activity; an untimed liveness requirement may insist only that an event is offered *eventually*; this may prove inadequate in the specification

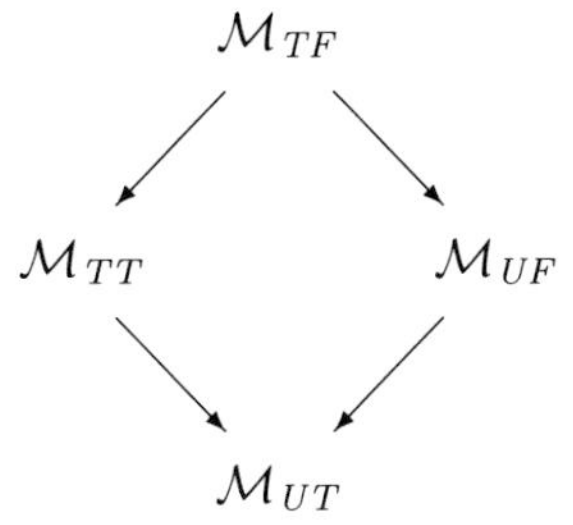

Figure 5.1 the models beneath $\mathcal{M}_{TF}$

of a real-time system. Nevertheless, a projection mapping from $\mathcal{M}_{TF}$ to $\mathcal{M}_{UF}$ might be used to establish important properties of a real-time system. For example, it may be possible to establish deadlock freedom using the algebraic properties of untimed CSP, instead of the satisfaction relation.

If a requirement can be established by reasoning within the untimed traces model, then we may employ a simple syntactic abstraction defined upon the syntax of CSP terms. Schneider (1989) has developed a theory of timewise refinement based upon the timed failures-stability model $\mathcal{M}_{TFS}$. In this section, we develop a similar theory for $\mathcal{M}_{TF}$ and exhibit a refinement proof rule for untimed safety specifications. We begin by presenting a syntax for untimed CSP, together with a semantic function for Reed's untimed traces model.

5.7.1 Traces model

We give an untimed syntax of CSP terms:

$$\begin{array}{lll} P & ::= & STOP \mid SKIP \mid X \mid & \text{atoms} \\ & & a \rightarrow P \mid P \,;\, P \mid P \not{\backslash} P & \text{sequential composition} \\ & & P \,\square\, P \mid P \sqcap P \mid a : A \rightarrow P_a \mid & \text{alternation} \\ & & P \parallel P \mid P \;{}_{A}\!\|_{B}\; P \mid P \,|||\, P \mid P \underset{A}{\parallel} P \mid & \text{parallel composition} \\ & & P \setminus A \mid f(P) \mid f^{-1}(P) \mid & \text{abstraction and renaming} \\ & & \mu\, X \bullet P \mid \langle X_i = P_i \rangle_j & \text{recursion} \end{array}$$

We define a semantic function from this syntax to the traces model $\mathcal{M}_{UT}$:

$$\mathcal{F}_{UT}[\![STOP]\!]\rho \mathrel{\widehat{=}} \{\langle\rangle\}$$

$$\mathcal{F}_{UT}[\![SKIP]\!]\rho \mathrel{\widehat{=}} \{\langle\rangle, \langle\checkmark\rangle\}$$

$$\mathcal{F}_{UT}[\![a \rightarrow P]\!]\rho \mathrel{\widehat{=}} \{\langle\rangle\} \cup \{\langle a\rangle^\frown tr \mid tr \in \mathcal{F}_{UT}[\![P]\!]\rho\}$$

$$\begin{aligned}\mathcal{F}_{UT}[\![P\,;\,Q]\!]\rho \mathrel{\widehat{=}} {} & \{tr \mid tr \in \mathcal{F}_{UT}[\![P]\!]\rho \wedge \checkmark \notin \sigma(tr)\,\} \\ & \cup \\ & \{tr_P{}^\frown tr_Q \mid tr_P{}^\frown\langle\checkmark\rangle \in \mathcal{F}_{UT}[\![P]\!]\rho \wedge tr_Q \in \mathcal{F}_{UT}[\![Q]\!]\rho\}\end{aligned}$$

$$\mathcal{F}_{UT}[\![P \mathbin{\not\!\downarrow} Q]\!]\rho \mathrel{\widehat{=}} \{tr_P{}^\frown tr_Q \mid tr_P \in \mathcal{F}_{UT}[\![P]\!]\rho \wedge tr_Q \in \mathcal{F}_{UT}[\![Q]\!]\rho\}$$

$$\mathcal{F}_{UT}[\![P \mathbin{\Box} Q]\!]\rho \mathrel{\widehat{=}} \mathcal{F}_{UT}[\![P]\!]\rho \cup \mathcal{F}_{UT}[\![Q]\!]\rho$$

$$\mathcal{F}_{UT}[\![P \sqcap Q]\!]\rho \mathrel{\widehat{=}} \mathcal{F}_{UT}[\![P]\!]\rho \cup \mathcal{F}_{UT}[\![Q]\!]\rho$$

$$\mathcal{F}_{UT}[\![a : A \rightarrow P_a]\!]\rho \mathrel{\widehat{=}} \{\langle a\rangle^\frown tr \mid a \in A \wedge tr \in \mathcal{F}_{UT}[\![P_a]\!]\rho\}$$

$$\mathcal{F}_{UT}[\![P \parallel Q]\!]\rho \mathrel{\widehat{=}} \mathcal{F}_{UT}[\![P]\!]\rho \cap \mathcal{F}_{UT}[\![Q]\!]\rho$$

$$\begin{aligned}\mathcal{F}_{UT}[\![P \;{}_A\|_B\; Q]\!]\rho \mathrel{\widehat{=}} {} & \{tr \mid tr \upharpoonright (A \cup B) = tr \wedge\, tr \upharpoonright A \in \mathcal{F}_{UT}[\![P]\!]\rho \\ & \qquad\qquad \wedge\, tr \upharpoonright B \in \mathcal{F}_{UT}[\![Q]\!]\rho\}\end{aligned}$$

$$\begin{aligned}\mathcal{F}_{UT}[\![P \mathbin{|||} Q]\!]\rho \mathrel{\widehat{=}} {} & \{tr \mid \exists\, tr_P, tr_Q \bullet tr \textit{ interleaves } (tr_P, tr_Q) \\ & \qquad tr_P \in \mathcal{F}_{UT}[\![P]\!]\rho \wedge tr_Q \in \mathcal{F}_{UT}[\![Q]\!]\rho\}\end{aligned}$$

$$\begin{aligned}\mathcal{F}_{UT}[\![P \underset{A}{\parallel} Q]\!]\rho \mathrel{\widehat{=}} {} & \{tr \mid \exists\, tr_P, tr_Q \bullet tr \setminus A \textit{ interleaves } (tr_P \setminus A, tr_Q \setminus A) \\ & \qquad tr \upharpoonright A = tr_P \upharpoonright A = tr_Q \upharpoonright A \\ & \qquad tr_P \in \mathcal{F}_{UT}[\![P]\!]\rho \wedge tr_Q \in \mathcal{F}_{UT}[\![Q]\!]\rho\}\end{aligned}$$

$$\mathcal{F}_{UT}[\![P \setminus A]\!]\rho \mathrel{\widehat{=}} \{tr \setminus A \mid tr \in \mathcal{F}_{UT}[\![P]\!]\rho\}$$

$$\mathcal{F}_{UT}[\![f(P)]\!]\rho \mathrel{\widehat{=}} \{f(tr) \mid tr \in \mathcal{F}_{UT}[\![P]\!]\rho\}$$

$$\mathcal{F}_{UT}[\![f^{-1}(P)]\!]\rho \mathrel{\widehat{=}} \{tr \mid f(tr) \in \mathcal{F}_{UT}[\![P]\!]\rho\}$$

$\mathcal{F}_{UT}[\![\mu X \bullet P]\!]\rho \mathrel{\widehat{=}}$ the unique fixed point of the mapping on $\mathcal{M}_{UT}$ corresponding to X, P and ρ

The untimed interrupt construct $P \mathbin{\not\!\downarrow} Q$ may transfer control from P to Q after any sequence of events; an arbitrary trace of this process may be any trace of P, followed by any trace of Q. The subsidiary relation *interleaves* is as defined by Hoare (1985): tr *interleaves* (tr_P, tr_Q) precisely when tr is an interleaving of tr_P and tr_Q.

If $S(tr)$ represents a behavioural specification on untimed traces, then we may define a satisfaction relation:

$$P \ \mathbf{sat}_\rho \ S(tr) \ \widehat{=} \ \forall\, tr \in UT \ \bullet \ tr \in \mathcal{F}_{UT}[\![P]\!]\rho \Rightarrow S(tr)$$

The choice of free variable identifies the model employed; we write tr to denote an arbitrary untimed trace. If the interpretation of **sat** is not obvious from the context, we will decorate it with the name of a semantic model. Using this relation, we may obtain a compositional proof system, similar to the $\mathcal{M}_{TF}$ proof system presented earlier in this chapter: e.g.

$$\frac{P \ \mathbf{sat}_\rho \ S(tr)}{a \rightarrow P \ \mathbf{sat}_\rho \ tr = \langle\rangle \vee tr = \langle a \rangle ^\frown tr' \wedge S(tr')}$$

The inference rules for the other operators are straightforward, except in the case of recursion. For a recursive process to have a well-defined semantics, the body of the recursive definition should be *guarded* for the recursive variable; a term P is guarded for a variable X if each occurrence of X in P is prefixed by some observable event. If term P is guarded for X, then the following rule may be applied:

$$\frac{X \ \mathbf{sat}_\rho \ S(tr) \Rightarrow P \ \mathbf{sat}_\rho \ S(tr)}{\mu\, X \bullet P \ \mathbf{sat}_\rho \ S(tr)} \quad [\ STOP \ \mathbf{sat} \ S(tr)\ ]$$

An untimed trace specification is satisfiable iff it is satisfied by $STOP$; this is a consequence of the following axiom for $\mathcal{M}_{UT}$:

$$\forall\, Y \in \mathcal{M}_{UT} \ \bullet \ \langle\rangle \in Y$$

The requirement that S is satisfiable is expressed by the side condition of the rule.

This proof system is considerably simpler than the proof system for $\mathcal{M}_{TF}$. If an untimed safety specification may be established within the untimed traces model, then we may remove the timing information from the syntax of the process and apply the inference rules for $\mathcal{M}_{UT}$.

5.7.2 Syntactic abstraction

We may define a syntactic abstraction Θ from the syntax of timed terms to the syntax of untimed terms. This removes timing information from the term, identifying any form of sequential composition with the immediate transfer of control. The abstraction mapping distributes through all of the standard operators:

$$\begin{aligned}
\Theta(\bot) &\mathrel{\widehat{=}} STOP \\
\Theta(STOP) &\mathrel{\widehat{=}} STOP \\
\Theta(SKIP) &\mathrel{\widehat{=}} SKIP \\
\Theta(WAIT\ t) &\mathrel{\widehat{=}} SKIP \\
\Theta(X) &\mathrel{\widehat{=}} X \\
\Theta(a \rightarrow P) &\mathrel{\widehat{=}} a \rightarrow \Theta(P) \\
\Theta(a \xrightarrow{t} P) &\mathrel{\widehat{=}} a \rightarrow \Theta(P) \\
\Theta(P\ ;\ Q) &\mathrel{\widehat{=}} \Theta(P)\ ;\ \Theta(Q) \\
\Theta(P\ ⨟\ Q) &\mathrel{\widehat{=}} \Theta(P)\ ;\ \Theta(Q) \\
\Theta(P \mathbin{\Box} Q) &\mathrel{\widehat{=}} \Theta(P) \mathbin{\Box} \Theta(Q) \\
\Theta(P \sqcap Q) &\mathrel{\widehat{=}} \Theta(P) \sqcap \Theta(Q) \\
\Theta(a : A \rightarrow P_a) &\mathrel{\widehat{=}} a : A \rightarrow \Theta(P_a) \\
\Theta(P \parallel Q) &\mathrel{\widehat{=}} \Theta(P) \parallel \Theta(Q) \\
\Theta(P\ {}_A\|_B\ Q) &\mathrel{\widehat{=}} \Theta(P)\ {}_A\|_B\ \Theta(Q) \\
\Theta(P \mathbin{|||} Q) &\mathrel{\widehat{=}} \Theta(P) \mathbin{|||} \Theta(Q) \\
\Theta(P \underset{A}{\parallel} Q) &\mathrel{\widehat{=}} \Theta(P) \underset{A}{\parallel} \Theta(Q) \\
\Theta(P \setminus A) &\mathrel{\widehat{=}} \Theta(P) \setminus A \\
\Theta(f(P)) &\mathrel{\widehat{=}} f(\Theta(P)) \\
\Theta(f^{-1}(P)) &\mathrel{\widehat{=}} f^{-1}(\Theta(P)) \\
\Theta(\mu X \bullet P) &\mathrel{\widehat{=}} \mu X \bullet \Theta(P) \\
\Theta(\mu X \circ P) &\mathrel{\widehat{=}} \mu X \bullet \Theta(P) \\
\Theta(\langle X_i = P_i \rangle_j) &\mathrel{\widehat{=}} \langle X_i = \Theta(P)_i \rangle_j
\end{aligned}$$

The timeout construct $P \overset{t}{\triangleright} Q$ may offer the user a choice between P and Q, or may behave as Q, depending on whether the timeout has occurred. Without timing information there is a nondeterministic choice between these two alternatives:

$$\Theta(P \overset{t}{\rhd} Q) \;\widehat{=}\; (\Theta(P) \,\Box\, \Theta(Q)) \sqcap \Theta(Q)$$

The timed interrupt operators are mapped to untimed interrupts:

$$\begin{aligned} \Theta(P \underset{t}{\lightning} Q) \;&\widehat{=}\; \Theta(P) \lightning \Theta(Q) \\ \Theta(P \underset{e}{\nabla} Q) \;&\widehat{=}\; \Theta(P) \lightning e \rightarrow \Theta(Q) \end{aligned}$$

The indexed nondeterministic choice and nondeterministic delay operators are mapped to the obvious targets:

$$\begin{aligned} \Theta(\textstyle\bigsqcap_{i \in I} P_i) \;&\widehat{=}\; \textstyle\bigsqcap_{i \in I} \Theta(P_i) \\ \Theta(\mathit{WAIT}\ T) \;&\widehat{=}\; \mathit{SKIP} \end{aligned}$$

5.7.3 Timewise refinement

If a specification $S(s)$ on timed traces is independent of timing information, then we may transform S into a behavioural specification on untimed traces. We define a simple projection mapping on elements of TT:

Definition 5.18

$$\begin{aligned} \mathit{tstrip}(\langle\rangle) \;&\widehat{=}\; \langle\rangle \\ \mathit{tstrip}(\langle(t, a)\rangle^\frown s) \;&\widehat{=}\; \langle a\rangle^\frown \mathit{tstrip}(s) \end{aligned}$$

The mapping *tstrip* removes the time values from the trace. If the truth of a behavioural specification S is independent of these values, we say that S is a *time-independent* specification.

Definition 5.19 A behavioural specification $S(s)$ is time-independent iff

$$\forall\, s_1, s_2 : TT \;\bullet\; \mathit{tstrip}(s_1) = \mathit{tstrip}(s_2) \;\Rightarrow\; S(s_1) \equiv S(s_2)$$

If $S(s)$ is a time-independent specification on timed traces, then it will prove convenient to define a corresponding condition upon untimed traces:

Definition 5.20 If $S(s)$ is a timed trace specification, then

$$\Phi S(tr) \;\widehat{=}\; \forall\, s \in TT \bullet \mathit{tstrip}(s) = tr \Rightarrow S(s)$$

An untimed trace tr meets the specification ΦS iff every assignment of time values to the events in tr produces a timed trace that meets S. Recall that the sequence of time values must be non-decreasing if the result is to be a valid timed trace.

Trace operators which do not refer to the times at which events occur may be applied to both timed and untimed traces. For example, the restriction and counting operators are defined on UT by

$$\begin{array}{rcll} \langle\rangle \upharpoonright A & \mathrel{\widehat{=}} & \langle\rangle & \\ (\langle a\rangle ^\frown tr) \upharpoonright A & \mathrel{\widehat{=}} & \langle a\rangle ^\frown (tr \upharpoonright A) & \text{if } a \in A \\ & & tr \upharpoonright A & \text{otherwise} \end{array}$$

$$tr \downarrow A \mathrel{\widehat{=}} \#(tr \upharpoonright A)$$

If a timed trace specification $S(s)$ is constructed using such operators, then the untimed trace condition will often be a consequence of $S(tr)$. As an example, consider the timed trace specification

$$S(s) \mathrel{\widehat{=}} (last(s) = a) \Rightarrow s \downarrow b = 0$$

A process satisfies this specification if whenever we record an a event, we find that no b events have been recorded. It is easy to establish that

$$(last(tr) = a) \Rightarrow tr \downarrow b = 0 \quad \Rightarrow \quad \Phi S(tr)$$

for any untimed trace tr.

If the image of S under Φ is satisfied by the untimed equivalent of a timed process P, then we might expect that P satisfies S. However, if we choose

$$P \mathrel{\widehat{=}} (a \rightarrow STOP \mathbin{|||} SKIP) \,;\, b \rightarrow STOP$$

then $\Theta(P)$ satisfies ΦS, where S is as defined above, but P does not satisfy S in $\mathcal{M}_{TF}$. With instantaneous sequential composition, events b may be observed at the same time as a, and so may appear first in the trace. The trace $\langle(0, b), (0, a)\rangle$ is a possible observation of P, and does not meet S.

This problem may occur whenever we use the instantaneous form of sequential composition. We could remove this operator from the syntax of timed CSP and use only the delayed form; this is the approach taken by Schneider (1989). We choose instead to retain it, for greater flexibility in process descriptions, and identify the situations in which it may be safely applied.

Definition 5.21 A process P is Θ-safe iff

$$\forall\, s, X \;\bullet\; (s, X) \in \mathcal{F}_{TF}[\![P]\!] \Rightarrow tstrip(s) \in \mathcal{F}_{UT}[\![P]\!]$$

A direct application of this definition would be impractical; fortunately, this property may be established by a simple inspection of the process syntax.

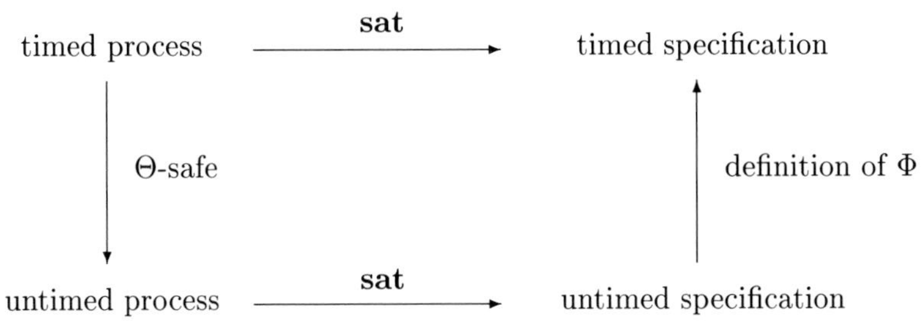

Figure 5.2 timewise refinement

Definition 5.22

- For any time t or set of times T, the terms $STOP$, $SKIP$, $\perp$, $WAIT\ t$, and X are all $\checkmark$-guarded.

- If P and Q are both $\checkmark$-guarded, then the terms $a \rightarrow P$, $a \xrightarrow{t} P$, $P \,\Box\, Q$, $P \sqcap Q$, $P \fatsemi Q$, $P \parallel Q$, $P \;{}_A\|_B\; Q$, $P \interleave Q$, $P \setminus A$, $f(P)$, $f^{-1}(P)$, $\mu X \bullet P$, $\mu X \circ P$, $P \overset{t}{\triangleright} Q$, $P \underset{t}{\lightning} Q$, and $P \underset{a \in A}{\nabla} Q_a$ are all $\checkmark$-guarded.

- If P_a and P_i are $\checkmark$-guarded, for each event $a \in A$ or index i, then the terms $a : A \rightarrow P_a$, $\bigsqcap_{i \in I} P_i$, and $\langle X_i = P_i \rangle_j$ are all $\checkmark$-guarded.

- If P and Q are both $\checkmark$-guarded and t is strictly positive, then the terms $WAIT\ t; P$, $P; WAIT\ t$, and $P; WAIT\ t\ ;\ Q$ are all $\checkmark$-guarded.

A term P is *$\checkmark$-guarded* if every instantaneous sequential composition is accompanied by a delay operator. This syntactic property is a sufficient condition for a process to be Θ-safe:

Lemma 5.23 For any timed CSP term P,

$$P \text{ is } \checkmark\text{-guarded} \quad \Rightarrow \quad P \text{ is } \Theta\text{-safe}$$

This result follows directly from the semantic equations for the timed failures and untimed traces models. We may now exhibit a refinement proof rule for untimed safety specifications:

Rule 5.24

$$\frac{\Theta(P) \ \textbf{sat} \ \Phi S(tr)}{P \ \textbf{sat} \ S(s)} \quad [\, P \text{ is } \Theta\text{-safe} \,]$$

If we can establish that the abstraction of a Θ-safe process P meets ΦS, then we may infer that P also satisfies S. The antecedent of the rule is a proof obligation in the untimed traces model, the consequent is a proof obligation in $\mathcal{M}_{TF}$.

Proof To see that this rule is sound, consider the commuting diagram of Figure 5.2. If s is a timed trace of a Θ-safe process, then $tstrip(s)$ will be a trace of $\Theta(P)$. If $\Theta(P)$ satisfies the behavioural specification $\Phi S(tr)$, then we may infer that S holds of trace s. The consequent part of the rule follows immediately. □

5.8 EXAMPLE

Consider the following implementation of a timed sensitive vending machine:

$$\begin{array}{rcl} TSVM & \mathrel{\widehat{=}} & coin \xrightarrow{t_1} (reset \xrightarrow{t_3} TSVM \\ & & \qquad\quad \overset{t_2}{\rhd} \\ & & \qquad\quad coke \xrightarrow{t_4} TSVM) \end{array}$$

The company that operates this machine requires that every drink is paid for in advance, and that the machine is ready to accept another order within a certain time t_4. In section 4.4, we formalised these requirements as separate behavioural specifications:

$$\begin{array}{rcl} SAFE(s) & \mathrel{\widehat{=}} & s \downarrow coke \leqslant s \downarrow coin \\[2ex] NEXT(s, X) & \mathrel{\widehat{=}} & \langle (t, coke) \rangle \ \underline{\text{in}}\ s \Rightarrow coin \notin \sigma(X \upharpoonright t + t_4) \\ & & \qquad\qquad\qquad\quad \vee \\ & & \qquad\qquad\qquad\quad coin \in \sigma(s \upharpoonright t) \end{array}$$

The machine is supplied with the following manufacturer's guarantee: if a coin is inserted at time t, then a drink is ready before time $t + t_5$, providing that the user does not trigger a *reset* during the interval $[t+t_1, t+t_1+t_2]$. This requirement corresponds to the following behavioural specification:

$$\begin{array}{rcl} OKAY(s, X) & \mathrel{\widehat{=}} & \langle (t, coin) \rangle \ \underline{\text{in}}\ s \wedge reset \notin \sigma(s \uparrow [t + t_1, t + t_1 + t_2]) \\ & & \Rightarrow \\ & & coke \notin \sigma(X \upharpoonright t + t_5) \vee coke \in \sigma(s \upharpoonright t) \end{array}$$

We would like to establish that the suggested implementation $TSVM$ meets the following behavioural specification:

$$SPEC(s, X) \;\widehat{=}\; SAFE(s) \wedge NEXT(s, X) \wedge OKAY(s, X)$$

5.8.1 Safety

The safety specification $SAFE$ is independent of timing considerations. Although it is possible to show that $TSVM$ satisfies this specification using the timed failures proof system, it will be easier to establish the result by timewise refinement. We observe that $TSVM$ is $\checkmark$-guarded and hence Θ-safe, and that

$$tr \downarrow coke \leqslant tr \downarrow coin \quad \Rightarrow \quad \Phi SAFE(tr)$$

Applying the abstraction mapping Θ reveals that

$$\Theta(TSVM) \;\equiv\; SVM$$

where SVM is the untimed vending machine of section 2.9:

$$\begin{aligned} SVM \;\widehat{=}\; coin \rightarrow (&PAID \,\Box\, reset \rightarrow SVM \\ &\sqcap \\ &coke \rightarrow SVM) \end{aligned}$$

An application of rule 5.24 reduces our proof obligation to

$$SVM \quad \mathbf{sat} \quad tr \downarrow coke \leqslant tr \downarrow coin$$

We observe that this recursion is guarded, and apply the inference rule for recursion in $\mathcal{M}_{UT}$. We have now to prove that

$$\begin{aligned} coin \rightarrow (&PAID \,\Box\, reset \rightarrow X \\ &\sqcap \qquad\qquad\qquad \mathbf{sat}_\rho \quad tr \downarrow coke \leqslant tr \downarrow coin \\ &coke \rightarrow X) \end{aligned}$$

under the assumption that

$$X \quad \mathbf{sat}_\rho \quad tr \downarrow coke \leqslant tr \downarrow coin$$

This result may be established using the inference rules for event prefix, deterministic choice, and nondeterministic choice in $\mathcal{M}_{UT}$.

5.8.2 Liveness

The rest of the proof must be conducted within the timed failures model. We begin by observing that the body of the recursion *SVM* is *constructive*, providing that $t_1 > 0$. We may then apply the inference rule for recursion, reducing our proof obligation to

$$\begin{array}{l} coin \xrightarrow{t_1} (reset \xrightarrow{t_3} X \\ \qquad\quad \overset{t_2}{\triangleright} \\ \qquad\quad coke \xrightarrow{t_4} X) \end{array} \quad \mathbf{sat}_\rho \quad NEXT(s, X) \wedge OKAY(s, X)$$

under the assumption that

$$X \quad \mathbf{sat}_\rho \quad NEXT(s, X) \wedge OKAY(s, X)$$

If we restrict our attention to the second of these specifications, we may apply the inference rule for event prefix to yield:

$$reset \xrightarrow{t_3} X \quad \mathbf{sat}_\rho \quad \begin{array}{l} s = \langle\rangle \\ \vee \\ s = \langle(t, reset)\rangle^\frown s' \wedge OKAY((s', X) - (t + t_3)) \end{array}$$

Similarly, we may easily establish that

$$coke \xrightarrow{t_4} X \quad \mathbf{sat}_\rho \quad \begin{array}{l} s = \langle\rangle \wedge coke \notin \sigma(X) \\ \vee \\ s = \langle(t, coke)\rangle^\frown s' \wedge coke \notin \sigma(X \restriction t) \\ \qquad\qquad\qquad\qquad \wedge\ OKAY((s', X) - (t + t_4)) \end{array}$$

Applying the inference rule for the timeout operator, we may deduce that

$$\begin{array}{l} reset \xrightarrow{t_3} X \\ \overset{t_2}{\triangleright} \\ coke \xrightarrow{t_4} X \end{array} \quad \mathbf{sat}_\rho \quad A(s, X) \vee B(s, X) \vee C(s, X)$$

where

$$\begin{array}{lcl} A(s, X) & \mathrel{\widehat=} & begin(s) \leqslant t_2 \\ & & s = \langle(t, reset)\rangle^\frown s' \\ & & OKAY((s', X) - (t_3 + t)) \\ B(s, X) & \mathrel{\widehat=} & s = \langle\rangle \ \wedge \ coke \notin \sigma(X - (t_2 + \delta)) \wedge \\ & & \\ C(s, X) & \mathrel{\widehat=} & s - (t_2 + \delta) = \langle(t, coke)\rangle^\frown s' \\ & & coke \notin \sigma(X - (t_2 + \delta) \restriction t) \\ & & OKAY((s', X) - (t_4 + t)) \end{array}$$

An application of the rule for event prefix reduces our proof obligation to

$$\left.\begin{array}{l} s = \langle\rangle \\ \vee \\ s = \langle(t', coin)\rangle^\frown s' \wedge \begin{array}[t]{l} A((s', X) - (t_1 + t')) \\ \vee \\ B((s', X) - (t_1 + t')) \\ \vee \\ C((s', X) - (t_1 + t')) \end{array} \end{array}\right\} \Rightarrow \quad OKAY(s, X)$$

The specification $OKAY$ is vacuous for the empty trace; we have only to prove

$$\left.\begin{array}{l} \langle(t_0, coin)\rangle \in s \\ reset \notin \sigma(s \uparrow [t_0 + t_1, t_0 + t_1 + t_2]) \\ s = \langle(t', coin)\rangle^\frown s' \;\wedge \begin{array}[t]{l} A((s', X) - (t_1 + t')) \\ \vee \\ B((s', X) - (t_1 + t')) \\ \vee \\ C((s', X) - (t_1 + t')) \end{array} \end{array}\right\} \Rightarrow \begin{array}{l} coke \notin \sigma(X \upharpoonright t_0 + t_5) \\ \vee \\ coke \in \sigma(s \upharpoonright t_0) \end{array}$$

If $t' \neq t_0$, then the result is easily established by expanding A, B, and C. Suppose then that $t' = t_0$; our assumption that

$$reset \notin \sigma(s \uparrow [t' + t_1, t' + t_1 + t_2])$$

contradicts $A(s, X)$, so we have only to show that

$$\left.\begin{array}{l} s = \langle(t', coin)\rangle^\frown s' \;\wedge \begin{array}[t]{l} B((s', X) - (t_1 + t')) \\ \vee \\ C((s', X) - (t_1 + t')) \end{array} \end{array}\right\} \Rightarrow \begin{array}{l} coke \notin \sigma(X \upharpoonright t' + t_5) \\ \vee \\ coke \in \sigma(s \upharpoonright t') \end{array}$$

From the definitions of B and C we obtain:

$$\begin{array}{l} s' = \langle\rangle \;\wedge\; coke \notin \sigma(X - (t_1 + t_2 + t' + \delta)) \\ \vee \\ s' - (t_1 + t_2 + t' + \delta) = \langle(t'', coke)\rangle^\frown s'' \end{array}$$

The result follows, providing that

$$t_5 \;\geqslant\; t_1 + t_2 + \delta$$

If a coin is inserted at time t, then we cannot guarantee to provide a drink any earlier than $t + t_1 + t_2 + \delta$. We must allow a delay of t_1 for the coin to be inserted, a delay of t_2 for the coin to drop, and a delay of at least δ for control to be passed to the dispensing process.

The proof of $NEXT(s, X)$ is similar, although an additional constraint must be added to ensure that this specification is preserved by each recursive call. We may conclude that the full specification is satisfied:

$$TSVM \quad \mathbf{sat} \quad SPEC(s, X)$$

providing that the above condition upon t_5 is observed.

6 STRUCTURING SPECIFICATIONS

6.1 ABSTRACTION

If we wish to produce a readable specification of a large system, then we must take care to present our description in a clear, structured fashion. At each level of abstraction, we identify the interfaces between system components and conceal any events which are not of interest. We express our specification as a series of *service* specifications, each describing the service provided by a particular component of the system. In this way, we may refine a description of the service provided by a system towards a satisfactory implementation.

The hiding operator provides the mechanism for abstraction in timed CSP; the expression $P \setminus A$ denotes a process that behaves as P, except that

- events from A occur as soon as they become available
- only events from outside A are observed

In section 5.2.8 we gave an inference rule for this operator that was easy to derive, but difficult to apply. We can achieve a significant reduction in complexity if we separate the concerns of concealment and scheduling. To this end, we define a predicate act_A which holds of any *A-active* behaviour:

Definition 6.1 $\quad \mathrm{act}_A(s, X) \mathrel{\widehat{=}} [0, end(s, X)) \times A \subseteq X$

A behaviour (s, X) is A-active if all events from set A occur as soon as they become available. If we wish to establish that $P \setminus A$ satisfies a specification $S(s, X)$, it is sufficient to show that

- $S(s, X)$ holds for all of the A-active behaviours of P
- $S(s, X)$ is unaffected by the concealment of events from A

The second condition is satisfied if the truth of the specification is unaffected by the removal of A's events from the trace and refusal.

Definition 6.2 A behavioural specification $S(s, X)$ is A-independent iff

$$\forall s : TT ; X : TR \bullet S(s, X \cup [0, end(s)) \times A) \Rightarrow S(s \setminus A, X)$$

If S describes a service provided across an interface that is disjoint from A, then S should be A-independent. The following abbreviation will prove convenient:

Definition 6.3 $S(s, X) \mathbin{\backslash\!\backslash} A \mathrel{\widehat{=}} \mathrm{act}_{\mathrm{A}}(s, X) \Rightarrow S(s, X)$

This states that the specification $S(s, X)$ holds whenever the current behaviour is A-active. We may now present a simple proof rule for the hiding operator:

Rule 6.4

$$\frac{P \ \mathbf{sat}_\rho \ S(s, X) \mathbin{\backslash\!\backslash} A}{P \setminus A \ \mathbf{sat}_\rho \ S(s, X)} \quad [\ S \text{ is } A\text{-independent}\ ]$$

If an A-independent specification S holds for all A-active behaviours of a term P, then we may infer that $P \setminus A$ satisfies $S(s, X)$.

6.1.1 Example

Suppose that process P satisfies the following specification:

$$\begin{aligned} T(s, X) \ \widehat{=}\ & a \notin \sigma(X \uparrow [1, 2)) \vee a \in \sigma(s \uparrow [0, 2)) \\ & \wedge \\ & \langle (t, a) \rangle \ \underline{\mathrm{in}}\ s \Rightarrow b \notin \sigma(X \uparrow [t + 1, t + 2)) \\ & \qquad\qquad \vee \\ & \qquad\qquad b \in \sigma(s \uparrow [t + 1, t + 2)) \end{aligned}$$

In this case, the event a is available from time 1 to time 2, unless it has already occurred. Further, if an a is observed at any time t, then b either occurs or is available during the interval $[t + 1, t + 2)$.

If we consider only the a-active behaviours of P, then a is present for the duration of refusal set X. If the behaviour (s, X) extends beyond time 1, we know that a must occur before time 2. We can show that

$$\begin{aligned} T(s, X) \mathbin{\backslash\!\backslash} a \ \equiv\ & end(s, X) \geqslant 1 \Rightarrow a \in \sigma(s \uparrow [0, 2)) \\ & \wedge \\ & \langle (t, a) \rangle \ \underline{\mathrm{in}}\ s \Rightarrow b \notin \sigma(X \uparrow [t + 1, t + 2)) \\ & \qquad\qquad \vee \\ & \qquad\qquad b \in \sigma(s \uparrow [t + 1, t + 2)) \end{aligned}$$

and it is easy to establish that

$$T(s, X) \mathbin{\backslash\!\backslash} a \Rightarrow S(s, X) \mathbin{\backslash\!\backslash} a$$

where

$$S(s,X) \mathrel{\widehat{=}} \exists t : [0,2) \bullet b \notin \sigma(X \uparrow [t+1, t+2)) \\ \vee \\ b \in \sigma(s \uparrow [t+1, t+2))$$

It is clear that $S(s,X)$ is an a-independent specification, so we may apply the new inference rule for the hiding operator to obtain

$$P \setminus a \quad \mathbf{sat} \quad \exists t : [0,2) \bullet b \notin \sigma(X \uparrow [t+1, t+2)) \\ \vee \\ b \in \sigma(s \uparrow [t+1, t+2))$$

The event b is either made available or observed, during the interval $[t+1, t+2)$, where $0 \leqslant t < 2$.

6.2 SCHEDULING

The form of liveness condition employed above is both awkward and inadequate if we wish to abstract from the events concerned. If we have that

$$P \quad \mathbf{sat} \quad a \notin \sigma(X \uparrow I) \vee a \in \sigma(s \uparrow J)$$

then we may infer only that $P \setminus a$ performs event a at some time during the interval J. If we intend to conceal an event a, then any liveness specification involving a should address the time at which a becomes available.

Instead of requiring that an event a is offered during a fixed interval *unless* it is observed, we may insist that a is available *until* it is observed.

Definition 6.5

$$a \text{ from } t\ (s,X) \mathrel{\widehat{=}} a \notin \sigma(X \uparrow [t, \mathit{begin}(s \uparrow [t,\infty) \downharpoonright a)))$$

The right-hand predicate states that event a is absent from refusal set X between time t and the time at which the next a is observed; it is easy to see that the process $WAIT\ t; a \rightarrow STOP$ will satisfy this specification.

This form of liveness specification allows us to determine the precise time of occurrence of hidden events. If a process P satisfies the liveness condition a from t, then we may infer that the event a occurs at time t in all a-active behaviours of P. If we define

Definition 6.6 $a \text{ at } t\ (s,X) \mathrel{\widehat{=}} \langle (t,a) \rangle \ \underline{\text{in}}\ s$

then we obtain

$$a \text{ from } t\ (s,X) \Rightarrow \mathit{end}(s,X) > t \Rightarrow a \text{ at } t\ (s,X) \mathbin{\setminus\!\!\setminus} a$$

If a becomes available at t, and it is hidden, then it will be observed at t, if the current observation extends far enough. This follows from:

Lemma 6.7 For any $S(s, X)$, if $end(s, X) > t$ then

$$
\begin{aligned}
(S(s, X) \vee a \text{ from } t\ (s, X)) \setminus\!\!\setminus a &\Rightarrow (S(s, X) \vee a \text{ at } t\ (s, X)) \setminus\!\!\setminus a \\
(S(s, X) \wedge a \text{ from } t\ (s, X)) \setminus\!\!\setminus a &\Rightarrow (S(s, X) \wedge a \text{ at } t\ (s, X)) \setminus\!\!\setminus a
\end{aligned}
$$

Proof From the definition of $\setminus\!\!\setminus$, we obtain

$$([0, end(s, X)) \times \{a\}) \subseteq X$$

Our assumption that $end(s, X) > t$ allows us to infer that $a \in \sigma(X \uparrow t)$. From definition 6.5, we deduce that

$$[t, begin(s \uparrow [t, \infty) \downharpoonleft a)) \quad = \quad \{\}$$

and hence that $\langle (t, a) \rangle \ \underline{\text{in}}\ s$. The result follows. □

We may allow a process to withdraw the offer of an event if it has not been accepted within a given period of time, or if another event has been observed.

Definition 6.8

$$a \text{ from } t \text{ until } t'\ (s, X) \quad \widehat{=} \quad a \notin \sigma(X \uparrow [t, min\{t', begin(s \uparrow [t, \infty) \downharpoonleft a)\}))$$

If the offer of event a has not been accepted by time t', the process may retract without violating the liveness specification. This corresponds to a simple application of the timeout operator.

$$WAIT\ t_1\ ;\ ((a \rightarrow STOP) \overset{t_2}{\rhd} STOP) \quad \textbf{sat} \quad a \text{ from } t_1 \text{ until } t_1 + t_2$$

Event a is enabled at t_1 and, if it has not been performed, disabled at $t_1 + t_2$.

Definition 6.9

$$a \text{ from } t \text{ until } b\ (s, X) \quad \widehat{=} \quad a \notin \sigma(X \uparrow [t, begin(s \uparrow [t, \infty) \downharpoonleft \{a, b\})))$$

If a process is to satisfy this specification, event a must become available at time t, and must remain available until either a or b is observed. We may combine this condition with the possibility of a timeout:

Definition 6.10

$$
\begin{aligned}
&a \text{ from } t \text{ until } t' \text{ or } b\ (s, X) \ \widehat{=} \\
&\qquad a \notin \sigma(X \uparrow [t, min\{t', begin(s \uparrow [t, \infty) \downharpoonleft \{a, b\})\}))
\end{aligned}
$$

It is worth observing that:

$$a \text{ from } t \text{ until } t' \text{ or } b \quad \equiv \quad a \text{ from } t \text{ until } t' \vee a \text{ from } t \text{ until } b$$

More usually, we will wish to insist that a becomes available at some time during a fixed interval I. We can capture this requirement with a simple quantification:

Definition 6.11

$$a \text{ from } I\ (s, X) \quad \hat{=} \quad \exists\, t : I \bullet a \text{ from } t$$

As an example, consider the process P defined by:

$$P \quad \hat{=} \quad (\mathit{WAIT}\,[1, 2)\,;(a \rightarrow \mathit{STOP} \,\Box\, b \rightarrow \mathit{STOP})) \overset{4}{\triangleright} \mathit{STOP}$$

We may use the timed failures proof system to show that

$$P \quad \textbf{sat} \quad a \text{ from } [1, 2) \text{ until } 4 \text{ or } b\ (s, X)$$

The event a is enabled at some time between 1 and 2, and disabled at time 4 or when b occurs, whichever is the sooner.

With another existential quantification, we may allow the offer of a to be withdrawn at any time during an interval J. Further, we may require that event a made available until some event from set B is observed:

Definition 6.12

$$a \text{ from } I \text{ until } J \text{ or } B \quad \hat{=} \quad \exists\, t : I\,;\, t' : J \bullet \exists\, b : B \bullet a \text{ from } t \text{ until } t' \text{ or } b$$

The following equivalence confirms that existential quantification over set B has captured the required constraint:

$$a \text{ from } t \text{ until } B\ (s, X) \quad \equiv \quad a \notin \sigma(X \uparrow [t, \mathit{begin}(s \uparrow [t, \infty) \restriction \{a\} \cup B)))$$

The offer of a may be withdrawn following the occurrence of any event from set B. This justifies the following definition:

Definition 6.13

$$A \text{ from } I \text{ until } J \text{ or } B \quad \hat{=} \quad \forall\, a : A \bullet a \text{ from } I \text{ until } J \text{ or } (A \cup B)$$

If a process is to satisfy this specification, the whole of set A must become available at some time t in I, and remain available until some time t' in J, unless an event from $A \cup B$ is observed. The sequence of quantifiers is the most appropriate for our needs; the specification "A from I (s, X)" is satisfied by any process that becomes ready for every event from A at some time during I. An example might be

$$WAIT\,[0, 1)\,;\, in.m : in.M \rightarrow P_m$$

This process becomes ready to accept any message m from set M on channel in at some time during interval $[0, 1)$.

A similar generalisation may be applied to the 'at' construct; we may replace the single event and time with a set and interval:

Definition 6.14 $\quad A \text{ at } I\ (s, X) \mathrel{\widehat{=}} \exists\, a : A\, ;\, t : I \bullet a \text{ at } t\ (s, X)$

This condition is true if some event from set A is observed at some time during the interval I.

We may generalise the statement of lemma 6.7. If (s, X) is an A-active behaviour, and every event from A is made available at some time during interval I, then some event from A must be observed during I.

Lemma 6.15 If $end(s, X) > end(I)$ then

$$(S(s, X) \vee A \text{ from } I\ (s, X)) \setminus\!\setminus A \quad \Rightarrow \quad (S(s, X) \vee A \text{ at } I\ (s, X)) \setminus\!\setminus A$$

$$(S(s, X) \wedge A \text{ from } I\ (s, X)) \setminus\!\setminus A \quad \Rightarrow \quad (S(s, X) \wedge A \text{ at } I\ (s, X)) \setminus\!\setminus A$$

Some care must be taken in the presence of an 'until' clause: if the interval in which an event is enabled intersects with the interval in which the offer may be withdrawn, then there is no guarantee that the event will occur.

Lemma 6.16 If $end(s, X) > end(I)$ and $begin(J) > end(I)$ then

$$(S(s, X) \vee A \text{ from } I \text{ until } J\ (s, X)) \setminus\!\setminus A \quad \Rightarrow \quad (S(s, X) \vee A \text{ at } I\ (s, X)) \setminus\!\setminus A$$

$$(S(s, X) \wedge A \text{ from } I \text{ until } J\ (s, X)) \setminus\!\setminus A \quad \Rightarrow \quad (S(s, X) \wedge A \text{ at } I\ (s, X)) \setminus\!\setminus A$$

If the offer of events from set A may be withdrawn on the observation of an event from B, then we know that some event from $A \cup B$ will occur in an A-active behaviour.

Lemma 6.17 If $end(s, X) > end(I)$ then

$$(S(s, X) \vee A \text{ from } I \text{ until } B\ (s, X)) \setminus\!\setminus A \quad \Rightarrow \quad (S(s, X) \vee A \cup B \text{ at } I\ (s, X)) \setminus\!\setminus A$$

$$(S(s, X) \wedge A \text{ from } I \text{ until } B\ (s, X)) \setminus\!\setminus A \quad \Rightarrow \quad (S(s, X) \wedge A \cup B \text{ at } I\ (s, X)) \setminus\!\setminus A$$

In each of these lemmas, we cannot assert that any event is observed unless the experiment is of sufficient duration: $end(s, X) > end(I)$.

6.3 A SPECIFICATION LANGUAGE

The 'at' and 'from' expressions are *macro* expressions. We may use such expressions to make our specifications more palatable, although it will often be necessary to expand them in the course of a proof. We may consider these expressions as functions acting on timed failures. If we lift the boolean operators to take functions as arguments, we may obtain a simple language for timed specifications. For example, the requirement that

$$P \quad \mathbf{sat} \quad a \text{ from } t\ (s, X) \wedge \neg\, (b \text{ at } t\ (s, X))$$

may be shortened to

$$P \quad \mathbf{sat} \quad a \text{ from } t \wedge \neg\, (b \text{ at } t)$$

Not only are such specifications easier to read, but also they are open to interpretation in other models. This language is a first order logic with time-valued variables, comparable to those of Hooman (1990) and Jahanian and Mok (1986).

There is no need to extend the satisfaction relation between processes and specifications. If F is defined upon the set of all timed failures, then

$$P \ \mathbf{sat}\ F(s, X) \quad \Leftrightarrow \quad \forall\, s, X \bullet (s, X) \in \mathcal{F}_{TF}[\![P]\!] \Rightarrow F(s, X)$$

In the case when F is applied to the typical failure (s, X), as in the example above, we will omit the function argument. We may employ the inference rules of the timed failures proof system to establish results expressed in our new language. We may also derive laws for reasoning about higher-order objects such as 'at' and 'from' expressions. If we define

$$\begin{aligned} \text{time } (s, X) \ &\mathrel{\widehat{=}}\ end(s, X) \\ \text{active } A\ (s, X) \ &\mathrel{\widehat{=}}\ [0, end(s, X)) \subseteq X \end{aligned}$$

then lemma 6.7 gives rise to a simple example

$$\text{active } A \ \wedge\ A \text{ from } t \ \wedge\ \text{time} > t \quad \Rightarrow \quad A \text{ at } t$$

If events from set A do not require the cooperation of the environment, and all events from A are made available at time t, then some event from A will be observed at time t.

In the course of chapter 7, we will require a number of functions to extract information from a timed trace. One such function has already been defined,

$$A \text{ at } I\ (s, X) \quad \equiv \quad \exists\, a : A \bullet a \in \sigma(s \uparrow I)$$

which returns a boolean expression whose value is *true* precisely when some event from set A is present in trace s restricted to interval I. The remaining functions will be defined using projection mappings upon timed failures.

If M is a projection mapping from timed failures to time values, and φ is a predicate upon time values, then

$$F(s, X) \mathrel{\widehat{=}} \varphi(M(s, X))$$

defines a behavioural specification on timed failures. A similar construction may be used for projection mappings whose results are timed events, sequences of events, or even components of events.

We will often wish to consider the sequence of data values passed along a certain channel c during a particular interval I. The following projection mapping yields precisely this information:

$$\text{data } c \text{ during } I\ (s, X) \mathrel{\widehat{=}} \mathit{data}(s \downharpoonright c.\Sigma \uparrow I)$$

where *data* is defined by

$$\begin{aligned} \mathit{data}(\langle\rangle) &\mathrel{\widehat{=}} \langle\rangle \\ \mathit{data}(\langle(t, c.a)\rangle^\frown s) &\mathrel{\widehat{=}} \langle a\rangle^\frown \mathit{data}(s) \end{aligned}$$

The result is a sequence drawn from the datatype of values permitted on channel c.

Another useful projection mapping returns the last timed event from set A observed during interval I, or strictly before time t:

$$\begin{aligned} \text{last } A \text{ during } I\ (s, X) &\mathrel{\widehat{=}} \mathit{foot}(s \downharpoonright A \uparrow I) \\ \text{last } A \text{ before } t\ (s, X) &\mathrel{\widehat{=}} \mathit{foot}(s \downharpoonright A \uparrow [0, t)) \end{aligned}$$

Similarly, we may define a projection mapping 'count' that yields the number of occurrences of events from a given set during a specified interval.

$$\begin{aligned} \text{count } A \text{ during } I\ (s, X) &\mathrel{\widehat{=}} \#(s \downharpoonright A \uparrow I) \\ \text{count } A \text{ before } t\ (s, X) &\mathrel{\widehat{=}} \#(s \downharpoonright A \uparrow [0, t)) \end{aligned}$$

Again, we may choose to count only the events observed before some time t.

It will prove convenient to give names to the projection mappings from timed events to times and events.

$$\begin{aligned} \text{time of } (t, a) &\mathrel{\widehat{=}} t \\ \text{name of } (t, a) &\mathrel{\widehat{=}} a \end{aligned}$$

for any timed event (t, a). We will add to this list of projection mappings and functions whenever we encounter constraints that cannot be expressed using our existing vocabulary.

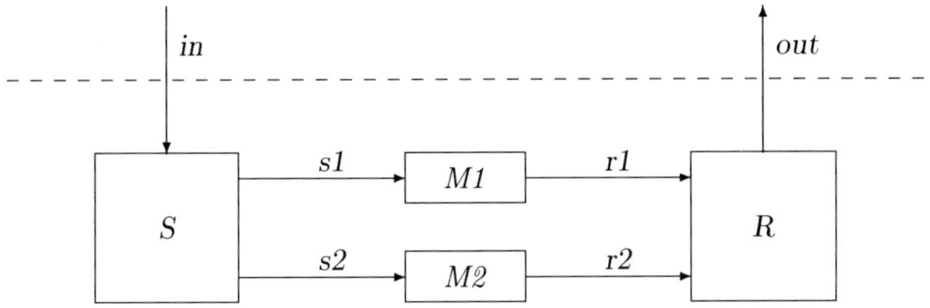

Figure 6.1 transmission with a choice of media

6.4 EXAMPLE

Consider a simple communications network—illustrated in Figure 6.1—consisting of a sender process S, a receiver process R, and two communications media, $M1$ and $M2$. The network accepts messages on channel *in*, and delivers messages on channel *out*. The sender transmits each message to the receiver using either $M1$ or $M2$. The choice of medium may depend upon message length, current load, or internal errors; in any case, the user is not informed.

Both transmission media are reliable, but each is associated with a different nondeterministic delay. The first will transmit messages from channel $s1$ to channel $r1$ with a delay of between 1 and 2 seconds, while the other will transmit messages from $s2$ to $t2$ with a delay of between 0.1 and 0.3 seconds. These channels are invisible to the network user. We assume that all messages are of message type M, and choose $c.M$ to denote the set of communications possible on channel c,

$$c.M \quad \widehat{=} \quad \{c.m \mid m \in M\}$$

where c is any of $s1$, $s2$, $r1$, $r2$.

We require that any implementation of this network should deliver a message within 3 seconds of its arrival on channel *in*. This requirement is captured by the following behavioural specification:

$$LIVE \quad \widehat{=} \quad in.m \text{ at } t \Rightarrow out.m \text{ from } (t, t+3)$$

If a message is input at time t, it will be available on channel *out* at some time between t and $t + 3$.

Each transmission medium is initially ready to accept a message, and is always prepared to accept a new message within 0.1 seconds. If medium $M1$ accepts a message m on channel $s1$ at time t, then it must begin to offer the communication $r1.m$ at some time between $t + 1$ and $t + 2$, and become ready for a new message before time $t + 0.1$. We may capture these requirements with the following behavioural specification upon medium $M1$:

$$\begin{array}{lll} M1 & \textbf{sat} & s1.M \text{ from } 0 \\ & & \wedge \\ & & s1.m \text{ at } t \Rightarrow r1.m \text{ from } (t+1, t+2) \\ & & \qquad\qquad\quad \wedge \\ & & \qquad\qquad\quad s1.M \text{ from } (t, t+0.1) \end{array}$$

The faster medium $M2$ satisfies a similar specification, undertaking to deliver a message after a delay of between 0.1 and 0.3 seconds:

$$\begin{array}{lll} M2 & \textbf{sat} & s2.M \text{ from } 0 \\ & & \wedge \\ & & s2.m \text{ at } t \Rightarrow r2.m \text{ from } (t+0.1, t+0.3) \\ & & \qquad\qquad\quad \wedge \\ & & \qquad\qquad\quad s2.M \text{ from } (t, t+0.1) \end{array}$$

For the purposes of this example, we have assumed adequate buffering of messages. This issue may be addressed separately, using timed safety specifications.

The sender process S passes each input to at least one of the transmission media within 0.2 seconds of its arrival on channel in:

$$\begin{array}{lll} S & \textbf{sat} & in.m \text{ at } t \Rightarrow s1.m \text{ from } (t, t+0.2) \\ & & \qquad\qquad\quad \vee \\ & & \qquad\qquad\quad s2.m \text{ from } (t, t+0.2) \end{array}$$

In order to guarantee the successful transmission of a specific message, we must insist that the sender process does not flood the media with spurious messages. This requirement corresponds to the the following untimed safety specification: for any message m, the number of transmissions of m is less than or equal to the number of times m is accepted on channel in.

$$S \quad \textbf{sat} \quad \forall\, m : M \bullet \text{count}\{s1.m, s2.m\} \leqslant \text{count } in.m$$

Even with a timed implementation, such a safety specification could probably be established by reasoning within the untimed traces model.

The receiver R behaves in a complementary fashion. It is always prepared to accept a new message from either medium within 0.1 seconds. Messages are ready for output on channel *out* within *0.2* seconds of arrival.

$$
\begin{array}{lll}
R & \textbf{sat} & r1.M \cup r2.M \text{ from } 0 \\
& & \wedge \\
& & r1.m \text{ at } t \Rightarrow out.m \text{ from } (t, t + 0.2) \\
& & \qquad\qquad\quad \wedge \\
& & \qquad\qquad\quad r1.M \cup r2.M \text{ from } (t, t + 0.1) \\
& & \wedge \\
& & r2.m \text{ at } t \Rightarrow out.m \text{ from } (t, t + 0.2) \\
& & \qquad\qquad\quad \wedge \\
& & \qquad\qquad\quad r1.M \cup r2.M \text{ from } (t, t + 0.1)
\end{array}
$$

If a message is received on either $r1$ or $r2$ at time t, it is made available on channel *out* before time $t + 0.2$.

We assume that the sender and receiver have disjoint alphabets, and that the named channels are distinct. With these assumptions, we may implement the network as a simple parallel combination:

$$NET \mathrel{\widehat{=}} (S \underset{\{s1,s2\}}{\|} (M1 \mathbin{|||} M2) \underset{\{r1,r2\}}{\|} R) \setminus \{s1, s2, r1, r2\}$$

To demonstrate that this meets our liveness requirement, we must show that

$$COMMS \;\; \textbf{sat} \;\; LIVE \setminus\!\!\setminus \{s1, s2, r1, r2\}$$

where *COMMS* is the process

$$S \underset{\{s1,s2\}}{\|} (M1 \mathbin{|||} M2) \underset{\{r1,r2\}}{\|} R$$

From the specifications of *M1* and *M2* and the inference rule for interleaving parallel combination, we may deduce that

$$
\begin{array}{lll}
M1 \mathbin{|||} M2 & \textbf{sat} & s1.M \text{ from } 0 \wedge s2.M \text{ from } 0 \\
& & \wedge \\
& & s1.m \text{ at } t \Rightarrow r1.m \text{ from } (t + 1, t + 2) \\
& & \qquad\qquad\quad \wedge \\
& & \qquad\qquad\quad s1.M \text{ from } (t, t + 0.1) \\
& & \wedge \\
& & s2.m \text{ at } t \Rightarrow r2.m \text{ from } (t + 0.1, t + 0.3) \\
& & \qquad\qquad\quad \wedge \\
& & \qquad\qquad\quad s2.M \text{ from } (t, t + 0.1)
\end{array}
$$

Using the inference rule for communicating parallel, we may establish that:

$$\begin{array}{lll} S \underset{\{s1,s2\}}{\|} (M1 \mid\mid\mid M2) & \textbf{sat} & in.m \text{ at } t \Rightarrow s1.m \text{ from } (t, t+0.3) \\ & & \qquad \vee \\ & & \qquad s2.m \text{ from } (t, t+0.3) \\ & & \wedge \\ & & s1.m \text{ at } t \Rightarrow r1.m \text{ from } (t+1, t+2) \\ & & \wedge \\ & & s2.m \text{ at } t \Rightarrow r2.m \text{ from } (t+0.1, t+0.3) \end{array}$$

Another application of the inference rule yields that:

$$\begin{array}{lll} COMMS & \textbf{sat} & in.m \text{ at } t \Rightarrow s1.m \text{ from } (t, t+0.3) \\ & & \qquad \vee \\ & & \qquad s2.m \text{ from } (t, t+0.3) \\ & & \wedge \\ & & s1.m \text{ at } t \Rightarrow r1.m \text{ from } (t+1, t+2.1) \\ & & \wedge \\ & & s2.m \text{ at } t \Rightarrow r2.m \text{ from } (t+0.1, t+0.4) \\ & & \wedge \\ & & \{r1.m\} \cup \{r2.m\} \text{ at } t \Rightarrow out.m \text{ from } (t, t+0.2) \end{array}$$

Under the assumption that the set $\{s1, s2, r1, r2\}$ is hidden from the environment, we may apply lemma 6.7 and infer that:

$$\begin{array}{lll} COMMS & \textbf{sat} & (in.m \text{ at } t \Rightarrow out.m \text{ from } (t+0.1, t+0.9) \\ & & \qquad \vee \\ & & \qquad out.m \text{ from } (t+1, t+2.6)) \setminus\!\!\setminus \{s1, s2, r1, r2\} \end{array}$$

The disjunction corresponds to the hidden choice of media. If the message is sent via medium $M2$, there will be a delay of between 0.1 and 0.9 seconds; a different range of delays is introduced by the slower medium $M1$.

The above behavioural specification is $\{s1, s2, r1, r2\}$-independent; we may apply the inference rule for the hiding operator given in section 6.1 to obtain

$$\begin{array}{lll} NET & \textbf{sat} & in.m \text{ at } t \Rightarrow out.m \text{ from } (t+0.1, t+0.9) \\ & & \qquad \vee \\ & & \qquad out.m \text{ from } (t+1, t+2.6) \end{array}$$

which is enough to establish our liveness requirement.

In this proof, we have omitted the details of the functional application and variable substitution necessary for the timed failures proof system. This cumbersome process can be avoided altogether if we derive inference rules for the direct manipulation of macro specification statements.

7 CASE STUDY

7.1 A LOCAL AREA NETWORK PROTOCOL

To illustrate the application of timed CSP to the specification of real-time systems, we will show how the functions presented in chapter 6 may used to describe the behaviour of a communications protocol at two different levels of abstraction. The protocol chosen for this purpose is based upon the Ethernet communication protocol, a standard protocol for local area networks.

The Ethernet protocol is a *broadcast* protocol: signals sent by one station may reach all of the stations upon the network. It is a *carrier-sense* protocol: stations listen for a carrier signal on the broadcast medium and act accordingly. Another important feature is *collision detection*. Each station must monitor the broadcast medium during transmission, and cease immediately if it becomes apparent that another station is also transmitting.

The protocol specification is divided into two parts, corresponding to the data link and physical layers of the ISO reference model described by Tanenbaum (1981). This model consists of seven layers, each representing a different level of abstraction, from the hardware of the physical layer to the user software of the application layer. Each layer provides a service to the layer above, facilitating virtual communication between peer processes on different machines. In this chapter, we will concern ourselves with the bottom three layers of the model: the *communication subnet* of figure 7.1.

The physical layer is the lowest layer in the model hierarchy, and transmits data as bits between the stations, or *nodes* of the network. We will provide a timed failures description of the service provided by this layer, but we will not attempt to describe its internal behaviour. Such a description would require a treatment of broadcast communication; our present model of computation is based upon synchronisation.

The data link layer accepts *packets* of data from the layer above, inserting the data into *frames* for transmission to the physical layer. Each frame is transferred to the physical layer as a stream of bits. The data link is responsible for handling any errors which arise in frame transmission, providing its client layer with an error-free

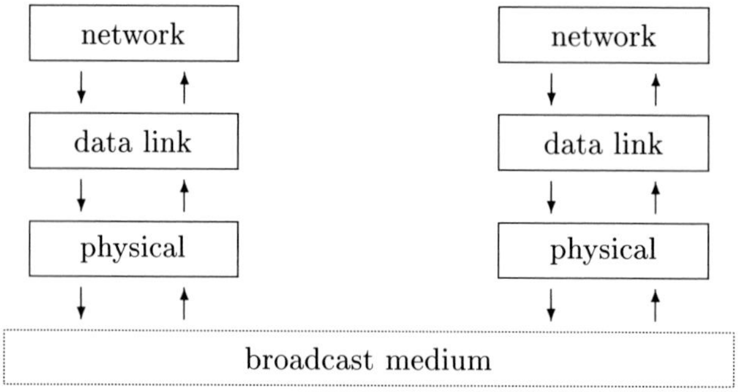

Figure 7.1 the communications subnet

virtual communication medium. To provide this service, the data link must be capable of detecting errors, retransmitting damaged frames, and sending acknowledgments.

The *network layer* is the third layer of the ISO model. This layer converts *messages* into packets, and uses the data link to transmit them to their destination. We will refer to the network layer as the *client* layer, reserving the term *network* for the communication system as a whole.

The data link component of the Ethernet protocol does not correspond precisely to the ISO model. The data link component of Ethernet will attempt to transmit each frame no more than sixteen times; if all of these attempts are interrupted by collision detect signals from the physical layer, then the current frame is abandoned. Further, although incoming frames are checked for errors, no facility is provided for retransmission or acknowledgment. Errors (other than those caused by collisions) are simply reported to the client layer at the current node.

In this chapter, we will specify the data link component of a protocol similar to the one defined by Xerox (1980). To simplify the presentation, we will assume that all errors are due to collisions on the broadcast medium. In this case, there is no need for error reporting at the destination node. We will also assume the existence of an implementation of the randomisation strategy employed in Ethernet, described at the end of section 7.7. With these assumptions, we may address the complex timing properties of the protocol within the framework of a short case study.

7.2 LAYERED PROTOCOLS

The layers of our protocol form a service hierarchy: each layer provides a service to the layer above, and makes demands upon the layer below. We will use timed failures specifications to capture the requirements at each level of hierarchy, and derive a correctness condition for any implementation of the protocol.

7.2.1 Specification

If a service is provided by layer L, it can be described in terms of the occurrence and availability of events from some set A_L. We will use H_L to denote the other actions performed by the layer, those hidden from the layer above. If L_i is a service hierarchy, then we require that

$$\begin{array}{lll} m \geqslant n+2 & \Rightarrow & \Sigma_{Ln} \cap \Sigma_{Lm} = \{\} \\ m = n+1 & \Rightarrow & \Sigma_{Ln} \cap \Sigma_{Lm} = A_{Ln} \end{array}$$

where Σ_L is the alphabet of layer L. Each layer should insulate the layer above from the service provided by the layer below. In the communication subnet, the data link layer *DL* should insulate the client layer *NL* from the service provided by the physical layer:

$$\begin{array}{lll} \Sigma_{NL} \cap \Sigma_{PL} & = & \{\} \\ \Sigma_{NL} \cap \Sigma_{DL} & = & A_{DL} \\ \Sigma_{DL} \cap \Sigma_{PL} & = & A_{PL} \end{array}$$

The data link and physical layers communicate across an interface A_{PL}.

Each layer is associated with a *service* specification and a *total* specification. The first describes the service provided to the layer above, while the second describes the internal activity necessary to provide such a service. We use S_L and T_L to denote the service and total specifications of layer L, respectively. If L' is the layer below L, then the conjunction of T_L and $S_{L'}$ must be enough to ensure that the service S_L is provided:

$$(T_L \wedge S_{L'}) \setminus\!\!\setminus H_L \quad \Rightarrow \quad S_L$$

The use of the $\setminus\!\!\setminus$ operator in the above implication corresponds to the assumption that the events from H_L are to be concealed. We require also that S_L is H_L-independent: any service specification must be independent of hidden events.

Returning to the communication subnet, a data link implementation will satisfy a total specification T_{DL}. The service to the client layer, S_{DL}, should be a consequence of this specification, given that the physical layer provides a service S_{PL} to the data link:

$$\begin{array}{rll} (S_{PL} \wedge T_{DL}) \setminus\!\!\setminus H_{DL} & \Rightarrow & S_{DL} \\ T_{PL} \setminus\!\!\setminus H_{PL} & \Rightarrow & S_{PL} \end{array}$$

The service provided by the physical layer must be a consequence of its own internal activity; there is no layer beneath it.

7.2.2 Implementation

A protocol hierarchy may be implemented as a parallel combination of node processes, one for each node on the network. A node process will be the parallel combination of layer processes, one for each layer in the protocol:

$$\begin{aligned} PROTOCOL &\mathrel{\widehat{=}} \|_{\Sigma_i}\ NODE_i & i \in NODE \\ NODE_i &\mathrel{\widehat{=}} \|_{\Sigma_{i,j}} LAYER_{i,j} & j \in LAYER \end{aligned}$$

where Σ_i is the set of possible events at node i, and $\Sigma_{i,j}$ is the set of possible events on layer j at node i. The disjoint nature of the event sets allow us to rewrite the protocol as a combination of layers:

$$\begin{aligned} PROTOCOL &\mathrel{\widehat{=}} \|_{\Sigma_j}\ LAYER_j & j \in LAYER & \\ LAYER_j &\mathrel{\widehat{=}} |||\ \ LAYER_{i,j} & i \in NODE & \quad (j \geqslant 1) \\ LAYER_0 &\mathrel{\widehat{=}} \|_{\Sigma_{i,0}} LAYER_{i,0} & i \in NODE & \end{aligned}$$

The lowest layer of the protocol has access to a physical communication medium; all of the others have only virtual communication, corresponding to an interleaved parallel combination.

The communication subnet is implemented as follows:

$$\begin{aligned} ETHERNET &\mathrel{\widehat{=}} DATALINK \underset{A_{PL}}{\|} PHYSICAL & \\ DATALINK &\mathrel{\widehat{=}} |||\ \ DL_i & i \in NODE \\ PHYSICAL &\mathrel{\widehat{=}} \|_{ALL_i} PL_i & i \in NODE \end{aligned}$$

The data link layer is an interleaving combination of node processes; any synchronisation is by virtue of the service provided by the physical layer. The processes in the physical layer must agree upon certain events, corresponding to the presence of signals on the broadcast medium.

An implementation of a protocol hierarchy may be judged correct if

$$PROTOCOL \setminus H \quad \mathbf{sat} \quad S_L(s, X)$$

where S_L is the service provided by the top layer, and H is the set of all internal events. If the protocol is implemented as a parallel combination of layers

$$PROTOCOL \mathrel{\widehat{=}} ((L_0 \underset{A_0}{\|} L_1) \underset{A_1}{\|} L_2) \underset{A_2}{\|} \ldots$$

then by the disjoint nature of our event sets and interfaces we have that

$$PROTOCOL \equiv (((L_0 \setminus H_0) \underset{A_0}{\|} L_1) \setminus H_1 \underset{A_1}{\|} L_2) \setminus H_2 \underset{A_2}{\|} \ldots$$

where H is the union of the hidden event sets H_j.

Applying the inference rules of chapter 5, it is sufficient to show that each layer j satisfies the corresponding total specification, and that an adequate service is provided at each stage:

$$\left.\begin{array}{l} S_j(s \lfloor \Sigma_j, X_j) \\ T_{j+1}(s \lfloor \Sigma_{j+1}, X_{j+1}) \\ X \lfloor A_j = (X_j \cup X_{j+1}) \lfloor A_j \\ X \setminus A_j = (X_j \cap X_{j+1}) \setminus A_j \end{array}\right\} \quad \Rightarrow \quad S_{j+1}(s, X) \mathbin{\backslash\!\backslash} H_{j+1}$$

The total specification of layer $j+1$, together with the service provided layer j, must be enough to provide the service S_{j+1}, given that the events from set H_{j+1} are to be hidden from the environment. The instantiation of trace and refusal sets in the left-hand side of the predicate comes from the inference rule for the communicating parallel operator.

To establish that our example protocol is correct, we must show that

$$\begin{array}{lll} DL & \textbf{sat} & T_{DL}(s, X) \\ PL & \textbf{sat} & T_{PL}(s, X) \end{array}$$

$$\left.\begin{array}{l} S_{PL}(s \lfloor \Sigma_{PL}, X_P) \\ T_{DL}(s \lfloor \Sigma_{DL}, X_D) \\ X \lfloor A_{PL} = (X_P \cup X_D) \lfloor A_{PL} \\ X \setminus A_{PL} = (X_P \cap X_D) \setminus A_{PL} \end{array}\right\} \quad \Rightarrow \quad S_{DL}(s, X) \mathbin{\backslash\!\backslash} H_{DL}$$

$$T_{PL}(s, X) \quad \Rightarrow \quad S_{PL}(s, X) \mathbin{\backslash\!\backslash} H_{PL}$$

There are no layers beneath the physical layer; the service specification S_{PL} must be a consequence of the total specification T_{DL}.

7.3 THE DATA LINK SERVICE

The data link layer accepts *packets* of data from the client layer at each node. It then attempts to transmit this data to all of the other nodes, via the broadcast medium of the physical layer. Each packet of data is encapsulated in a *frame* before transmission, and transmitted to the physical layer. We assume that collisions are the only source of data corruption; if the data link succeeds in transmitting the whole frame, then the data link component of any receiving node will be able to pass the data to its client.

If the data link is interrupted by a collision during the transmission of a frame, it will *back off* and attempt to send the entire frame again. If sixteen consecutive transmissions are interrupted, the frame is discarded and the data link informs the client layer of its failure. Successful transmissions are also reported by the transmitter. Our assumption that collisions are the only source of corruption means that there is no need for error reporting at the receiver; collision-damaged frame fragments are simply discarded.

Figure 7.2 the service provided by the data link layer

The data link is always ready to receive data from the physical layer, decapsulating whole frames and passing them to the client layer whenever the packet is addressed to the current node. The data link does not store packets: any buffering of data is the responsibility of the client layer. As a result, there is a limit on the time between the successful transmission of a frame and its delivery to the client layer at the destination node. There are also upper limits upon the time spent waiting to start a transmission, and the time spent transmitting. These are determined by the time taken to transmit one bit and the cable propagation delay, both parameters of the system.

7.3.1 Abstraction

We must establish which of the observable events in a possible history of the system are of interest. Our service specification will be expressed as a constraint on the occurrence and availability of these events. The data link layer is an interleaving of data link processes, one for each node on the network. The set of nodes in the network and the datatype of packets are parameters of the system.

$$
\begin{array}{llll}
i \in NODE & & \text{nodes in the network} \\
p \in PKT & & \text{data packets} \\
r \in REP & ::= & succ \mid fail
\end{array}
$$

The datatype of reports has two elements, representing success and failure. The interface between the data link layer and the client layer at node i will consist of three channels: $i.in$, $i.rep$, and $i.out$. Packets of data are received from the client layer at node i along channel $i.in$, and successful transmission is reported on channel $i.rep$. Valid frames received from the physical layer at node i will be decapsulated and passed as packets to the client layer, along channel $i.out$.

7.3.2 Formal specification

The service specification of the data link will consist of constraints upon the behaviour at a single node—*local* requirements—and constraints upon the behaviour of the entire layer—*network* requirements. Each class of constraint will include both safety and liveness conditions. This classification is largely for the convenience of the reader; in section 7.4, we will employ a more systematic approach.

The alphabet of the interface between the data link and client layers, across the whole network, is given by

$$A_{DL} \mathrel{\widehat{=}} \{i.in.p, i.rep.r, i.out.p \mid i : NODE \,;\, r : REP \,;\, p : PKT\}$$

The following subsets of A_{DL} will be useful in our service specification:

$$\begin{aligned} IN_i &\mathrel{\widehat{=}} \{i.in.p \mid p : PKT\} \\ REP_i &\mathrel{\widehat{=}} \{i.rep.r \mid r : REP\} \\ OUT_i &\mathrel{\widehat{=}} \{i.out.p \mid p : PKT\} \end{aligned}$$

These denote the set of all possible input events at node i, the set of possible reports at node i, and the set of possible output events at node i, respectively.

The service provided by the data link layer to the client is parameterised by the following time constants:

t_{in}	maximum delay between report and readiness for input
t_{rep}	maximum delay between input and availability of report
t_{out}	client layer maximum response time for output
t_{cs}	maximum delay in preparing a frame for transmission
t_{con}	length of the contention interval
t_{max}	maximum delivery delay for a successful transmission

The length of the contention interval, t_{con}, is an upper bound on the time taken to *acquire* the broadcast medium: if a node i transmits for time t_{con} without detecting a collision, then we can be sure that the other nodes will wait for i to finish before attempting to transmit.

We will assume the existence of a function *dest*, which returns the destination of a packet or frame. This will be a single node, although we could model broadcast packets by making the result of *dest* a set of nodes.

Local Conditions. We wish to ensure that the data link layer at each node alternates between accepting packets and reporting on their transmission. We can capture this requirement as a simple specification on the traces of the system, by counting the occurrences of events from the sets IN_i and REP_i:

$$DS1 \mathrel{\widehat{=}} \forall\, i \bullet (\text{count } IN_i = \text{count } REP_i + 1) \vee (\text{count } IN_i = \text{count } REP_i)$$

There must be an input before each report, and there can be no more than one report following each input.

If the data link layer at node i accepts a packet at time t, it should be prepared to report the success or failure of its transmission within time t_{rep}.

$$DS2 \mathrel{\widehat{=}} \forall\, i, t \bullet IN_i \text{ at } t \Rightarrow i.rep.succ \text{ from } (t, t + t_{rep}) \lor i.rep.fail \text{ from } (t, t + t_{rep})$$

We also require that the data link should be ready for input, unless it is currently attempting to transmit a packet or waiting for a report to be collected.

$$DS3 \mathrel{\widehat{=}} \forall\, i, t \bullet IN_i \text{ from } 0 \land (REP_i \text{ at } t \Rightarrow IN_i \text{ from } (t, t + t_{in}))$$

At each node i, the data link is willing initially to accept any valid packet on channel $i.in$. Subsequently, the data link becomes ready for a new packet on this channel within time t_{in} of any report on channel $i.rep$.

Network Conditions. If a success is reported at node i, then the last packet input at i will be safely delivered to its destination.

$$DS4 \mathrel{\widehat{=}} \forall\, i, j, t, t' \bullet \; i.rep.succ \text{ at } t \;\; dest(p) = j \;\; \text{last } IN_i \text{ during } [0, t) = (t', i.in.p) \;\; \Rightarrow j.out.p \text{ from } (t', t' + t_{max})$$

If the value *succ* is passed to the client layer at node i, and the last packet input at that node was p at time t', with destination j, then that packet is made available for output at node j within time t_{max}.

Without a probabilistic argument, we can *guarantee* a successful transmission only when no other node is entrusted with a packet for the length of the contention interval. If a packet is input at node i at time t, and no other node is entrusted with a packet during the interval $(t - t_{rep}, t + t_{con} + t_{cs})$, then that packet will be delivered safely, and a success report will be available within time t_{rep}.

$$DS5 \mathrel{\widehat{=}} \forall\, i, p, t \bullet \; i.in.p \text{ at } t \;\; \forall\, k \bullet k \neq i \Rightarrow \neg\,(IN_k \text{ at } (t - t_{rep}, t + t_{con} + t_{cs})) \;\; \Rightarrow i.rep.succ \text{ from } (t, t + t_{rep})$$

The bounds of the time interval ensure that all previous packets have been dealt with, and that no other frames are ready until the period of contention is over.

Environmental Assumptions. The data link cannot provide the service specified above without the cooperation of the client layer, in the following respect. At each node, the client layer is responsible for the buffering of output packets; if the data link offers a packet to the client layer on channel $i.out$, the client will accept it within time t_{out}. To express this environmental assumption, we define the following projection mapping on timed failures:

$$\text{response}\, A\ (s, X)\ \widehat{=}$$
$$inf\{t \mid \forall t', I \bullet I \subseteq [0, end(s,X)) \wedge (t' \in I \Rightarrow A \not\subseteq X \uparrow t') \Rightarrow length(I) < t\}$$

This function yields the least value for t such that, if I is an interval contained in $[0, end(s,X))$ and there is no time t' during I at which the whole of A is offered by the environment, then I must be shorter than t. Observe that

$$\text{response}\, A < t\ \ (s, X)\ \ \equiv$$
$$\forall I \bullet I \subseteq [0, end(s,X)) \wedge length(I) \geqslant t \Rightarrow \exists t' \in I \bullet A \subseteq X \uparrow t'$$

If the response time is less than t, then the whole of A must be offered by the environment at least once during any interval of length t.

Our assumption about the client layer may be expressed as follows:

$$EA\ \ \widehat{=}\ \ \forall i \bullet \text{response}\, OUT_i < t_{out}$$

We assume that the data link at node i never has to wait longer than t_{out} for an offer of output to be accepted. Our specification of the data link service is

$$S_{DL}\ \ \widehat{=}\ \ EA \Rightarrow DS1 \wedge DS2 \wedge DS3 \wedge DS4 \wedge DS5$$

This is not a complete specification, by any means. We have shown that certain important aspects of the data link service may be rendered as timed failures specifications. In the following sections, we will see how the data link and physical layers interact to provide this service.

7.4 THE DATA LINK SPECIFICATION

The data link layer accepts packets from the client layer, and adds framing information. If the physical layer signals that the broadcast medium is clear, then the data link begins transmission. If the physical layer signals a collision, then the transmission is interrupted as soon as possible. In this case, another attempt is made after a random period of time has elapsed. If sixteen attempts have been made to transmit the same frame, the data link signals that the transmission has failed, and awaits a new packet. If no collision occurs during the transmission of a frame, then the data link signals a success.

Reception is less complicated. The data link receives bits of data from the physical layer, and stores them until the broadcast medium falls silent. When this occurs, the data

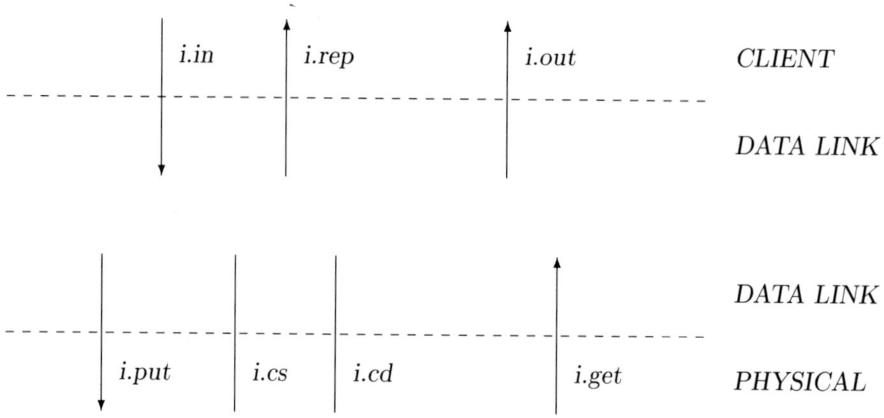

Figure 7.3 the two interfaces of the data link layer

stored is tested to see whether it corresponds to a valid frame intended for the current node. If this is so, then the data is stripped of its framing information and passed to the client layer. If not, then the data is discarded. In either case, the data link should be ready to receive new data before the inter-frame spacing time has elapsed.

7.4.1 Abstraction

The data link layer at node i accepts data packets along channel $i.in$, and passes the data to the physical layer along channel $i.put$ as a stream of bits. Data is collected from the physical layer at node i along channel $i.get$, and passed to the client layer along channel $i.out$. Reports are made available to the client layer on channel $i.rep$.

The physical layer is ready to synchronise upon the event $i.cs$ whenever the broadcast medium is clear at node i. Similarly, whenever a collision is detected at node i, the physical layer will make the event $i.cd$ available to the data link. If this event is observed, then the data link has been informed that a collision is taking place. The alphabet of the data link layer is thus

$$\begin{aligned}\Sigma_{DL} \ \widehat{=}\ & \{i.in.p, i.rep.r, i.out.p \mid i : NODE\ ; p : PKT\ ; r : REP\} \\ & \cup \\ & \{i.put.b, i.get.b, i.cs, i.cd \mid i : NODE\ ; b : BIT\}\end{aligned}$$

where the datatype of bits is given by

$$BIT \ ::= \ 0 \mid 1$$

Any other events considered during implementation must be hidden before the data link is combined with the physical and client layers. Such events will not form a part of the data link specification.

7.4.2 Formal specification

The total specification of the data link must be satisfiable by the data link layer itself, without the cooperation of the physical layer. The data link layer has only virtual communication between nodes, so our constraints must not require interaction between data link components at different nodes. All of our specifications will correspond to local requirements.

The following subsets of Σ_{DL} will be used in our specification:

$$\begin{aligned}
IN_i &\mathrel{\widehat=} \{i.in.p \mid p : PKT\} \\
PUT_i &\mathrel{\widehat=} \{i.put.b \mid b : BIT\} \\
GET_i &\mathrel{\widehat=} \{i.get.b \mid b : BIT\}
\end{aligned}$$

These denote the set of possible inputs at node i, the set of possible bit transmissions at node i, and the set of possible bit receptions at node i, respectively.

We abbreviate a set of functions, each of which returns the time of occurrence of the most recent event from a particular set. If no event from that set has been observed, they will return the value 0.

$$\begin{aligned}
lastin_i(t) &\mathrel{\widehat=} \text{time of last } IN_i \text{ before } t \\
lastcs_i(t) &\mathrel{\widehat=} \text{time of last } i.cs \text{ before } t \\
lastcd_i(t) &\mathrel{\widehat=} \text{time of last } i.cd \text{ before } t \\
lastput_i(t) &\mathrel{\widehat=} \text{time of last } PUT_i \text{ before } t \\
lastget_i(t) &\mathrel{\widehat=} \text{time of last } GET_i \text{ before } t
\end{aligned}$$

and assume the existence of a function $frame : PKT \rightarrow \text{seq } BIT$ such that $frame(p)$ is the sequence of bits corresponding to packet p, together with the framing information required for transmission.

The following abbreviations will also appear in our specification:

$$\begin{aligned}
lastpacket_i(t) &\mathrel{\widehat=} \text{name of last } IN_i \text{ before } t \\
lastframe_i(t) &\mathrel{\widehat=} frame(lastpacket_i(t)) \\
lasttrans_i(t) &\mathrel{\widehat=} \text{data } i.put \text{ during } (lastcs_i(t), t) \\
attempts_i(t) &\mathrel{\widehat=} \text{count } i.cs \text{ during } (lastin_i(t), t)
\end{aligned}$$

These correspond to: the last packet input at node i; the last frame prepared for transmission at node i; the sequence of bits transmitted since the last cs signal at node i; the number of attempts made by node i to transmit the current frame.

Our specification of the data link layer will be parameterised by a number of time constants. The correct operation of the protocol will depend upon the relationships between these and the constants defined in the previous section.

t_{succ}	maximum delay between a successful transmission and the offer of a report
t_{fail}	maximum delay between a failed transmission and the offer of a report
t_{slot}	minimum backoff delay — the *slot time* is the scheduling quantum for retransmission of a frame — $512\mu s$
t_{back}	maximum backoff delay — $524ms$
t_{bit}	time taken to transmit one bit — $100ns$
t_{int}	inter-frame spacing delay — $9.6\mu s$
t_{rec}	maximum delay between reception of a valid frame and the offer of an output

Each of these constants will be discussed in greater detail in section 7.6, where we discuss the interaction between the data link and physical layers. The values listed above are those given in the Ethernet specification document.

Inputs. The first constraint of our data link specification has already been presented as part of the data link service:

$$DT1 \;\widehat{=}\; DS1$$

This stated that, at any node, inputs and reports should occur in strict alternation. The data link layer should be able to provide this part of the service without the assistance of the physical layer. This is true of another of our local conditions, which required that the input channel at any node is ready within time t_{in} of a report being collected.

$$DT2 \;\widehat{=}\; DS3$$

Reports. If a success is reported at node i, then the last packet input at that node must have been transmitted successfully.

$$DT3 \;\widehat{=}\; \forall\, i, t \bullet i.rep.succ \text{ at } t \Rightarrow lasttrans_i(t) = lastframe_i(t)$$

A success may be reported only if the sequence of bits transmitted since the last $i.cs$ event is equal to the last frame readied for transmission at i. Conversely, if this packet has been successfully transmitted, a report should be made available:

$$
\begin{aligned}
DT4 \;\widehat{=}\;& \forall\, i, t \bullet PUT_i \text{ at } t \wedge \mathit{lasttrans}_i(t) = \mathit{lastframe}_i(t) \\
& \Rightarrow \\
& i.\mathit{rep}.\mathit{succ} \text{ from } (t, t + t_{succ})
\end{aligned}
$$

If a bit is passed along channel $i.put$ at time t to complete the transmission of a frame, then a success will be reported on channel $i.rep$ within time t_{succ}.

For a failure to be reported at node i, sixteen attempts must have been made to transmit the current packet.

$$
\begin{aligned}
DT5 \;\widehat{=}\;& \forall\, i, t \bullet i.\mathit{rep}.\mathit{fail} \text{ at } t \\
& \Rightarrow \\
& \mathit{attempts}_i(t) = 16
\end{aligned}
$$

Conversely, if the sixteenth consecutive attempt to transmit the same packet is interrupted, then the data link should report a failure:

$$
\begin{aligned}
DT6 \;\widehat{=}\;& \forall\, i, t \bullet i.cd \text{ at } t \wedge \mathit{attempts}_i(t) = 16 \\
& \Rightarrow \\
& i.\mathit{rep}.\mathit{fail} \text{ from } (t, t + t_{fail})
\end{aligned}
$$

If the sixteenth attempt to transmit the current frame at node i is interrupted by the observation of a collision at time t, then the data link should offer a failure report on channel $i.rep$ within time t_{fail}.

Carrier-Sense. If the data link at node i requests the carrier-sense information, then one of two conditions must hold:

- a packet has been received since the last report at node i, or
- a transmission has been interrupted, the minimum backoff period has expired, and fewer than sixteen attempts have been made to transmit the current frame.

This requirement may be expressed as follows:

$$
\begin{aligned}
DT7 \;\widehat{=}\;& \forall\, i, t \bullet i.cs \text{ at } t \Rightarrow \mathit{lastin}_i(t) > \mathit{lastput}_i(t) \\
& \qquad\qquad\qquad\qquad \vee \\
& \qquad\qquad\qquad\qquad \mathit{lastcd}_i(t) < t - t_{slot} \wedge \mathit{attempts}_i(t) < 16
\end{aligned}
$$

The event $i.cs$ may be observed only if a packet has been input since the last bit transmission, or time t_{slot} has elapsed since the last collision was detected. Recall that, in our interpretation of the protocol, carrier-sense information is requested only as a prelude to bit transmission.

Conversely, the data link at each node should be ready to synchronise upon the *cs* event within time t_{cs} of receiving a packet for transmission, and within time t_{back} of a transmission being interrupted.

$$\begin{aligned} DT8 \;\widehat{=}\;& \forall\, i, t \bullet IN_i \text{ at } t \Rightarrow i.cs \text{ from } (t, t + t_{cs}) \\ & \wedge \\ & i.cd \text{ at } t \wedge attempts_i(t) < 16 \Rightarrow i.cs \text{ from } (t + t_{slot}, t + t_{back}) \end{aligned}$$

If a packet is input at node i at time t, then the event $i.cs$ should be made available by time $t + t_{cs}$. Further, if a collision is observed at node i, and fewer than sixteen attempts have been made to transmit the current frame, then $i.cs$ will be made available within time t_{back}.

Collision Detection. For a collision to be observed at node i, that node must be currently transmitting. We say that a node i is transmitting at t if a bit is broadcast at some time during the interval $(t - t_{bit}, t + t_{bit})$. This constraint is captured by the following behavioural specification:

$$\begin{aligned} DT9 \;\widehat{=}\;& \forall\, i, t \bullet i.cd \text{ at } t \\ & \Rightarrow \\ & lastput_i(t) > t - 2t_{bit} \end{aligned}$$

Conversely, the data link should be ready to observe a collision at any time during frame transmission:

$$\begin{aligned} DT10 \;\widehat{=}\;& \forall\, i, t \bullet PUT_i \text{ at } t \\ & \Rightarrow \\ & i.cd \text{ from } t \text{ until } t + 2t_{bit} \end{aligned}$$

Transmission. The data link should not pause during a transmission. If a bit is transmitted by node i, then either another bit was sent exactly t_{bit} ago, or the signal $i.cs$ was observed exactly time t_{int} ago. This constraint may be expressed as follows:

$$\begin{aligned} DT11 \;\widehat{=}\;& \forall\, i, t \bullet PUT_i \text{ at } t \Rightarrow lastcs_i(t - 2t_{bit}) > lastcd_i(t - 2t_{bit}) \\ & \wedge \\ & PUT_i \text{ at } t - t_{bit} \vee i.cs \text{ at } t - t_{int} \end{aligned}$$

Note that the data link should not continue the transmission if a collision has occurred since the last *cs* event; we allow a short period of time ($2t_{bit}$) for transmission to cease. Further, we require that

$$DT12 \;\widehat{=}\; \forall\, i, t \bullet lasttrans_i(t) \leqslant lastframe_i(t)$$

The sequence of data transmitted at node i must be a prefix of the last packet framed at node i.

The data link should be ready to transmit the first bit of a sequence time t_{int} after observing the cs event, and the subsequent bits at intervals of t_{bit}, providing that no collision is observed.

$$
\begin{array}{lll}
DT13 & \mathrel{\widehat{=}} & \forall\, i, t \bullet i.cs \text{ at } t \Rightarrow \exists\, b \bullet i.put.b \text{ from } t + t_{int} \\
 & & \qquad \wedge \\
 & & \qquad (PUT_i \text{ at } t \\
 & & \qquad\ lastcs_i(t) > lastcd_i(t) \\
 & & \qquad\ lasttrans_i(t) \neq lastframe_i(t)) \Rightarrow \exists\, b \bullet i.put.b \text{ from } t + t_{bit}
\end{array}
$$

The data link may stop transmitting as soon as a collision is observed, or when the transmission is complete.

Reception. The data link should be ready to receive data within one bit time of the last bit arriving, unless two bit times have expired without a signal. If two bit times have elapsed since the last *get* event, then the data link receiver does not need to be ready until time t_{int} has passed.

$$
\begin{array}{lll}
DT14 & \mathrel{\widehat{=}} & \forall\, i, t \bullet GET_i \text{ at } t \Rightarrow GET_i \text{ from } (t, t + t_{bit}) \text{ until } t + 2t_{bit} \\
 & & \qquad\qquad\qquad\quad \wedge \\
 & & \qquad\qquad\qquad\quad GET_i \text{ from } (t + 2t_{bit}, t + t_{int})
\end{array}
$$

The data link becomes ready for a bit on channel $i.get$ within time t_{bit} of the last bit being received at i. The offer of GET_i may be withdrawn after two bit times have elapsed, but must be renewed before time t_{int} has elapsed; the data link must be ready before the next frame arrives.

Output. For a packet to be output at a node, it must have been received as an intact frame with the correct address. Valid frames will be preceded by an inter-frame space of duration t_{int}, and a transmission has ceased once two bit times have elapsed since the last *get* event. With these assumptions, we may identify the last frame fragment received by node i.

$$lastrec_i(t) \mathrel{\widehat{=}} \text{data } i.get \text{ during } [lastspace_i(t), lastgap_i(t)]$$

where $lastspace_i(t)$ is the endpoint of the last inter-frame space at node i:

$$lastspace_i(t) \mathrel{\widehat{=}} max\{t' \mid t' < t \wedge \neg\,(GET_i \text{ at } (t' - t_{int}, t')) \wedge GET_i \text{ at } t'\}$$

and $lastgap_i(t)$ denotes the beginning of the last gap of length $> 2t_{bit}$ observed at that node before time t.

$$lastgap_i(t) \mathrel{\widehat{=}} max\{t' \mid t' < t - 2t_{bit} \wedge \neg\,(GET_i \text{ at } (t', t' + 2t_{bit})) \wedge GET_i \text{ at } t'\}$$

This marks the end of the last contiguous bit sequence received at node i. Observe that both $lastspace_i$ and $lastgap_i$ are undefined if no data has arrived at the node i. We may complete the definitions by setting both to 0 in this case, assuming that predicate *validframe* is defined upon the empty trace of data values.

If we output a packet to the client layer, then we have received a stream of data on the *get* channel that corresponds to a valid frame with the correct address.

$$
\begin{aligned}
DT15 \;\widehat{=}\; \forall\, i, t, p \bullet i.out.p \text{ at}.t \Rightarrow \exists\, t', f \bullet\; & t - t_{int} < t' < t \\
& lastrec_i(t') = f \\
& validframe(f) \\
& address(f) = i \\
& unframe(f) = p
\end{aligned}
$$

If a packet is output at time t, then the last bit of the corresponding frame must have arrived at some time during the interval $(t - 2t_{bit}, t)$. The data link layer should not buffer frames or packets.

The data link should be ready to output a valid frame within time t_{rec} of the last bit being received:

$$
\begin{aligned}
DT16 \;\widehat{=}\; \forall\, i, t, t', f, p \bullet (& lastrec_i(t) = f \\
& validframe(f) \\
& unframe(f) = p \\
& dest(p) = i \\
& lastgap_i(t) = t' \;) \\
& \quad \Rightarrow i.out.p \text{ from } (t', t' + t_{rec}) \text{ until } t' + t_{int}
\end{aligned}
$$

Note that we are assuming the existence of a suitable function for testing the validity of a data frame.

We may now present the total specification of the data link layer. With no environmental assumptions to consider, it is simply the conjunction of the requirements specified above:

$$
T_{DL} \;\widehat{=}\; \bigwedge_{n:1..16} DTn
$$

7.5 THE PHYSICAL SERVICE

The physical layer provides a means of communication between distinct data link processes. The data link layer at a node may pass bits to the physical layer at at a rate of 10 megabits per second; the physical layer at that node will place a corresponding signal upon the broadcast medium, transmitting the data to the other nodes. Signals received without interference are decoded and passed to the data link layer.

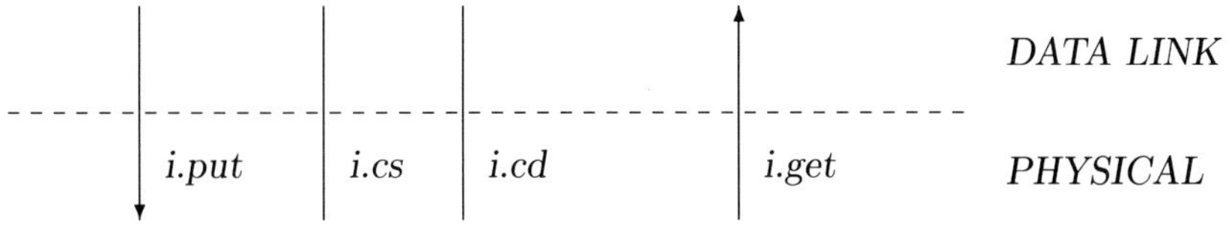

Figure 7.4 the service provided by the physical layer

The physical layer also provides information about the state of the broadcast medium. A *carrier-sense* signal allows the data link layer to determine whether or not there is activity on the broadcast medium at the current node. Further, if a node i is transmitting bit signals, and interference is detected upon the broadcast channel, the physical layer will report that a *collision* is taking place.

7.5.1 Abstraction

The physical layer accepts bits from the data link layer at node i along channel $i.put$. Bit signals received from other nodes are passed to the data link along channel $i.get$. If a collision is occurring at node i, then the physical layer will make the event $i.cd$ available to the data link.

The presence of a signal upon the broadcast medium at node i will be represented by the *unavailability* of the event $i.cs$. This choice of abstraction is compatible with our representation of the data link layer; we wish to synchronise with the physical layer when there is *no* activity upon the broadcast medium, as a prelude to data transmission. The alphabet of the data link–physical interface is given by

$$A_{PL} \;\widehat{=}\; \{i.put.b, i.cs, i.cd, i.get.b \mid i : NODE\,;\, b : BIT\}$$

7.5.2 Formal specification

We present a formal description of the service provided by the physical layer, in terms of the occurrence and availability of the events in the set A_{PL}. To reason about the availability of collision detect and carrier-sense signals, we must identify the time at which the last signal arrived at a particular node. Recall that $lastput_i(t)$ denotes the time of the last signal transmitted at node i. We define

$$lastsig_i(t) \;\widehat{=}\; max\{lastput_j(t - t_{ij}) + t_{ij} \mid j : NODE\}$$

where t_{ij} is the time taken for a signal to travel from node i to node j on the broadcast medium. With this definition, $lastsig_i(t)$ is the arrival time of the last signal at node i before time t.

Transmission. The medium should be capable of receiving bits as fast as the data link layer can transmit them:

$$PS1 \ \widehat{=} \ \forall i, t \bullet PUT_i \text{ from } 0 \ \wedge \ PUT_i \text{ at } t \Rightarrow PUT_i \text{ from } (t, t + t_{bit})$$

At each node i, the physical layer is prepared initially to accept a bit signal. Further, if a bit is accepted at time t, then the physical layer must be ready for another before time $t + t_{bit}$.

Carrier-Sense. We intend that the physical and data link layers should synchronise upon the event $i.cs$ only when the broadcast medium is silent at node i. The physical layer may take up to two bit times to respond to the presence of signals on the broadcast medium; if a synchronisation occurs, then the broadcast medium must have been silent less than two bit times ago.

$$PS2 \ \widehat{=} \ \forall i, t \bullet i.cs \text{ at } t \Rightarrow \exists t' \bullet t' > t - 2t_{bit} \ \wedge \ lastsig_i(t') < t' - 2t_{bit}$$

If an $i.cs$ synchronisation occurs at time t, then there must be a time $t' > t - 2t_{bit}$ such that the last signal before t' arrived before $t' - 2t_{bit}$.

The physical layer should make the event $i.cs$ available within two bit times of activity ceasing on the broadcast medium at node i. This offer should remain open at least until activity resumes.

$$PS3 \ \widehat{=} \ \forall i, t, t' \bullet lastsig_i(t) = t' \wedge t' < t - 2t_{bit} \ \Rightarrow \ i.cs \text{ from } (t', t' + 2t_{bit}) \text{ until } t$$

If the last signal to arrive at node i before time t arrives at time t', then event $i.cs$ should be made available before time $t' + 2t_{bit}$, and remain available at least until time t.

Collision Detection. A collision should be reported at node i only if a signal arrives from another node during a transmission.

$$PS4 \ \widehat{=} \ \forall i, t \bullet i.cd \text{ at } t \Rightarrow lastput_i(t) > t - 2t_{bit} \ \wedge \ lastsig_i(t) > t - 2t_{bit}$$

If a collision is reported at time t, then the interval $(t - 2t_{bit}, t)$ must contain a transmission, and the arrival of a signal from another node. Conversely, if a signal arrives from another node during transmission, then the physical layer should make $i.cd$ available within two bit times.

$$PS5 \;\widehat{=}\; \forall\, i, t \bullet lastput_i(t) > t - t_{bit} \;\wedge\; lastsig_i(t) > t - t_{bit} \;\Rightarrow\; i.cd \text{ from } (lastcd_i(t), t + 2t_{bit}) \text{ until } t + 3t_{bit}$$

If node i has transmitted a data bit less than time t_{bit} ago, and another node j transmitted approximately time t_{ij} ago, then $i.cd$ should be offered to the data link. This signal may already be available, hence the lower bound of $lastcd_i(t)$. Unless the collision continues, the offer may be withdrawn after one additional bit time.

Reception. In our idealised description of the physical layer, no bit should be received unless it has previously been transmitted at the appropriate time.

$$PS6 \;\widehat{=}\; \forall\, i, t \bullet i.get.b \text{ at } t \;\Rightarrow\; \exists\, j \bullet j.put.b \text{ at } t - t_{ij}$$

For data to be received without corruption, the receiving node must synchronise with the incoming sequence of bits. To facilitate this synchronisation, nodes observing the Ethernet protocol must transmit a fixed bit sequence as a preamble to each frame. This is a responsibility of the physical layer, and will not form part of our service specification.

The corresponding liveness condition is given by:

$$\begin{aligned} PS7 \;\widehat{=}\; & \forall\, i, j, t \bullet i.put.b \text{ at } t - t_{ij} \\ & \wedge \\ & \forall\, k, t' \bullet (k \neq i \;\wedge\; PUT_k \text{ at } t' \;\wedge\; t' \in [t - t_{ij}, t]) \\ & \qquad \Rightarrow t' \geqslant t - t_{ij} + 2t_{bit} \;\wedge\; t_{jk} > t_{ij} \\ & \Rightarrow \\ & j.get.b \text{ from } t \text{ until } t + 0.1t_{bit} \end{aligned}$$

The reception of a bit signal b at destination node j is guaranteed if any transmission that occurs during its journey takes place

- at least two bit times after b was transmitted
- at a node further away from j than the sender i

Under these conditions, no signal can interfere with the reception of bit signal b. Note that we have assumed that the broadcast medium is reliable, and that signals propagate at a constant rate.

7.6 COMBINATION

We are obliged to demonstrate that the service provided by the data link layer is a consequence of that layer's total specification, together with the service provided by the physical layer, under the assumption that synchronisations from the set H_{DL} are concealed from the client layer. Our proof requirement is given by:

$$\left.\begin{array}{l} S_{PL}(s \upharpoonright \Sigma_{PL}, X_P) \\ T_{DL}(s \upharpoonright \Sigma_{DL}, X_D) \\ X \upharpoonright A_{PL} = (X_P \cup X_D) \upharpoonright A_{PL} \\ X \setminus A_{PL} = (X_P \cap X_D) \setminus A_{PL} \end{array}\right\} \Rightarrow \quad S_{DL}(s, X) \setminus\!\!\setminus H_{DL}$$

It is sufficient to show that this result holds for each conjunct of the service specification S_{DL}; we will provide a brief justification in each case.

Each specification is given in terms of functions of timed failures, e.g. 'count', 'from', and 'response'. In these specifications, the connectives are *lifted* operators, whose actions on functions are defined by extension:

$$(\mathrm{f}\ op_{\uparrow}\ \mathrm{g})\ (s, X) \quad \widehat{=} \quad \mathrm{f}\,(s, X)\ op\ \mathrm{g}\,(s, X)$$

where $op_{\uparrow}$ is the lifted form of connective op. The interpretation of connectives such as $+$, $=$, and $\wedge$ is obvious from the context; we have written $op_{\uparrow}$ as op.

7.6.1 Local safety

Recall the first component of the data link service specification:

$$\begin{array}{lcl} DS1\ (s, X) & \widehat{=} & (\forall\, i \bullet \text{count}\ IN_i = \text{count}\ REP_i + 1 \\ & & \qquad \vee \\ & & \quad \text{count}\ IN_i = \text{count}\ REP_i\ )\quad (s, X) \end{array}$$

We are given that $(IN_i \cup REP_i) \subseteq \Sigma_{DL}$, and that

$$\begin{array}{lcl} DT1\ (s \upharpoonright \Sigma_{DL}, X_D) & \equiv & (\forall\, i \bullet \text{count}\ IN_i = \text{count}\ REP_i + 1 \\ & & \qquad \vee \\ & & \quad \text{count}\ IN_i = \text{count}\ REP_i\ )\quad (s \upharpoonright \Sigma_{DL}, X_D) \end{array}$$

It is easy to see that, for any s and X,

$$A \subseteq B \quad \Rightarrow \quad \text{count}\ A\ (s, X) = \text{count}\ A\ (s \upharpoonright B, X)$$

and hence that

$$DT1\ (s \upharpoonright \Sigma_{DL}, X_D) \quad \Rightarrow \quad DS1\ (s, X)$$

7.6.2 Input

The second requirement in the data link specification was

$$DS2 \;\widehat{=}\; \forall\, i, t \bullet IN_i \text{ at } t \Rightarrow i.rep.succ \text{ from } (t, t + t_{rep}) \;\vee\; i.rep.fail \text{ from } (t, t + t_{rep})$$

In the total specification of the data link layer, we insisted that no failure may be reported without sixteen attempts at transmission. As a result, the provision of this part of the data link service relies upon the following lemma:

Lemma 7.1 At any particular node i, the data link never has to wait more than t_{long} for a carrier-sense synchronisation $i.cs$, where t_{long} is the duration of the longest valid frame. This is *1.2ms* for the Ethernet protocol.

Proof Suppose that the event $i.cs$ is not available at time t. From *PS3* we may deduce that $lastsig_i(t) > t - 2t_{bit}$, and hence that there is at least one other node j on the network already transmitting. There are two possibilities to consider:

- node j transmits without contention for time t_{con}, and *acquires* the broadcast channel, or
- node j is interrupted by another node k

If node j transmits a bit once every t_{bit} during an interval length t_{con} without interruption, then the *cs* synchronisation must be unavailable at every node on the network. This is because the length of the contention interval is greater than the round-trip signal propagation time for the network:

$$t_{con} \;>\; 2\; max\{t_{ij} \mid i, j : NODE\}$$

Suppose that node j has been transmitting for t_{con} at time t, with no collisions observed at j thus far. Then by *PS5* we know that $lastsig_j(t) < t - t_{con}$, and hence that

$$\forall\, k \;\bullet\; lastput_k(t - t_{jk}) < t - t_{jk} - t_{con}$$

Recall that the data link layer at each node must satisfy the requirement

$$PUT_k \text{ at } t \;\Rightarrow\; PUT_k \text{ at } t - t_{bit} \vee k.cs \text{ at } t - t_{int}$$

and observe that it is not possible for node k to begin transmission after $t - t_{jk}$, as $k.cs$ will not be available until time t_{jk} after j ceases transmission, by *PS2*. Hence j will not be interrupted.

In this case, *DT13* guarantees that node j will continue transmission until it has exhausted the current frame. It must then wait at least t_{int} before transmitting another bit, because of requirement *DT11*. If j transmits the last bit of the current frame at time t, then for each node k on the network we may assume that

$$\neg\ PUT_k \text{ at } (t + t_{jk} - t_{short}, t + t_{jk} + t_{int})$$

where t_{short} is the length of the shortest valid transmission; this is $57.6\mu s$ in the Ethernet protocol. From this we infer that

$$\forall k \bullet lastput_k(t + t_{jk} + t_{int}) < t + t_{jk} - t_{short}$$

It is an obvious property of the network that

$$t_{ij} - t_{ik} \leqslant t_{jk}$$

and from the definition of *lastput* we may deduce that

$$\forall k, t_1, t_2, t_3 \bullet t_3 < t_2 \leqslant t_1 \wedge lastput_k(t_1) < t_3 \Rightarrow lastput_k(t_2) < t_3$$

Recalling the definition of $lastsig_i$, we observe

$$lastsig_i(t + t_{ij} + t_{int}) \equiv max\{lastput_k(t + t_{ij} + t_{int} - t_{ik}) + t_{ik} \mid k : NODE\}$$

If we assume that $t_{short} > t_{con}$, remembering that t_{con} is more than twice t_{ij} for any i and j, then we may combine these results to yield

$$lastsig_i(t + t_{ij} + t_{int}) \leqslant t + t_{ij}$$

Given that $t_{int} > 2t_{bit}$, requirement *PS3* guarantees that the carrier-sense signal is made available at node i before $t + t_{ij} + 2t_{bit}$. Our assumption that such events are hidden from the client layer means that this signal will occur.

Now consider the other possibility: that j is interrupted within t_{con} of starting to transmit. In this case, no node will acquire the broadcast channel during the current time slot, and the event *cs* will be offered at node i within time t_{con}, the length of the contention interval. If j is to be interrupted, then at least one other node k must begin transmission before signals from j reach it, by *DT11* and *PS2*. Suppose that j and k start to transmit at times t_j and t_k, respectively. Observe that these nodes cause signals to arrive at i during the interval

$$[min\{t_j + t_{ij}, t_k + t_{ik}\}, max\{t_k + t_{jk} + t_{ij}, t_j + t_{jk} + t_{ik}\}]$$

Node j is interrupted by k, and thus ceases transmission, at time $t_k + t_{jk}$, and vice versa. This follows from requirements *PS5*, *DT10* and *DT11*.

If the medium at i does not fall silent at or before the end of this interval, then another node l must have started to transmit before signals from j or k could reach it. Signals from this node will cease to arrive at i before time

$$max\{t_j + t_{jl} + t_{il}, t_k + t_{kl} + t_{il}\}$$

A brief sketch of the situation should reassure the reader that l must be further from node i than j or k. An inductive argument will confirm that activity on the medium at node i must cease within time t_{con}, under the assumption that the network is finite, and $t_{con} > 2\ max\{t_{ij} \mid i, j : NODE\}$. □

Having justified the lemma, we may deduce that, if the data link at node i is entrusted with a packet for transmission at time t, then the *cs* synchronisation is available at time $t + t_{cs}$, or will be offered for at least two bit times before time $t + t_{cs} + t_{long}$.

$$\begin{array}{lll} \forall\, i, t & \bullet & IN_i \text{ at } t \Rightarrow \exists\, t' \bullet t + t_{cs} < t' < t + t_{cs} + t_{long} \\ & & \qquad\qquad\qquad \wedge \\ & & \qquad\qquad\qquad i.cs \text{ from } (lastcs_i(t + t_{cs}), t') \text{ until } t' + 2t_{bit} \end{array}$$

Recall that t_{cs} is the maximum delay between the input of a packet and readiness for transmission, from *DT8*.

Similarly, if a transmission is interrupted and rescheduled for time t, then $i.cs$ will occur within time t_{long}, allowing another attempt to begin after the inter-frame spacing t_{int}. During the proof of the previous lemma, we established that if a node has been transmitting for time t_{con}, then it will not be interrupted. The worst case delay for status reporting may be calculated as follows:

	t_{cs}	preparing frame for transmission
$16\ \times$	t_{long}	waiting for the channel to clear
$16\ \times$	t_{int}	inter-frame spacing
$15\ \times$	t_{con}	almost succeeding
$15\ \times$	t_{back}	backing off
	t_{long}	successful transmission
	t_{succ}	delay in reporting success to data link
	$< t_{rep}$	in total, if we are to provide service S_{DL}

The response time may be reduced by increasing the backoff delay with each collision. The Ethernet protocol insists that a node cannot delay for time t_{back} unless the current frame has been interrupted at least nine times.

7.6.3 Reports

The third component of the data link service specification is more easily established. Recall that this insisted that

$$\forall\, i, t \quad \bullet \quad IN_i \text{ from } 0 \wedge REP_i \text{ at } t \Rightarrow IN_i \text{ from } (t, t + t_{in})$$

At any node i, the data link layer must initially be ready to accept any packet on channel $i.in$. Further, should a report be accepted at time t, the data link will be ready to accept another packet before time $t + t_{in}$.

Recall that the total specification of the data link layer included precisely the same requirement:

$$DT2 \;\widehat{=}\; \forall\, i, t \bullet IN_i \text{ from } 0 \wedge REP_i \text{ at } t \Rightarrow IN_i \text{ from } (t, t + t_{in})$$

We must show that, if this requirement is true of the data link layer, then it must remain true when the data link is placed in parallel combination with the physical layer. We may assume that

$$DT2\ (s \upharpoonright \Sigma_{DL}, X_D)$$

$$IN_i \cup REP_i \;\subseteq\; \Sigma_{DL}$$

$$X \setminus A_{PL} \;=\; (X_P \cap X_D) \setminus A_{PL}$$

From the alphabet constraints, we may infer that

$$\begin{aligned}\forall\, i, t, a \bullet a \in IN_i \cup REP_i \Rightarrow\; & (a \notin \sigma(X_D \uparrow t) \;\Rightarrow\; a \notin \sigma(X \uparrow t) \\ & \wedge \\ & \langle (t, a) \rangle \;\underline{\text{in}}\; s \;\Leftrightarrow\; \langle (t, a) \rangle \;\underline{\text{in}}\; (s \upharpoonright \Sigma_{DL}))\end{aligned}$$

If an event from $IN_i \cup REP_i$ is offered by the data link layer, then it must be offered by the parallel combination. Further, the data link layer will perform an event from this set whenever the parallel combination does so. From the definitions of 'from' and 'at' given in chapter 6, we may infer that, for any time t

$$IN_i \text{ from } t\ (s \upharpoonright \Sigma_{DL}, X_D) \;\Rightarrow\; IN_i \text{ from } t\ (s, X)$$

$$REP_i \text{ at } t\ (s \upharpoonright \Sigma_{DL}, X_D) \;\Rightarrow\; REP_i \text{ at } t\ (s, X)$$

The result follows easily from the laws of the predicate calculus.

It will not always be necessary to expand the definitions of functions such as 'at' and 'from'. The timed failures proof system may be used to derive rules for reasoning about specifications expressed using these functions. For example, the proof of *DS3* could have made use of the following rule:

$$\frac{P \;\mathbf{sat}\; e \text{ from } t}{P \underset{A}{\|} Q \;\mathbf{sat}\; e \text{ from } t} \quad [\, e \notin \sigma(Q),\ A = \sigma(P) \cap \sigma(Q)\,]$$

A useful library of derived inference rules like this could be built up by pursuing further case studies in specification with timed CSP.

7.6.4 Network considerations

If a success is reported at node i, then the last packet input at i will be safely delivered to its destination.

$$
\begin{aligned}
DS4 \;\widehat{=}\;& \forall\, i, j, t, t' \bullet \\
& \quad i.rep.succ \text{ at } t \\
& \quad dest(p) = j \\
& \quad \text{last } IN_i \text{ during } [0, t) = (t', i.in.p) \\
& \qquad \Rightarrow j.out.p \text{ from } (t', t' + t_{max})
\end{aligned}
$$

We establish that the parallel combination of the data link and physical layers meets this requirement with the following argument.

For a success to be reported at node i, the last frame input at i must have been transmitted to the physical layer without interruption. Recall that

$$
\begin{aligned}
DT3 \;\equiv\;& \forall\, i, t \bullet i.rep.succ \text{ at } t \\
& \quad \Rightarrow \\
& \quad lasttrans_i(t) = lastframe_i(t)
\end{aligned}
$$

From requirement $PS5$, we know that any other transmissions would cause the event $i.cd$ to be offered to the data link layer. However, requirement $DT10$ insists that the data link layer be ready to accept $i.cd$ whenever i is transmitting, and $DT11$ insists that transmission should cease if $i.cd$ is observed.

We may conclude that no other node k transmits before $t_1 - t_{ik}$, where t_1 is the time at which the last bit of the frame was transmitted:

$$t_1 \;\widehat{=}\; \text{last } PUT_i \text{ before } t$$

Assuming that the minimum frame length t_{short} is greater than the length of the contention interval t_{con}, we may infer that node i acquired the broadcast medium during the transmission of the current frame. We may apply the argument used in the proof of lemma 7.1 to establish that no other node k can begin transmission before time $t_1 + t_{ik} + t_{int}$. Thus for any bit b of the frame in question,

$$
\begin{aligned}
i.put.b \text{ at } t \;\Rightarrow\;& \forall\, k, t' \bullet k \neq i \wedge PUT_k \text{ at } t' \wedge t' \in [t - t_{ij}, t] \\
& \quad \Rightarrow \\
& \quad t' \geqslant t - t_{ij} + t_{int} \wedge t_{jk} > t_{ij}
\end{aligned}
$$

From component $PS7$ of the physical layer service, we know that any bit transmitted by node i is received by any node j, providing that the above condition is met:

$$\begin{aligned} PS7 \;\equiv\; & \forall\, i, j, t \bullet i.put.b \text{ at } t - t_{ij} \\ & \wedge \\ & \forall\, k, t' \bullet (k \neq i \;\wedge\; PUT_k \text{ at } t' \;\wedge\; t' \in [t - t_{ij}, t]) \\ & \qquad \Rightarrow t' \geqslant t - t_{ij} + 2t_{bit} \;\wedge\; t_{jk} > t_{ij} \\ & \Rightarrow \\ & j.get.b \text{ from } t \text{ until } t + 0.1t_{bit} \end{aligned}$$

We may conclude that each bit of the frame was received by the physical layer at node j, and passed to the data link layer along channel $j.get$.

We now appeal to the output part of the data link specification. At time $t_1 + t_{ij}$, the last bit of the frame arrived at node j. We must establish that

$$lastrec_j(t_1 + 3t_{bit} + t_{ij}) \;=\; lasttrans_i(t_1)$$

The last frame fragment received at node j up to and including time $t_1 + t_{ij}$ should be identical to the last frame fragment transmitted at i. Recall that

$$lastrec_j(t) \;\widehat{=}\; \text{data } i.get \text{ during } [lastspace_j(t), lastgap_j(t)]$$

where $lastspace_j(t)$ is the endpoint of the last inter-frame space at node i:

$$lastspace_j(t) \;\widehat{=}\; max\{t' \mid t' < t \wedge \neg\,(GET_j \text{ at } (t' - t_{int}, t')) \wedge GET_j \text{ at } t'\}$$

and $lastgap_j(t)$ denotes the beginning of the last gap of length $> 2t_{bit}$ observed at that node before time t.

$$lastgap_j(t) \;\widehat{=}\; max\{t' \mid t' < t - 2t_{bit} \wedge \neg\,(GET_j \text{ at } (t', t' + 2t_{bit})) \wedge GET_j \text{ at } t'\}$$

From our observations above, we know that no other node k transmits during the interval $[t_0 - t_{ik}, t_1 + t_{ik} + t_{int}]$, where t_0 is the time at which node i began to transmit the frame in question:

$$t_0 \;\widehat{=}\; t_{int} + \text{time of last } i.cs \text{ before } t_1$$

If another node k had transmitted after $t_0 - t_{ik}$, then a collision would have been observed at i. From the bounds of this interval, and requirements *PS6* and *PS7*, we may infer that

$$\begin{aligned} lastgap_j(t_1 + t_{ij} + 3t_{bit}) &= t_1 + t_{ij} \\ lastspace_j(t_1 + t_{ij} + 3t_{bit}) &= t_0 + t_{ij} \end{aligned}$$

providing that $t_{int} > 3t_{bit}$. We may then prove, by induction upon the length of the bit sequence transmitted at node i from time t_0 onwards, that

$$\begin{aligned} lastrec_j(t_1 + 3t_{bit} + t_{ij}) &= lasttrans_i(t_1) \\ &= lastframe_i(t_1) \\ &= frame(lastpacket_i(t_1)) \end{aligned}$$

The last contiguous bit sequence received at node j before time $t_1 + t_{ij} + 3t_{bit}$ is a valid frame containing the last packet input at node i before time t_1.

We appeal to property *DT16* of the data link layer:

$$\begin{aligned} \forall\, t, t', f, p \bullet (&lastrec_j(t) = f \\ &validframe(f) \\ &unframe(f) = p \\ &dest(p) = j \\ &lastgap_j(t) = t'\ ) \\ &\quad \Rightarrow j.out.p \text{ from } (t', t' + t_{rec}) \text{ until } t' + t_{int} \end{aligned}$$

We know that $dest(p) = j$, and we may assume that the function *frame* always yields valid frames for transmission. Hence we have that

$$j.out.p \text{ from } (t_1 + t_{ij}, t_1 + t_{ij} + t_{rec}) \text{ until } t_1 + t_{ij} + t_{int}$$

However, our data link service requirement states that this output should remain available until it occurs. Fortunately, this service is provided subject to an environmental assumption:

$$EA \quad \equiv \quad \forall\, i \bullet \text{response } OUT_i < t_{out}$$

If we assume that

$$t_{out} \quad < \quad t_{int} - t_{rec}$$

then this assumption allows us to infer that $j.out.p$ is observed before $t_1 + t_{ij} + t_{int}$:

- we have shown that this event is available during $[t_1 + t_{ij} + t_{rec}, t_1 + t_{ij} + t_{int}]$, and
- we may infer from *EA* that the data link is seen to refuse $j.out.p$ at some time during any interval of length $> t_{out}$, corresponding to our knowledge that the event is offered by the environment.

We may conclude that

$$j.out.p \text{ from } (t_1 + t_{ij}, t_1 + t_{ij} + t_{rec})$$

If a packet p input at time t is to be successfully transmitted by node i, then the successful attempt at transmission may end no later than

$$\begin{array}{rrll} t\,+ & & t_{cs} & \text{preparing frame for transmission} \\ + & 16\,\times & t_{long} & \text{waiting for the channel to clear} \\ + & 16\,\times & t_{int} & \text{inter-frame spacing} \\ + & 15\,\times & t_{con} & \text{almost succeeding} \\ + & 15\,\times & t_{back} & \text{backing off} \\ + & & t_{long} & \text{successful transmission of longest valid frame} \end{array}$$

This places an upper bound upon the value of t_1. We conclude that this component of the data link service is provided if

$$t_{max} > t_{cs} + 17t_{long} + t_{rec} + 15t_{con} + 16t_{int} + 15t_{back} + max\{t_{ij} \mid i, j : NODE\}$$

The maximum delay between input and the offer of output for a successful transmission will be less than t_{max}, providing that t_{max} is greater than the value of the expression to the right.

7.6.5 Success

The data link at node i guarantees to deliver a packet at time t, providing that no other nodes are entrusted with a packet during the interval

$$[t - t_{rep}, t + t_{con} + t_{cs}]$$

The lower bound of this interval allows us to infer that no signals arrive at node i during the packet transmission. We know that

$$\forall k \bullet k \neq i \Rightarrow lastin_k(t) < t - t_{rep}$$

In the proof of requirement $DS2$, we established that no node will ever wait for longer than time t_{con} for a chance to begin transmission. From requirement $DT7$, we know that the latest time that a carrier-sense synchronisation may be observed at each node k is given by

$$\begin{array}{rrll} lastin_k(t)\,+ & & t_{cs} & \text{preparing frame for transmission} \\ + & 16\,\times & t_{long} & \text{waiting for the channel to clear} \\ + & 16\,\times & t_{int} & \text{inter-frame spacing} \\ + & 15\,\times & t_{con} & \text{almost succeeding} \\ + & 15\,\times & t_{back} & \text{backing off} \end{array}$$

From requirement $DT12$, we know that the last bit sequence transmitted at node k must be a subsequence of the last packet framed at that node:

$$\forall k, t \bullet lasttrans_k(t) \leqslant lastframe_k(t)$$

From this we may infer that each node k must cease transmission before time t_k, where t_k is given by

$$t_k \mathrel{\widehat{=}} lastin_k(t) + t_{cs} + 15t_{con} + 16t_{int} + 15t_{back} + 17t_{long}$$

No more bits may be transmitted if the current frame is exhausted, or has been interrupted sixteen times, by *DT7*, *DT8*, and *DT11*. Assuming that t_{rep} exceeds the lower bound placed upon it earlier, we may infer that

$$lastsig_i(t + t_{con} + t_{cs}) < t$$

Appealing to the argument of lemma 7.1 yet again, we conclude that node i acquires the broadcast medium and thus succeeds in transmitting the frame. The lower bound upon the value of t_{rep} is enough to ensure that this success is reported before time $t + t_{rep}$.

This completes our semi-formal proof that the parallel combination of the data link and physical layers is enough to satisfy the data link service specification, under the following assumptions:

$$\begin{array}{rcl} t_{short} & > & t_{con} \\ t_{con} & > & 2\ max\{t_{ij} \mid i,j : NODE\} \\ t_{rep} & > & t_{cs} + 15t_{con} + 16t_{int} + 15t_{back} + 17t_{long} + t_{succ} \\ t_{int} & > & 3t_{bit} \\ t_{out} & < & t_{int} - t_{rec} \\ t_{max} & > & t_{cs} + 15t_{con} + 16t_{int} + 15t_{back} + 17t_{long} + t_{rec} + \max\{t_{ij} \mid i,j : NODE\} \end{array}$$

Similar constraints are applied in the Ethernet specification document: e.g., Appendix E of that document states that

> *It is important that data link controller implementations be able to receive a frame that arrives immediately after another frame has been transmitted or received. Here, "immediately" means 9.6µs, based on the minimum inter-frame spacing provided as recovery time for the data link. It is important that the data link controller be able to resume reception within that time.*

This particular requirement corresponds to the following component of the data link total specification:

$$\begin{array}{lcl} DT14 & \mathrel{\widehat{=}} & \forall\, i,t \bullet GET_i \text{ at } t \Rightarrow GET_i \text{ from } (t, t + t_{bit}) \text{ until } t + 2t_{bit} \\ & & \qquad\qquad\qquad\qquad \wedge \\ & & \qquad\qquad\qquad\qquad GET_i \text{ from } (t + 2t_{bit}, t + t_{int}) \end{array}$$

If a bit signal is received at any node i, then the data link should offer to accept another within time t_{bit}. This offer may be withdrawn if no bit arrives within two bit times, which will be the case if a valid frame has just arrived, providing that the data link is ready to resume reception within time t_{int}.

7.7 IMPLEMENTATION

The Xerox (1980) specification document makes no recommendation about the implementation of the Ethernet protocol, stating that it may consist of any combination of hardware, firmware, or software. However, a concurrent variant of the language Pascal is used to describe the behaviour of the data link layer. The resulting program is presented as a definitive statement of the intended behaviour of the data link layer.

The precision of our specification language means that we have no need of an algorithmic description for specification purposes. However, such a description is useful as a guide to implementation, and as an aid to understanding the details of the timed failures specification. Accordingly, we represent the data link layer as a timed CSP process, which must satisfy the data link total specification.

7.7.1 Structure

The data link layer at a single node will be implemented as a parallel combination of four processes: two sending, and two receiving. The transmit data encapsulation process inserts a packet of data into an appropriate data frame and hands it to the transmit link manager. This process connects to the physical layer at the node, receiving collision and carrier-sense signals, and sending bits for transmission.

The receiver processes complement this action: the receive link manager collects bits from the physical layer, and passes complete frames to the data decapsulation process for validation. Valid frames intended for the current node are stripped and passed to the client layer. The labelled arrows in figure 7.5 correspond to channels of communication between the processes, while the two lines labelled *cd* and *cs* represent synchronisations with the physical layer.

7.7.2 Implementation

The data link layer is an interleaving parallel combination of data link processes, one for each node in the network:

$$DL \;\widehat{=}\; |||_{i:NODE}\, DL_i$$

At each node, there are processes to receive and transmit data. There is no reason for the two processes to synchronise with each other in an ideal implementation.

$$DL_i \;\widehat{=}\; i : (TRANSMIT \;|||\; RECEIVE)$$

We label the processes with the appropriate *NODE* identifier. The process descriptions below are independent of the node identity.

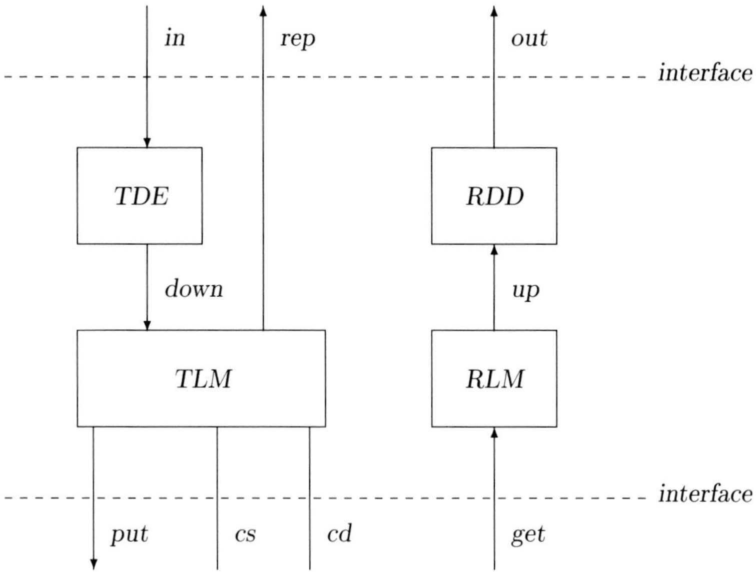

Figure 7.5 the internal structure of the data link layer

Transmission. Data transmission is handled by two processes, sharing a single private channel:

$$TRANSMIT \mathrel{\widehat{=}} (TDE \underset{down}{\|} TLM) \setminus down$$

The data encapsulation process accepts a packet from the client layer, frames it, and passes the frame to the link management process:

$$TDE \mathrel{\widehat{=}} in?m \xrightarrow{t_1} down!frame(m) \xrightarrow{t_2} TDE$$

Once the link manager has accepted a frame for transmission, it waits for a signal from that the medium is clear, and then passes the frame to the physical layer, bit by bit. Initially the process must listen for a frame on the appropriate channel:

$$TLM \mathrel{\widehat{=}} down?f \xrightarrow{t_3} HOLD_{f,1}$$

The cs event is hidden from the layers above, so it will occur as soon as both layers are ready. Once cs has been observed, transmission may begin.

$$HOLD_{f,n} \mathrel{\widehat{=}} cs \xrightarrow{t_{int}} (SEND_f \underset{cd}{\nabla} HANDLE_{f,n}) \; ; \; TLM$$

Recall that the data link must wait for time t_{int}, the inter-frame spacing, before starting to transmit. The process $HOLD_{f,n}$ holds a frame f until the cs synchronisation occurs, and the subsequent transmission is performed by a process $SEND_f$. The second subscript to the holding process is used to record the number of attempts made to transmit the current frame.

The sending process transmits the bits of the frame at intervals of t_{bit} to the physical layer, terminating successfully if it should succeed in transmitting the entire frame.

$$SEND_{\langle\rangle} \mathrel{\widehat{=}} rep!succ \xrightarrow{t_4} SKIP$$

$$SEND_{\langle x\rangle ^\frown s} \mathrel{\widehat{=}} send!x \xrightarrow{t_{bit}} SEND_s$$

Before terminating, the process informs the client layer that a successful transmission has occurred. If the sending process terminates without being interrupted, or the handler terminates, then the transmitter returns to its original state.

The transmission of a frame f may be interrupted at any time by the collision detect signal. If this occurs during the nth attempt to transmit the frame, then control is passed to the process $HANDLE_{f,n}$.

$$HANDLE_{f,n} \mathrel{\widehat{=}} BACKOFF_n \,;\, HOLD_{f,n+1} \quad \text{if } n < 16$$

$$HANDLE_{f,16} \mathrel{\widehat{=}} rep!fail \xrightarrow{t_5} SKIP$$

If fewer than sixteen attempts have been made to transmit the current frame, then the transmitter will wait for a certain period of time before making another attempt to transmit the frame. If the sixteenth attempt is interrupted, then the transmitter informs the client layer of its failure, and terminates.

According to our data link specification, the $BACKOFF_n$ process may be implemented by any delay between t_{slot} and t_{back}. In Ethernet, it is implemented by a random delay process, terminating at time $r * t_{slot}$ after being started, where time r is taken from a uniform distribution of integers in the range $1 \leqslant r \leqslant 2^{max\{10,n\}}$, where n is the number of the current attempt. This allows the data link to modify its behaviour as the load upon the broadcast medium varies.

Reception. Data reception is handled by two process, also connected by a single private channel:

$$RECEIVE \mathrel{\widehat{=}} (RLM \underset{up}{\|} RDD) \setminus up$$

The receive link manager accepts from the physical layer, and passes plausible frame fragments to the data decapsulation process. A fragment is plausible if its length exceeds 64 octets, the minimum frame size. The data decapsulation passes valid frames intended for the current node to the client layer along channel out.

The bit reception component of the link manager is prepared to accept bits from the physical layer at intervals of t_{bit}. If some bits have been received and no bits arrive for two bit times, control transferred to a simple validation process by a timeout operator:

$$RLM \mathrel{\widehat{=}} rec?x \xrightarrow{t_{bit}} LISTEN_{\langle x \rangle}$$

$$LISTEN_s \mathrel{\widehat{=}} (rec?x \xrightarrow{t_{bit}} LISTEN_{s \frown \langle x \rangle}) \overset{2t_{bit}}{\triangleright} PASS_s$$

The length of bit sequence s determines the behaviour of $PASS_s$.

$$PASS_s \mathrel{\widehat{=}} \text{if } \#(s) \geqslant 512 \text{ then } up!s \xrightarrow{t_6} RLM \text{ else } RLM$$

If the sequence is longer than *64* octets then it is passed to the decapsulation process via channel *up*. Shorter sequences should be discarded without further consideration.

If a bit sequence is passed to the decapsulation process, then the address field is matched against the current address. We assume the existence of a function *address* that returns the appropriate information. If a frame is intended for the current node, then it is stripped of framing information and offered to the client layer.

$$\begin{aligned} RDD \mathrel{\widehat{=}} up?f \xrightarrow{t_7} \text{if } address(f) = here \text{ then } out!unframe(f) \xrightarrow{t_8} RDD \\ \text{else } RDD \end{aligned}$$

We have assumed that all errors are due to collisions, and our assumption that $t_{short} > t_{con}$ means that all collision-damaged frame fragments, which take less than time t_{con} to transmit, will be shorter than *64* octets. With this assumption, no error checks are required during the decapsulation process.

By applying the inference rules of the timed failures proof system, we may confirm that our implementation meets the requirements of the data link total specification, providing that

$$\begin{aligned} t_1 + t_3 &< t_{cs} & t_6 &< t_{int} \\ t_2 &< t_{rep} + t_{in} & t_7 &< t_{rec} \\ t_4 &< t_{in} & t_8 &< t_{short} - t_{out} \\ t_5 &< t_{in} \end{aligned}$$

If all the above constraints are satisfied, then we have produced a satisfactory implementation of the data link layer.

7.8 DISCUSSION

The specification in this chapter is not a complete description of the service provided by the Ethernet protocol. We have captured some of the most important aspects of this service, and suggested a suitable implementation of the data link component of the protocol; this was sufficient to demonstrate the specification and design qualities of our notation. Furthermore, we can produce a more detailed study of the protocol without changing the method of specification employed in this chapter.

- We may expand our description of the data link by adopting a more systematic approach to the capture of requirements, as illustrated by the service specification of the physical layer. For each event a visible at the current level of abstraction, we considered the conditions under which a may occur, and the circumstances in which it must be offered to the environment. The resulting conjunction of safety and liveness constraints produced a more detailed specification.

- We may address other aspects of the data link service by adding new events to our interface. For example, to include error detection at receiving nodes, we might add a channel *err* to the datalink interface:

$$\{i.err.e \mid i : NODE\,;\, e : ERR\} \quad \subset \quad A_{DL}$$

  where *ERR* is a datatype of error reports. Alternatively, we may choose to consider the events on the channels *in* and *out* in greater detail, specifying the format of data and addressing information in packets and frames.

The lack of a suitable model for CSP prevents us from addressing the probabilistic aspects of the Ethernet protocol within our formal specification. However, the data link implementation and the physical service provide a basis for reasoning about the performance of the protocol. For example, results such as lemma 7.1 could be used to estimate the probability of a successful frame transmission, given suitable probability distributions for the length of packets, and the frequency at which they are submitted for transmission.

8 BROADCAST COMMUNICATION

8.1 SIGNALS

When describing the behaviour of a real-time process, we may wish to include instantaneous observable events that are not synchronisations. These *signals* may make it easier to describe and analyse certain aspects of behaviour, providing useful reference points in a history of the system. For example, an audible bell might form part of the user interface to a telephone network, even though the bell may ring without the cooperation of the user. This is incompatible with our existing view of communication.

In some cases, suitable environmental assumptions will allow us to describe such behaviour within the existing timed failures model. However, if we intend that these signals should be used to trigger other events or behaviours, then we must extend our semantic model to include an element of broadcast communication: some output events may occur without the cooperation of the environment.

In our model, signal events will occur as soon as they become available, and will propagate through parallel combination. A process may ignore any signal $\widehat{a}$ performed by another process, unless it is waiting to perform the corresponding synchronisation a. If this is the case, then both $\widehat{a}$ and a will occur. Of these, only the signal will be observed outside the parallel combination; it makes no sense to propagate a synchronisation.

We will define a denotational semantic model, representing each process as a set of possible behaviours. Each behaviour is represented by a triple (s, X, t), corresponding to the knowledge that the process may perform trace s while refusing set X, if observed up until time t. The time is included to simplify the semantic equations for parallel combination. Two component behaviours may give rise to a behaviour of a parallel combination only if they represent observations up until the same moment in time.

8.1.1 Notation

We will represent signals as distinguished events in a extended alphabet, adopting a *hatting* convention to differentiate a signal from the corresponding synchronisation. If we use $\widehat{\Sigma}$ to denote the set of all signal events, then the set of all events is given by

$$\widetilde{\Sigma} \ \widehat{=} \ \Sigma \cup \widehat{\Sigma}$$

For each synchronisation event a in Σ, we add a signal event $\widehat{a}$.

We use $T\widetilde{\Sigma}$ to denote the set of all timed events: synchronisations and signals labelled with times of occurrence. We use $\widetilde{TT}$ to denote the set of all timed traces: chronologically-ordered sequences of timed events.

$$T\widetilde{\Sigma} \ \widehat{=} \ \mathit{TIME} \times \widetilde{\Sigma}$$

$$\widetilde{TT} \ \widehat{=} \ \{s \in \operatorname{seq} T\widetilde{\Sigma} \mid (t, e) \text{ precedes } (t', e') \text{ in } s \Rightarrow t \leqslant t'\}$$

Signal events do not require the participation of any process other than the originator, and occur as soon as the originator is ready to perform them. Hence all availability information concerning signal events is recorded by the trace semantics. Our notion of refusal set remains unchanged from the timed failures model:

$$\mathit{TI} \ \widehat{=} \ \{[b, e) \mid 0 \leqslant b < e < \infty\}$$

$$\mathit{RT} \ \widehat{=} \ \{I \times A \mid I \in \mathit{TI} \wedge A \in \mathbb{P}\Sigma\}$$

$$\mathit{TR} \ \widehat{=} \ \{\bigcup C \mid C \in \mathbb{F}\,\mathit{RT}\}$$

The set of possible refusal sets in the timed signals model is given by TR, as before. The set of possible observations in this model is given by $\mathcal{O}_{SIG}$, where

$$\mathcal{O}_{SIG} \ \widehat{=} \ \widetilde{TT} \times \mathit{TR} \times \mathit{TIME}$$

Each possible behaviour is a triple, consisting of a timed trace from $\widetilde{TT}$, a timed refusal set, and a time value.

We will give a new semantics to our language of timed CSP terms, mapping each construct to an element of $\mathcal{S}_{SIG}$, where

$$\mathcal{S}_{SIG} \ \widehat{=} \ \mathbb{P}\,\mathcal{O}_{SIG}$$

As before, we employ a domain of environments to record the values of term variables, and define a semantic function for terms:

$$\widetilde{\mathit{ENV}} \ \widehat{=} \ \mathit{VAR} \to \mathcal{S}_{SIG}$$

$$\mathcal{F}_{SIG} \ \in \ \mathit{CSP} \to \widetilde{\mathit{ENV}} \to \mathcal{S}_{SIG}$$

We write $\mathcal{F}_{SIG}[\![P]\!]\rho$ to denote the semantics of term P in an environment ρ. As in the timed failures model, we omit the environment parameter when we give the semantics of a closed term.

We define an event set operator for timed traces; this is a projection mapping which returns the set of all timed signals which are mentioned in the trace. The event set operator defined in chapter 2 may also be applied to timed traces with signals, returning the set of all timed synchronisations.

$$\widehat{\sigma}(s) \;\widehat{=}\; \{\widehat{a} \in \widehat{\Sigma} \mid \exists\, t \bullet \langle(t, \widehat{a})\rangle \;\underline{\text{in}}\; s\}$$

$$\sigma(s) \;\widehat{=}\; \{\widehat{a} \in \Sigma \mid \exists\, t \bullet \langle(t, a)\rangle \;\underline{\text{in}}\; s\}$$

We overload the definition of these operators, applying them to process terms:

$$\widehat{\sigma}(P) \;\widehat{=}\; \{\widehat{a} \in \widehat{\Sigma} \mid \exists(s, X, t) \in \mathcal{F}_{SIG}[\![P]\!] \bullet \widehat{a} \in \widehat{\sigma}(s)\}$$

$$\sigma(P) \;\widehat{=}\; \{\widehat{a} \in \Sigma \mid \exists(s, X, t) \in \mathcal{F}_{SIG}[\![P]\!] \bullet a \in \sigma(s)\}$$

The result is the set of signal events that may be performed by a process P.

In order to give a semantics to parallel combination in a model with broadcast communication, we will need to identify the set of synchronisations which may be affected by a trace or interface set. We define a function *sync*, which returns a set of synchronisation events: for any $s \in \widetilde{TT}$ or $A \subseteq T\widetilde{\Sigma}$,

$$\begin{aligned} sync(\langle\rangle) &\;\widehat{=}\; \langle\rangle \\ sync(\langle(t, a)\rangle^\frown s) &\;\widehat{=}\; \langle(t, a)\rangle^\frown sync(s) \\ sync(\langle(t, \widehat{a})\rangle^\frown s) &\;\widehat{=}\; \langle(t, a)\rangle^\frown sync(s) \\ sync(A) &\;\widehat{=}\; \{a \in \Sigma \mid a \in A \vee \widehat{a} \in A\} \end{aligned}$$

This operator returns the set of synchronisation events which are mentioned—either as synchronisations or signals—in a sequence or set of timed events.

The semantics of parallel combination in the timed signals model will require a new subsequence relation between timed traces:

$$s_1 \subseteq s_2 \quad\Leftrightarrow\quad \forall\, t, a \bullet \langle(t, a)\rangle \;\underline{\text{in}}\; s_1 \Rightarrow \langle(t, a)\rangle \;\underline{\text{in}}\; s_2$$

We say that a trace s_1 is a subset of trace s_2 if and only if each timed event in s_1 is also present in s_2.

The failure subtraction operator may be applied to behaviours in this model:

$$(s, X, t) - t' \;\widehat{=}\; \begin{cases} (s \dot{-} t', X \dot{-} t', t - t') & \text{if } t \geqslant t' \\ (\langle\rangle, \{\}, 0) & \text{otherwise} \end{cases}$$

Subtracting time t from a behaviour discards the part of the behaviour that lies before time t; the remaining part is shifted backwards through time.

8.1.2 A semantic model

The timed signals model $\mathcal{M}_{SIG}$ is defined to be those elements S of $\mathcal{S}_{SIG}$ which satisfy a set of eight healthiness conditions, enshrined as axioms of the model:

1. $(s, X, t) \in S \Rightarrow t \geqslant end(s, X)$

2. $(s, X, t) \in S \wedge t' \geqslant t \Rightarrow \exists\, s' \bullet \sigma(s') \subseteq \widehat{\Sigma} \wedge (s^\frown(s' + t), X, t') \in S$

3. $(\langle\rangle, \{\}, 0) \in S$

4. $(s^\frown w, X, t) \in S \wedge end(s) \leqslant t' \leqslant min\{t, begin(w)\} \Rightarrow (s, X \upharpoonright t', t') \in S$

5. $(s, X, t) \in S \wedge s \cong w \Rightarrow (w, X, t) \in S$

6. $(s, X, t) \in S \Rightarrow \exists\, X' \in TR \bullet X \subseteq X' \wedge (s, X', t) \in S$
$\forall\, t' : TIME\,;\, a : \Sigma \bullet (t' \leqslant t \wedge (t', a) \notin X')$
$\Rightarrow (s \upharpoonright t'^\frown\langle(t', a)\rangle, X' \upharpoonright t', t') \in S$

7. $\forall\, t : TIME \bullet \exists\, n(t) \in \mathbb{N} \bullet (s, X, t) \in S \Rightarrow \#(s) \leqslant n(t)$

8. $(s, X, t) \in S \wedge X' \in TR \wedge X' \subseteq X \Rightarrow (s, X', t) \in S$

The first axiom insists that no trace or refusal information is recorded after the end of the current observation. The second states that any observation can be extended into the future; the only events that *must* be observed are signals. The remaining six conditions are inherited from the underlying timed failures model, modified slightly to reflect the possible presence of signal events in a process trace.

The third axiom allows us to infer that all processes have at least one possible behaviour: the empty failure, observed until time *0*. The fourth axiom states that any behaviour of S gives rise to another if truncated, while the fifth states that the set of traces of a process should be closed under timed trace equivalence.

The sixth axiom is a finitary condition upon refusal information. For any observation (s, X, t), there exists a maximal refusal set X' such that any timed synchronisation (t', a) not in X' is a possible extension of $s \upharpoonright t'$. The seventh axiom places a similar condition upon traces, asserting the existence of an upper bound $n(t)$ upon the number of events that may be observed before time t in any behaviour of S. The final axiom states that if a process may refuse X, then it may refuse any subset of X.

We define a distance metric upon the space of semantic sets:

$$\tilde{d}(S, T) \;\widehat{=}\; \inf\{\{2^{-t} \mid S(t) = T(t)\} \cup \{1\}\}$$

where $S(t)$ is the observation set $\{(s, X, t') \in S \mid t' \leqslant t\}$, the set of all observations in semantic set S which end at or before time t.

Theorem 8.1 The model $\mathcal{M}_{SIG}$ is a complete metric space under the metric $\tilde{d}$.

Proof A sequence $\{S_n\}$ in a metric space (M, d) is a *Cauchy sequence* if given $\epsilon > 0$, there exists N such that $d(S_n, S_m) < \epsilon$ for any $m, n > N$. A metric space (M, d) is said to be *complete* iff every Cauchy sequence in (M, d) converges to a point in M.

Suppose that $\{S_n\}$ is a Cauchy sequence in metric space $(\mathcal{M}_{SIG}, \widetilde{d})$, and let $\{n_i\}$ be a sequence of positive integers such that

$$\forall\, i \geqslant 0 \;\bullet\; i < n_i < n_{i+1}$$
$$\forall\, m \geqslant n \;\bullet\; \widetilde{d}(S_m, S_{n_i})$$

Under metric $\widetilde{d}$, the limit of sequence S_n is equal to

$$S \;\widehat{=}\; \bigcup_{i \geqslant 0} S_{n_i}(i)$$

By our choice of sequence n_i we have that

$$0 \leqslant t \leqslant i \;\Rightarrow\; S(t) = S_{n_i}(t)$$

For each axiom ax given in section 8.1, we must show that

$$\forall\, n \bullet S_n \in \mathcal{M}_{SIG} \;\Rightarrow\; S \text{ satisfies } ax$$

We consider the case of the second axiom:

$$(s, X, t) \in S \wedge t' \geqslant t \Rightarrow \exists\, s' \bullet \sigma(s') \subseteq \widehat{\Sigma} \wedge (s\frown(s' + t), X, t') \in S$$

Suppose that

$$(s, X, t) \in S \;\wedge\; t' \geqslant t$$

If we choose i such that

$$S(t') = S_{n_i}(t')$$

then we may infer that

$$(s, X, t) \in S_{n_i}$$

and hence that

$$\exists\, s' \;\bullet\; \sigma(s') \subseteq \widehat{\Sigma} \wedge (s\frown(s' + t), X, t') \in S_{n_i}$$

However

$$\begin{aligned}(s\frown(s' + t), X, t') \in S_{n_i} &\Rightarrow (s\frown(s' + t), X, t') \in S_{n_i}(t')\\ &\Rightarrow (s\frown(s' + t), X, t') \in S(t')\\ &\Rightarrow (s\frown(s' + t), X, t') \in S\end{aligned}$$

We may conclude that

$$(s, X, t) \in S \wedge t' \geqslant t \Rightarrow \exists\, s' \bullet \sigma(s') \subseteq \widehat{\Sigma} \wedge (s \frown (s' + t), X, t') \in S$$

and hence that the limit S satisfies the axiom. Similar reasoning allows us to establish that the limit satisfies the other seven axioms, and hence that the model $\mathcal{M}_{SIG}$ is a complete metric space. □

8.2 SEQUENTIAL PROCESSES

8.2.1 Livelock and deadlock

As in the timed failures model, the livelock process $\perp$ is identified with the deadlock process $STOP$. Any trace of either process will be empty,

$$\begin{aligned} \mathcal{F}_{SIG}[\![\, \perp \,]\!]\rho &\ \widehat{=}\ \{(s, X, t) \mid s = \langle\rangle \wedge t \geqslant end(X)\} \\ \mathcal{F}_{SIG}[\![STOP]\!]\rho &\ \widehat{=}\ \{(s, X, t) \mid s = \langle\rangle \wedge t \geqslant end(X)\} \end{aligned}$$

and any refusals must be recorded before the observation ends.

8.2.2 Termination and delay

The synchronising termination process $SKIP$ is ready to perform a single instance of the special event $\checkmark$ at any time.

$$\begin{aligned} \mathcal{F}_{SIG}[\![SKIP]\!]\rho \ \widehat{=}\ & \{(\langle\rangle, X, t) \mid \checkmark \notin \sigma(X) \wedge t \geqslant end(X)\} \\ & \cup \\ & \{(\langle(t, \checkmark)\rangle, X, t') \mid \checkmark \notin \sigma(X \upharpoonright t) \\ & \qquad\qquad \wedge \\ & \qquad\qquad t' \geqslant max\{t, end(X)\}\} \end{aligned}$$

If no events have been observed, then $\checkmark$ is available, and any refusals were recorded before the end of the observation. Otherwise, $\checkmark$ is observed at some time t and was available beforehand.

We may wish to use a signal to indicate that the successful termination of a process. Such an event would be propagated to the environment, causing termination in any process that is waiting to synchronise upon $\checkmark$. We define

$$\mathcal{F}_{SIG}[\![\widehat{SKIP}]\!]\rho \ \widehat{=}\ \{(\langle\rangle, \{\}, 0)\} \cup \{(\langle(0, \widehat{\checkmark})\rangle, X, t) \mid t \geqslant end(X)\}$$

If no events have been observed, then we have watched only until time 0. If our observation extends beyond this time, then a termination signal will be observed.

We also define two forms of delayed termination:

$$
\begin{aligned}
\mathcal{F}_{SIG}[\![WAIT\ t]\!]\rho \ \widehat{=}\ & \{(\langle\rangle, X, t') \mid \checkmark \notin X \upharpoonright t \wedge t' \geqslant end(X)\} \\
& \cup \\
& \{(\langle(t'', \checkmark)\rangle, X, t') \mid t'' \geqslant t \\
& \qquad \wedge \\
& \qquad t' \geqslant max\{t'', end(X)\} \\
& \qquad \wedge \\
& \qquad \checkmark \notin X \uparrow [t, t'')\}
\end{aligned}
$$

If the process is to synchronise upon the termination event, then $\checkmark$ is made available from time t onwards. If the process is to signal termination, then the termination signal will be observed at time t.

$$
\begin{aligned}
\mathcal{F}_{SIG}[\![\widehat{WAIT}\ t]\!]\rho \ \widehat{=}\ & \{(\langle\rangle, X, t') \mid end(X) \leqslant t' \leqslant t\} \\
& \cup \\
& \{(\langle(t, \widehat{\checkmark})\rangle, X, t') \mid t' \geqslant max\{t, end(X)\}\}
\end{aligned}
$$

8.2.3 Prefix

The event prefix operator transfers control to a process following the observation of an event. A synchronisation should be continuously available until it occurs:

$$
\begin{aligned}
\mathcal{F}_{SIG}[\![a \rightarrow P]\!]\rho \ \widehat{=}\ & \{(\langle\rangle, X, t) \mid a \notin \sigma(X) \wedge t \geqslant end(X)\} \\
& \cup \\
& \{(\langle(t, a)\rangle^\frown s, X, t') \mid a \notin \sigma(X \upharpoonright t) \\
& \qquad \wedge \\
& \qquad begin(s) \geqslant t + \delta \\
& \qquad \wedge \\
& \qquad t' \geqslant max\{t, end(s, X)\} \\
& \qquad \wedge \\
& \qquad (s, X, t') - (t + \delta) \in \mathcal{F}_{SIG}[\![P]\!]\rho\}
\end{aligned}
$$

A signal should occur immediately:

$$
\begin{aligned}
\mathcal{F}_{SIG}[\![\widehat{a} \rightarrow P]\!]\rho \ \widehat{=}\ & \{(\langle\rangle, \{\}, 0)\} \\
& \cup \\
& \{(\langle(0, \widehat{a})\rangle^\frown s, X, t) \mid t \geqslant end(s, X) \\
& \qquad \wedge \\
& \qquad begin(s) \geqslant \delta \\
& \qquad \wedge \\
& \qquad (s, X, t) - \delta \in \mathcal{F}_{SIG}[\![P]\!]\rho\}
\end{aligned}
$$

A delay of time δ is associated with the transfer of control to P.

8.2.4 Sequential composition

In the sequential composition $P\ ;\ Q$ control passes from P to Q as soon as P offers to synchronise upon the termination event $\checkmark$, or sends a termination signal $\widehat{\checkmark}$. In either case, there is no delay associated with the transfer of control, and the termination event is concealed from the environment.

$$
\begin{aligned}
&\mathcal{F}_{SIG}[\![P\ ;\ Q]\!]\rho \ \widehat{=} \\
&\qquad \{(s, X, t) \mid \checkmark \notin \sigma(s) \\
&\qquad\qquad\qquad \wedge \\
&\qquad\qquad\qquad \widehat{\checkmark} \notin \widehat{\sigma}(s) \\
&\qquad\qquad\qquad \wedge \\
&\qquad\qquad\qquad (s, X \cup ([0, t) \times \{\checkmark\}), t) \in \mathcal{F}_{SIG}[\![P]\!]\rho\} \\
&\qquad \cup \\
&\qquad CL_{\cong}\{(s^\frown w, X, t) \mid \checkmark \notin \sigma(s) \\
&\qquad\qquad\qquad\qquad \wedge \\
&\qquad\qquad\qquad\qquad \widehat{\checkmark} \notin \widehat{\sigma}(s) \\
&\qquad\qquad\qquad\qquad \wedge \\
&\qquad\qquad\qquad\qquad (w, X, t) - t' \in \mathcal{F}_{SIG}[\![Q]\!]\rho \\
&\qquad\qquad\qquad\qquad \wedge \\
&\qquad\qquad\qquad\qquad ((s^\frown\langle(t', \checkmark)\rangle, X \upharpoonright t' \cup ([0, t') \times \{\checkmark\}), t') \in \mathcal{F}_{SIG}[\![P]\!]\rho \\
&\qquad\qquad\qquad\qquad\ \vee \\
&\qquad\qquad\qquad\qquad\ (s^\frown\langle(t', \widehat{\checkmark})\rangle, X \upharpoonright t' \cup ([0, t') \times \{\checkmark\}), t') \in \mathcal{F}_{SIG}[\![P]\!]\rho)\}
\end{aligned}
$$

Any observation is either an observation of P in which no termination events occur, or a terminating observation of P followed by an observation of Q.

The sequential composition operator does not distinguish between the two forms of the termination event. This is illustrated by the following equivalence:

$$(P \mid\mid\mid WAIT\ t)\ ;\ Q \quad \equiv \quad (P \mid\mid\mid \widehat{WAIT}\ t)\ ;\ Q$$

In the presence of the sequential composition operator, the termination event $\checkmark$ occurs as soon as it is made available, and is concealed from the environment.

8.2.5 Choice

The semantics of the nondeterministic choice operator is the usual union of possible component behaviours:

$$\mathcal{F}_{SIG}[\![P \sqcap Q]\!]\rho \ \widehat{=}\ \mathcal{F}_{SIG}[\![P]\!]\rho \cup \mathcal{F}_{SIG}[\![Q]\!]\rho$$

and can be extended to give a meaning to indexed nondeterministic choice provided that the set of alternatives is *uniformly bounded*, in the sense of section 2.5.

If either of the components of a deterministic choice is ready to perform a signal event, then that choice will be resolved immediately.

$$
\begin{aligned}
&\mathcal{F}_{SIG}[\![P \;\Box\; Q]\!]\rho \;\widehat{=} \\
&\qquad \{(\langle\rangle, X, t) \mid (\langle\rangle, X, t) \in \mathcal{F}_{SIG}[\![P]\!]\rho \cap \mathcal{F}_{SIG}[\![Q]\!]\rho\} \\
&\qquad \cup \\
&\qquad \{(s, X, t) \mid s \neq \langle\rangle \\
&\qquad\qquad \wedge \\
&\qquad\qquad (s, X, t) \in \mathcal{F}_{SIG}[\![P]\!]\rho \cup \mathcal{F}_{SIG}[\![Q]\!]\rho \\
&\qquad\qquad \wedge \\
&\qquad\qquad (\langle\rangle, X \upharpoonright begin(s), begin(s)) \in \mathcal{F}_{SIG}[\![P]\!]\rho \cap \mathcal{F}_{SIG}[\![Q]\!]\rho\}
\end{aligned}
$$

Any event refused by a deterministic choice before any events have been observed must be refused by both components, and the behaviour following the first event must stem from just one of the components.

As an example, consider a process which is initially prepared to participate in the synchronisation a,

$$(a \rightarrow SKIP) \quad \Box \quad (WAIT\; t\, ; \widehat{b} \rightarrow STOP)$$

If this event occurs, the process terminates successfully. However, if a has not been observed by time t, the process sends a signal $\widehat{b}$ and then deadlocks. The occurrence of the signal event resolves the choice, and withdraws the offer of a.

The prefix choice operator may be used to offer the environment an infinite choice of inputs to a process. Signals correspond to output events; there is no reason to include signals in a prefix choice construct.

$$
\begin{aligned}
\mathcal{F}_{SIG}[\![a : A \rightarrow P_a]\!]\rho \;\widehat{=}\; & \{(\langle\rangle, X, t) \mid A \cap \sigma(X) = \{\}\} \\
& \cup \\
& \{(\langle(t', a)\rangle^\frown s, X, t) \mid a \in A \\
& \qquad\qquad\qquad\qquad \wedge \\
& \qquad\qquad\qquad\qquad t' \geqslant 0 \\
& \qquad\qquad\qquad\qquad \wedge \\
& \qquad\qquad\qquad\qquad A \cap \sigma(X \upharpoonright t') = \{\} \\
& \qquad\qquad\qquad\qquad \wedge \\
& \qquad\qquad\qquad\qquad (s, X, t) - (t' + \delta) \in \mathcal{F}_{SIG}[\![P_a]\!]\rho\}
\end{aligned}
$$

We assume that the set A contains only synchronisation events, and that the set of alternatives $\{P_a \mid a \in A\}$ is uniformly bounded.

8.2.6 Relabelling

The relabelling functions may be used to rename the events in a process, while preserving aspects of the control structure. We do not permit the use of such functions to transform signals into synchronisations, or vice versa:

$$\forall a : \Sigma \bullet f(a) \in \Sigma \qquad \forall \widehat{a} : \widehat{\Sigma} \bullet f(\widehat{a}) \in \widehat{\Sigma}$$

With this restriction, the effect of applying such a function is given by

$$\begin{aligned} \mathcal{F}_{SIG}[\![f^{-1}(P)]\!]\rho &\mathrel{\widehat=} \{(s, X, t) \mid (f(s), f(X), t) \in \mathcal{F}_{SIG}[\![P]\!]\rho\} \\ \mathcal{F}_{SIG}[\![f(P)]\!]\rho &\mathrel{\widehat=} \{(f(s), X, t) \mid (s, f^{-1}(X), t) \in \mathcal{F}_{SIG}[\![P]\!]\rho\} \end{aligned}$$

where $f^{-1}(X)$ denotes the inverse image of refusal set X under f.

8.2.7 Abstraction

We may conceal signal events from the environment by removing them from the trace. Because the process cannot stop signals occurring, the internal behaviour is independent of any signals performed. We extend the definition of the hiding operator on traces:

$$\begin{aligned} \langle\rangle \setminus A &\mathrel{\widehat=} \langle\rangle \\ (\langle(t, a)\rangle^\frown s) \setminus A &\mathrel{\widehat=} s \setminus A && \text{if } a \in A \\ & \qquad \langle(t, a)\rangle^\frown(s \setminus A) && \text{otherwise} \\ (\langle(t, \widehat{a})\rangle^\frown s) \setminus A &\mathrel{\widehat=} s \setminus A && \text{if } \widehat{a} \in A \\ & \qquad \langle(t, \widehat{a})\rangle^\frown(s \setminus A) && \text{otherwise} \end{aligned}$$

We may hide any combination of signals and synchronisations from the environment of a process:

$$\mathcal{F}_{SIG}[\![P \setminus A]\!]\rho \mathrel{\widehat=} \{(s \setminus A, X, t) \mid (s, X \cup ([0, t) \times (A \downharpoonright \Sigma)), t) \in \mathcal{F}_{SIG}[\![P]\!]\rho\}$$

Observe that only synchronisations may be added to the refusal set; signal events already occur as soon as they become available.

8.2.8 Recursion

As before, we may regard the semantics of a term P with free variable X as a function defined upon $\mathcal{S}_{SIG}$, mapping a set of behaviours S to the semantics of P in an environment obtained by associating X with S.

Definition 8.2 If P is a timed CSP term, and X and Y are variables such that Y does not occur free in P, then

$$\begin{aligned} \widetilde{M}(X, P)\rho &\mathrel{\widehat=} \lambda\, Y \bullet \mathcal{F}_{SIG}[\![P]\!]\rho[Y/X] \\ \widetilde{M_\delta}(X, P)\rho &\mathrel{\widehat=} \widetilde{W_\delta} \cdot \lambda\, Y \bullet \mathcal{F}_{SIG}[\![P]\!]\rho[Y/X] \end{aligned}$$

where $\widetilde{W_\delta}$ is the mapping defined by

$$\widetilde{W_\delta} \;\widehat{=}\; \lambda\, Y \bullet \mathcal{F}_{SIG}[\![\, WAIT\,\delta \,;\, X]\!]\rho[Y/X]$$

The definition of $\widetilde{W_\delta}$ reflects the delay associated with the second form of recursion operator. The semantics of each recursion operator is given by the fixed point of the corresponding mapping:

$$\mathcal{F}_{SIG}[\![\, \mu\, X \circ P]\!]\rho \;\widehat{=}\; \text{the unique fixed point of the mapping } \widetilde{M}(X, P)\rho$$

$$\mathcal{F}_{SIG}[\![\, \mu\, X \bullet P]\!]\rho \;\widehat{=}\; \text{the unique fixed point of the mapping } \widetilde{M_\delta}(X, P)\rho$$

The signals model $\mathcal{M}_{SIG}$ is a complete metric space under the metric $\tilde{d}$ defined earlier in this chapter. Following the arguments of chapter 3, we can show that the semantics of delayed recursion is always well-defined.

Further, the addition of signals to our computational model does not affect the notion of a constructive term. As in section 3.3, we may establish that the semantics of the immediate recursion $\mu\, X \bullet P$ is well-defined whenever term P is constructive for variable X.

8.3 SIGNALS AND CONCURRENCY

We intend that signals should be propagated through a parallel combination, and that available synchronisations are *triggered* by the corresponding signal events: if a signal $\widehat{a}$ is observed, then any process waiting to perform synchronisation a will be allowed to proceed. Observable synchronisations require the participation of the environment, so if a signal forms part of the interface between two processes then the corresponding synchronisation must be concealed.

It would be enough to conceal only those synchronisations which occur at the same time as the corresponding signal events, allowing a process to signal and synchronise upon the same event. For example, we might define a process

$$a \rightarrow STOP \;\stackrel{t}{\rhd}\; \widehat{a} \rightarrow STOP$$

which waits to synchronise upon event a, but will send a signal $\widehat{a}$ instead if no progress has been made by time t. However, it can be argued that no process may signal and synchronise upon the same event; we obtain a simpler, more intuitive, semantics for concurrency if we proscribe dynamic reconfiguration of input and output channels.

Accordingly, we place a simple restriction upon the sets presented as arguments to the alphabet parallel operator. In the parallel combination $P\; {}_A\|_B\; Q$ the sets A and B determine which synchronisations may be performed by processes P and Q, respectively. By adding signals to these sets, we may also determine which signals are propagated. We insist that

$$\begin{aligned} A \cap sync(A \cap \widehat{\Sigma}) &= \{\} \\ B \cap sync(B \cap \widehat{\Sigma}) &= \{\} \end{aligned}$$

No event a may appear in the same set as a synchronisation a and a signal $\widehat{a}$.

As an example, consider the following choices for A and B:

$$\begin{aligned} A &\mathrel{\widehat{=}} \{a, b, \widehat{c}\} \\ B &\mathrel{\widehat{=}} \{\widehat{a}, b, \widehat{c}\} \end{aligned}$$

In this case, either component may broadcast signal $\widehat{c}$ to the environment, and Q may broadcast $\widehat{a}$. If Q broadcasts $\widehat{a}$, then P may perform synchronisation a, but only the signal will be propagated to the environment. As before, both components must cooperate upon any synchronisation in $A \cap B$.

We may now derive the semantic equation for $P \;{}_A\|_B\; Q$. Suppose that the traces performed by components P and Q are s_P and s_Q respectively. Any synchronisation common to both sets must be performed by both components:

$$s \upharpoonright \Sigma \upharpoonright (A \cap B) \;=\; s_P \upharpoonright \Sigma \upharpoonright (A \cap B) \;=\; s_Q \upharpoonright \Sigma \upharpoonright (A \cap B)$$

and any synchronisation that is exclusive to one component will be observed if it is performed by that component, and not hidden by a corresponding signal. If we identify the sets of signals

$$\begin{aligned} C &\mathrel{\widehat{=}} A \cap \widehat{\Sigma} \\ D &\mathrel{\widehat{=}} B \cap \widehat{\Sigma} \end{aligned}$$

then we may capture this requirement as

$$\begin{aligned} s \upharpoonright \Sigma \upharpoonright (A - B) &= s_P \upharpoonright (\Sigma - sync(D)) \upharpoonright (A - B) \\ s \upharpoonright \Sigma \upharpoonright (B - A) &= s_Q \upharpoonright (\Sigma - sync(C)) \upharpoonright (B - A) \end{aligned}$$

Synchronisations of P that are also signals of Q are removed from the trace, and can only occur when Q performs the corresponding signal:

$$\begin{aligned} s_P \upharpoonright (A \cap sync(D)) &\subseteq sync(s_Q \upharpoonright D) \\ s_Q \upharpoonright (B \cap sync(C)) &\subseteq sync(s_P \upharpoonright C) \end{aligned}$$

If a is such a synchronisation, then (t, a) may appear in s_P only if $(t, \widehat{a})$ appears in s_Q. This will be true whenever (t, a) appears in the trace $sync(s_Q \upharpoonright D)$. A similar condition applies for synchronisations of Q.

The parallel combination will propagate any signals that lie in A or B and are performed by the corresponding process:

$$s \downharpoonright \widehat{\Sigma} \;\in\; s_P \downharpoonright C \;|||\; s_Q \downharpoonright D$$

Each component may perform signals from outside these sets, but they will not be passed to the other components, nor to the environment of the parallel combination. Combining these conditions, we obtain that

$$\begin{aligned} s \in s_P \;{}_A\widetilde{\|}_B\; s_Q \quad \Leftrightarrow \quad & s \downharpoonright \Sigma \downharpoonright (A \cap B) = s_P \downharpoonright \Sigma \downharpoonright (A \cap B) = s_Q \downharpoonright \Sigma \downharpoonright (A \cap B) \\ & s \downharpoonright \Sigma \downharpoonright (A - B) = s_P \downharpoonright (\Sigma - sync(D)) \\ & s \downharpoonright \Sigma \downharpoonright (B - A) = s_Q \downharpoonright (\Sigma - sync(C)) \\ & s_P \downharpoonright (A \cap sync(D)) \subseteq sync(s_Q) \\ & s_Q \downharpoonright (B \cap sync(C)) \subseteq sync(s_P) \\ & s \downharpoonright \widehat{\Sigma} \in s_P \downharpoonright C \;|||\; s_Q \downharpoonright D \;\;\wedge\;\; s \downharpoonright \Sigma = s \downharpoonright \Sigma \downharpoonright (A \cup B) \end{aligned}$$

If P performs a signal $\widehat{a}$ at time t, then the corresponding synchronisation should be offered to component Q. We may examine the effect of such an offer by including (t, a) in the appropriate refusal set. If s_P and s_Q are the traces performed by components P and Q, then we insist that for any time t'

$$\begin{aligned} sync(\sigma(s_Q \downharpoonright D \uparrow t')) \;&\subseteq\; \sigma(X'_P \downharpoonright A \uparrow t') \\ sync(\sigma(s_P \downharpoonright C \uparrow t')) \;&\subseteq\; \sigma(X'_Q \downharpoonright B \uparrow t') \end{aligned}$$

The synchronisations corresponding to the signals performed by Q at time t must be offered to component P at time t, if they are contained in set A. A similar condition applies to signals performed by P.

The behaviours of each component will take the following form:

$$\begin{aligned} (s_P, X_P \cup X'_P, t) \;&\in \mathcal{F}_{SIG}[\![P]\!]\rho \\ (s_Q, X_Q \cup X'_Q, t) \;&\in \mathcal{F}_{SIG}[\![Q]\!]\rho \end{aligned}$$

Any synchronisation from A that is refused by component P must be refused by the parallel combination. A similar condition applies to events from B.

$$\begin{aligned} X_P \;&\subseteq\; X \downharpoonright A \\ X_Q \;&\subseteq\; X \downharpoonright B \end{aligned}$$

We consider only those refusals of P and Q which correspond to events from A and B: any other synchronisation will be impossible. Conversely, any event refused from $A \cup B$

must be refused by at least one of the components, or concealed by the inclusion of the corresponding signal in the interface set.

$$X \downharpoonright (A \cup B) \setminus sync(C \cup D)) \quad = \quad (X_P \setminus sync(D)) \cup (X_Q \setminus sync(C))$$

For convenience, we define

$$\begin{aligned} X \in X_P \ {}_A\widetilde{\|}_B \ X_Q \ \Leftrightarrow \ & X_P \subseteq X \downharpoonright A \ \wedge \ X_Q \subseteq X \downharpoonright B \\ & X \downharpoonright (A \cup B) \setminus sync(C \cup D)) \\ & \quad = (X_P \setminus sync(D)) \cup (X_Q \setminus sync(C)) \end{aligned}$$

We may now give the semantic equation for alphabet parallel combination:

$$\begin{aligned} \mathcal{F}_{SIG}[\![P \ {}_A\|_B \ Q]\!]\rho \ \widehat{=} \ \{(s, X, t) \mid & \exists \, s_P, X_P, X'_P, s_Q, X_Q, X'_Q \bullet \forall \, t' \bullet \\ & s \in s_P \ {}_A\widetilde{\|}_B \ s_Q \ \wedge \ X \in X_P \ {}_A\widetilde{\|}_B \ X_Q \\ & sync(\sigma(s_Q \downharpoonright D \uparrow t')) \subseteq \sigma(X'_P \downharpoonright A \uparrow t') \\ & sync(\sigma(s_P \downharpoonright C \uparrow t')) \subseteq \sigma(X'_Q \downharpoonright B \uparrow t') \\ & (s_P, X_P \cup X'_P, t) \in \mathcal{F}_{SIG}[\![P]\!]\rho \\ & (s_Q, X_Q \cup X'_Q, t) \in \mathcal{F}_{SIG}[\![Q]\!]\rho \ \} \end{aligned}$$

If the two components are to synchronise upon every event from Σ, then no signals may be propagated to the environment. The semantics of a lockstep parallel construct $P \parallel Q$ is thus

$$\begin{aligned} \mathcal{F}_{SIG}[\![P \parallel Q]\!]\rho \ \widehat{=} \ \{(s, X_P \cup X_Q, t) \mid s = s \downharpoonright \Sigma \wedge (s, X_P, t) \in \mathcal{F}_{SIG}[\![P]\!]\rho \\ \wedge \ (s, X_Q, t) \in \mathcal{F}_{SIG}[\![Q]\!]\rho\} \end{aligned}$$

No such restriction need be applied to the interleaving parallel operator:

$$\begin{aligned} \mathcal{F}_{SIG}[\![P \ ||| \ Q]\!]\rho \ \widehat{=} \ \{(s, X, t) \mid \exists \, s_P, s_Q \bullet s \in s_P \ ||| \ s_Q \wedge (s_P, X, t) \in \mathcal{F}_{SIG}[\![P]\!]\rho \\ \wedge \ (s_Q, X, t) \in \mathcal{F}_{SIG}[\![Q]\!]\rho\} \end{aligned}$$

Signals and synchronisations are simply interleaved.

8.4 CONSISTENCY

The timed signals model is an extension of the timed failures model. If a process description P does not mention signal events, the semantics of P in $\mathcal{M}_{SIG}$ will be equivalent to the semantics of P in $\mathcal{M}_{TF}$. If we use π to denote the natural projection mapping between the two models, we may assert that

$$\mathcal{F}_{TF}[\![P]\!] \quad = \quad \pi(\mathcal{F}_{SIG}[\![P]\!])$$

for any closed term P constructed without signal events.

Definition 8.3 A timed CSP term is said to be signal-free if it contains no occurrences of events from $\widehat{\Sigma}$. This will be true whenever the term contains no subterms which match any of the following:

$$\widehat{SKIP}\ ,\ \widehat{WAIT}\ t,\ \widehat{a} \rightarrow P\ ,\ \text{or}\ \ P\ {}_A\|_B\ Q$$

where $(A \cup B) \cap \widehat{\Sigma} \neq \{\}$.

With this definition, our consistency result is expressed by the theorem below:

Theorem 8.4 If P is closed and signal-free, and any recursive subterms in P are constructive for the corresponding variables, then

$$\mathcal{F}_{TF}[\![P]\!] \quad = \quad \pi(\mathcal{F}_{SIG}[\![P]\!])$$

where projection mapping $\pi : \mathcal{M}_{SIG} \rightarrow \mathcal{M}_{TF}$ is given by

$$\pi(S) \quad \widehat{=} \quad \{(s, X) \mid \exists\, t \bullet (s, X, t) \in S\}$$

Proof We proceed by structural induction. To show that our result is true for recursively-defined processes, we must adopt a slightly stronger result for our inductive hypothesis. We begin by extending our definition of *signal-free* to semantic sets and environments:

Definition 8.5 If S is an element of $\mathcal{S}_{SIG}$, we say that S is signal-free if

$$\forall (s, X, t) \in S \quad \bullet \quad \widehat{\sigma}(s) = \{\}$$

Further, if $\rho \in \widetilde{ENV}$, we say that ρ is signal-free if

$$\forall\, X \in VAR \quad \bullet \quad \rho[\![X]\!] \text{ is signal-free}$$

It is easy to see that the semantic set $\mathcal{F}_{SIG}[\![P]\!]\rho$ will be signal-free whenever both P and ρ are signal-free. If we extend our projection mapping to environments with

$$\pi\rho \quad \widehat{=} \quad \{X \mapsto \pi(\rho[\![X]\!]) \mid X \in VAR\}$$

for any ρ in $\widetilde{ENV}$, we may also conclude that

$$\rho \text{ is signal-free} \quad \Rightarrow \quad \pi\rho \in ENV$$

We may now state our inductive hypothesis: if P is a signal-free term, then

$$\forall\, \rho \in \widetilde{ENV} \quad \bullet \quad \rho \text{ is signal-free} \Rightarrow \mathcal{F}_{TF}[\![P]\!](\pi\rho) = \pi(\mathcal{F}_{SIG}[\![P]\!]\rho)$$

Base case. It is sufficient to consider the case of the deadlock process. For any environment ρ in $\widetilde{ENV}$, we have

$$\mathcal{F}_{SIG}[\![STOP]\!]\rho \;\widehat{=}\; \{(s, X, t) \mid s = \langle\rangle \wedge t \geqslant end(X)\}$$

whence

$$\begin{aligned}\pi(\mathcal{F}_{SIG}[\![STOP]\!]) &= \pi(\{(s, X, t) \mid s = \langle\rangle \wedge t \geqslant end(X)\}) \\ &= \{(s, X) \mid s = \langle\rangle\} \\ &= \mathcal{F}_{TF}[\![STOP]\!]\end{aligned}$$

Although trace s is an element of $\widetilde{TT}$, we know that $s \upharpoonright \widehat{\Sigma} = \langle\rangle$, and hence that $s \in TT$.

Inductive step. Consider the case of the alphabet parallel operator. If the parallel combination $P \;_A\|_B\; Q$ is signal-free, then the same must be true of components P and Q. If s_P and s_Q are the traces corresponding to each component, we may conclude that $s_P = s_P \upharpoonright \Sigma$ and $s_Q = s_Q \upharpoonright \Sigma$. In this case,

$$\begin{aligned} s \in s_P \;_A\widetilde{\|}_B\; s_Q \;\Leftrightarrow\;\; & s \upharpoonright \Sigma \upharpoonright (A \cap B) = s_P \upharpoonright (A \cap B) = s_Q \upharpoonright (A \cap B) \\ & s \upharpoonright \Sigma \upharpoonright (A - B) = s_P \setminus sync(D) \\ & s \upharpoonright \Sigma \upharpoonright (B - A) = s_Q \setminus sync(C) \\ & s_P \upharpoonright (A \cap sync(D)) \subseteq sync(s_Q) \\ & s_Q \upharpoonright (B \cap sync(C)) \subseteq sync(s_P) \\ & s \upharpoonright \widehat{\Sigma} = \langle\rangle \;\wedge\; s \upharpoonright \Sigma = s \upharpoonright \Sigma \upharpoonright (A \cup B) \end{aligned}$$

From our assumption that the parallel combination is signal-free, we may conclude that the sets C and D are empty. From this, we deduce that

$$\begin{aligned} s \in s_P \;_A\widetilde{\|}_B\; s_Q \;&\Leftrightarrow\; s \upharpoonright (A - B) = s_P \wedge s \upharpoonright (B - A) = s_Q \wedge s = s \upharpoonright (A \cup B) \\ &\Leftrightarrow\; s \in s_P \;_A\|_B\; s_Q \end{aligned}$$

We may also infer that

$$\begin{aligned} X \in X_P \;_A\widetilde{\|}_B\; X_Q \;\Leftrightarrow\;\; & X_P \subseteq X \upharpoonright A \;\wedge\; X_Q \subseteq X \upharpoonright B \;\wedge \\ & \quad X \upharpoonright (A \cup B) \setminus sync(C \cup D)) = \\ & \qquad (X_P \setminus sync(D)) \cup (X_Q \setminus sync(C)) \\ \Leftrightarrow\;\; & X_P \subseteq X \upharpoonright A \;\wedge\; X_Q \subseteq X \upharpoonright B \;\wedge \\ & \quad X \upharpoonright (A \cup B) = X_P \cup X_Q \end{aligned}$$

We may use these results to simplify the semantics given for alphabet parallel combination in the signals model:

$$\begin{aligned}\mathcal{F}_{SIG}[\![P\ {}_A\|_B\ Q]\!]\rho \;\equiv\; \{(s,X,t) \mid \exists\, s_P, X_P, s_Q, X_Q \bullet s \in s_P\ {}_A\|_B\ s_Q \\ X \downharpoonright (A \cup B) = X_P \cup X_Q \\ X_P \subseteq X \downharpoonright A \wedge X_Q \subseteq X \downharpoonright B \\ (s_P, X_P, t) \in \mathcal{F}_{SIG}[\![P]\!]\rho \\ (s_Q, X_Q, t) \in \mathcal{F}_{SIG}[\![Q]\!]\rho\}\end{aligned}$$

If we assume that ρ is signal-free, we may apply our inductive hypothesis to components P and Q, yielding

$$\begin{aligned}\pi(\mathcal{F}_{SIG}[\![P\ {}_A\|_B\ Q]\!]\rho) \;=\; \{(s,X) \mid \exists\, s_P, X_P, s_Q, X_Q \bullet s \in s_P\ {}_A\|_B\ s_Q \\ X \downharpoonright (A \cup B) = X_P \cup X_Q \\ X_P \subseteq X \downharpoonright A \wedge X_Q \subseteq X \downharpoonright B \\ (s_P, X_P) \in \mathcal{F}_{TF}[\![P]\!]\pi\rho \\ (s_Q, X_Q) \in \mathcal{F}_{TF}[\![Q]\!]\pi\rho\} \\ \equiv\; \mathcal{F}_{TF}[\![P\ {}_A\|_B\ Q]\!]\pi\rho\end{aligned}$$

The case of the recursion operator requires the following lemma:

Lemma 8.6 The set of signal-free semantic sets,

$$SF \;\widehat{=}\; \{S \in \mathcal{S}_{SIG} \mid S \text{ is signal-free}\}$$

is a complete subspace of $\mathcal{S}_{SIG}$ under metric $\widetilde{d}$.

Proof of lemma 8.6 Suppose that $\{S_n\}$ is a Cauchy sequence in metric space $(SF, \widetilde{d})$, and let $\{n_i\}$ be a sequence of positive integers such that

$$\begin{aligned}\forall\, i \geqslant 0 \;&\bullet\; i < n_i < n_{i+1} \\ \forall\, m \geqslant n \;&\bullet\; \widetilde{d}(S_m, S_{n_i})\end{aligned}$$

Recall that the metric $\widetilde{d}$ was given by

$$\widetilde{d}(S,T) \;\widehat{=}\; \mathit{inf}\{\{2^{-t} \mid S(t) = T(t)\} \cup \{1\}\}$$

where $S(t)$ denotes the set of observations from S that end no later than time t. With this metric, the limit of the Cauchy sequence S_n is equal to

$$S \;\widehat{=}\; \bigcup_{i \geqslant 0} S_{n_i}(i)$$

By our choice of sequence n_i we have that

$$0 \leqslant t \leqslant i \;\Rightarrow\; S(t) = S_{n_i}(t)$$

and each S_n is signal-free. Hence we may observe that

$$\begin{aligned}(s, X, t) \in S \;&\Rightarrow\; (s, X, t) \in S(t)\\ &\Rightarrow\; \exists\, i \bullet (s, X, t) \in S_{n_i}(t)\\ &\Rightarrow\; \exists\, i \bullet (s, X, t) \in S_{n_i}\\ &\Rightarrow\; \widehat{\sigma}(s) = \{\}\end{aligned}$$

and conclude that the limit S is also signal-free. The set TF is thus a complete subspace of $\mathcal{S}_{SIG}$. □

The semantics of immediate recursion in the signals model is given by:

$$\mathcal{F}_{SIG}[\![\, \mu\, X \circ P]\!]\rho \;\widehat{=}\; \text{the unique fixed point of the mapping } \widetilde{M}(X, P)\rho$$

where the mapping $\widetilde{M}(X, P)\rho$ is given by

$$\widetilde{M}(X, P)\rho \;\widehat{=}\; \lambda\, Y \bullet \mathcal{F}_{SIG}[\![P]\!]\rho[Y/X]$$

In our inductive hypothesis, we have assumed that $\mu\, X \circ P$ and ρ are both signal-free. From this, we deduce that

$$Y \text{ is signal-free} \;\Rightarrow\; \mathcal{F}_{SIG}[\![P]\!]\rho[Y/X] \text{ is signal-free}$$

and hence that subspace SF is closed under the mapping $\widetilde{M}(X, P)\rho$. If we suppose that P is constructive for variable X, then this mapping has a unique fixed point, and this fixed point must lie in SF. We may conclude that the semantic set $\mathcal{F}_{SIG}[\![\, \mu\, X \circ P]\!]\rho$ is signal-free.

Applying the fixed point property, we may obtain that

$$\begin{aligned}\mathcal{F}_{SIG}[\![\, \mu\, X \circ P]\!]\rho &= \widetilde{M}(X, P)\rho\, (\mathcal{F}_{SIG}[\![\, \mu\, X \circ P]\!]\rho)\\ &= \mathcal{F}_{SIG}[\![P]\!]\rho[\mathcal{F}_{SIG}[\![\, \mu\, X \circ P]\!]\rho/X]\end{aligned}$$

Term P, environment ρ, and semantic set $\mathcal{F}_{SIG}[\![\, \mu\, X \circ P]\!]\rho$ are all signal-free, so we may apply our inductive hypothesis to yield that

$$\begin{aligned}\pi(\mathcal{F}_{SIG}[\![\, \mu\, X \circ P]\!]\rho) &= \mathcal{F}_{TF}[\![P]\!]\pi(\rho[\mathcal{F}_{SIG}[\![\, \mu\, X \circ P]\!]\rho/X])\\ &= \mathcal{F}_{TF}[\![P]\!]\pi\rho[\pi(\mathcal{F}_{SIG}[\![\, \mu\, X \circ P]\!]\rho)/X]\\ &= M(X, P)\pi\rho\, (\pi(\mathcal{F}_{SIG}[\![\, \mu\, X \circ P]\!]\rho)\end{aligned}$$

where the mapping $M(X, P)\pi\rho$ is as defined in chapter 3:

$$M(X, P)\pi\rho \quad = \quad \lambda\, Y \bullet \mathcal{F}_{TF}[\![P]\!]\pi\rho[Y/X]$$

We have shown that $\pi(\mathcal{F}_{SIG}[\![\, \mu\, X \circ P]\!]\rho)$ is a fixed point of this mapping, but there is also the fact that

$$\mathcal{F}_{TF}[\![\, \mu\, X \circ P]\!]\pi\rho \quad = \quad \text{the } \textit{unique} \text{ fixed point of the mapping } M(X, P)\pi\rho$$

so we may conclude that, provided that P is constructive for variable X,

$$\pi(\mathcal{F}_{SIG}[\![\, \mu\, X \circ P]\!]\rho) \quad = \quad \mathcal{F}_{TF}[\![\, \mu\, X \circ P]\!]\pi\rho$$

The remaining cases for the inductive step are comparatively simple.

We conclude that the inductive hypothesis holds for all terms: if P is a signal-free term in timed CSP, then

$$\forall\, \rho \in \widetilde{ENV} \quad \bullet \quad \rho \text{ is signal-free} \Rightarrow \mathcal{F}_{TF}[\![P]\!](\pi\rho) = \pi(\mathcal{F}_{SIG}[\![P]\!]\rho)$$

under the assumption that any recursive terms are constructive for the corresponding variables. The conclusion of theorem 8.4 follows immediately: if P is closed and signal-free, then $\mathcal{F}_{TF}[\![P]\!] = \pi(\mathcal{F}_{SIG}[\![P]\!])$. □

Furthermore, it is easy to see that the defining axioms of $\mathcal{M}_{SIG}$ are consistent with those of $\mathcal{M}_{TF}$, in the sense that

$$S \in \mathcal{M}_{SIG} \quad \Rightarrow \quad \pi(S) \in \mathcal{M}_{TF}$$

If a set S satisfies the axioms of the signals model, the projection $\pi(S)$ satisfies those of the timed failures model. We conclude that the semantics given in this chapter are consistent with the equations and axioms presented earlier, and hence that the signals model may be regarded as an extension of the timed failures model.

8.5 EXAMPLE

As an application of the signals model, we consider a timed CSP implementation of the physical layer of an Ethernet-like protocol. This layer provides a means of communication between the nodes of a local area network; data bits are accepted from the data link at each node, and passed along a broadcast medium. In section 7.5, we saw that the service provided by the physical layer could be captured as a timed failures specification. With the addition of signal events, we can produce a timed CSP description to satisfy that specification.

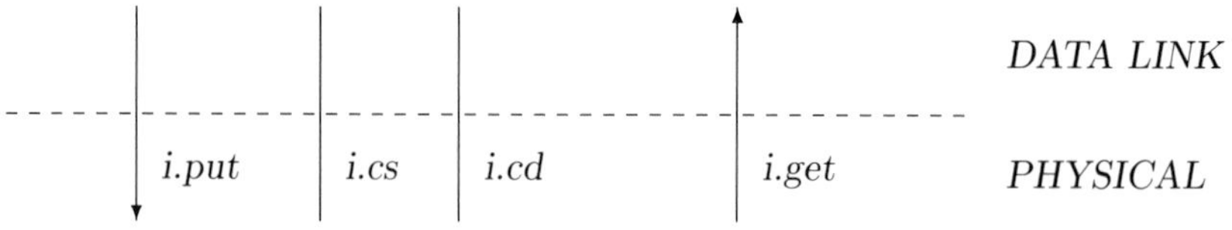

Figure 8.1 the service provided by the physical layer at node i

The service provided by the physical layer was described in terms of the availability and occurrence of synchronisation events from the following set:

$$A_{DL} \mathrel{\widehat{=}} \{i.put.b, i.cs, i.cd, i.get.b \mid i : NODE \,;\, b : BIT\}$$

At each node i, the physical layer shares two channels and two simple synchronisations with the data link component. The channels carry data bits between the two layers: bits are accepted from the data link layer along channel $i.put$, and transmitted to the data link along channel $i.get$. The synchronisation $i.cs$ is made available to the data link whenever activity ceases on the broadcast medium, and the synchronisation $i.cd$ is offered whenever a collision is taking place.

The event $i.put.b$ models the acceptance of a data bit b by the physical layer at node i. If the physical layer is to meet the specification given in chapter 7, a corresponding signal must be placed upon the broadcast medium at this node. Even so, there is no guarantee that the data bit will be received at another node j; if other nodes are transmitting, then this bit signal may be lost. This behaviour is easy to model if we introduce a set of signal events:

$$\widehat{\Sigma}_{PL} \mathrel{\widehat{=}} \{i.\widehat{at}.b \mid i : NODE \,;\, b : BIT\}$$

The event $j.\widehat{at}.b$ models the arrival of a bit b on the broadcast medium at node j.

Transmission. If a data bit b is passed to the physical layer along channel $i.put$, it should be broadcast to every other node on the network.

$$\begin{aligned} TRANS_i \mathrel{\widehat{=}} i.put.b \xrightarrow{t_{bit}} (&TRANS_i \\ &\interleave \\ &\interleave_{j \neq i} WAIT\ d_{ij} \,;\, j.\widehat{at}.b \rightarrow STOP\ ) \end{aligned}$$

We have decided that signal $j.\widehat{at}.b$ should occur at a time $d_{ij} + t_{bit}$ after the input event $i.put.b$. The bit time t_{bit} is the duration of a bit transmission on the broadcast medium.

The behaviour following an input event is an interleaving of two processes. The first is a fresh copy of the broadcast process: the physical layer at node i is ready to accept a new bit for transmission once time t_{bit} has elapsed. The second is an interleaving of simple transmission processes: each of these will produce a signal $j.\widehat{at}.b$ at the correct time, and then terminate.

Reception. The arrival of a data bit b at node i is modelled by the signal event $i.\widehat{at}.b$. If the physical layer at node i is ready, it will synchronise upon this event, and offer data bit b to the data link.

$$LISTEN_i \;\widehat{=}\; i.at.b : AT_i \xrightarrow{t_1} i.get.b \xrightarrow{t_2} LISTEN_i$$

where

$$AT_i \;\widehat{=}\; \{i.at.0, i.at.1\}$$

The combination of delays $t_1 + t_2$ must be strictly less than t_{bit} if the physical layer is to function correctly. In a valid frame sequence, a data bit is transmitted every t_{bit}; the physical component must be capable of decoding a data bit signal and passing it to the data link within this time. If the above process is not ready to observe signal $i.\widehat{at}.b$, then data bit b will not be received.

Carrier Sense. If more than two bit times have elapsed since the last bit arrived at node i, then the synchronisation $i.cs$ should be offered to the client layer. This offer should be withdrawn if another event from AT_i is observed. The following process will meet these requirements:

$$SENSE_i \;\widehat{=}\; (i.cs \rightarrow STOP) \underset{AT_i}{\nabla} NOISE_i$$

Once an at event is observed, control is passed to a process which offers to synchronise upon events from AT_i.

$$NOISE_i \;\widehat{=}\; (a : AT_i \xrightarrow{t_3} NOISE_i) \overset{2t_{bit}}{\triangleright} SENSE_i$$

If more than two bit times have elapsed since the last at event, this process withdraws the offer, and passes control to a copy of the original process $SENSE_i$.

Collision Detection. If a data bit arrives from another node while node i is transmitting, then synchronisation $i.cd$ should be offered to the data link layer. Accordingly, we define a process $DETECT_i$ which waits for i to start transmitting.

$$DETECT_i \;\widehat{=}\; a : PUT_i \xrightarrow{t_4} (MONITOR_i \underset{AT_i}{\nabla} COLLISION_i) \,;\, DETECT_i$$

Once a transmission has begun, control is passed to a monitor process. Observe that the delays t_4 and t_5 must be less than t_{bit}, or this process will interfere with frame transmission.

$$MONITOR_i \;\widehat{=}\; (a : PUT_i \xrightarrow{t_5} MONITOR_i) \overset{2t_{bit}}{\rhd} SKIP$$

This process offers to engage in events from $\{i.put.0, i.put.1\}$, until two bit times elapse without a *put* event. When this happens, the monitor process terminates successfully. If a bit arrives during a transmission, control is passed to the process $COLLISION_i$, which behaves as $MONITOR_i$, except that it is ready to engage in the event $i.cd$.

$$COLLISION_i \;\widehat{=}\; MONITOR_i \;|||\; i.cd \rightarrow STOP$$

As this is an interleaved parallel combination, it will terminate successfully when transmission ceases, and $MONITOR_i$ terminates. When this happens, control is passed to another copy of the original process.

Combination. The physical layer component at node i is the parallel combination of the processes defined above:

$$PL_i \;\widehat{=}\; (TRANS_i \underset{PUT_i}{\|} DETECT_i) \;|||\; SENSE_i \;|||\; LISTEN_i$$

The transmission and collision detect processes must agree on each occurrence of an event from PUT_i, but no other synchronisation is required. The physical layer itself is a parallel combination of node processes

$$PHYSICAL \;\widehat{=}\; \|_{ALL_i} PL_i$$

where ALL_i is the set of all events that are possible for node i:

$$ALL_i \;\widehat{=}\; PUT_i \cup GET_i \cup AT_i \cup \{i.cs, i.cd\} \cup \{j.\widehat{at}.b \mid j \in NODE \wedge j \neq i\}$$

Only the broadcast signal events are seen by more than one node.

9 DISCUSSION

9.1 OTHER APPROACHES

A wide variety of formal methods have been proposed for the specification and development of real-time systems, based upon process algebras, temporal logics, and timed programming languages. Although much research has been carried out, a consensus has yet to emerge concerning the applicability of the various formalisms to different types of system. A successful development method is likely to involve some combination of the features mentioned above. A notation that is well-suited to requirements capture is unlikely to be an efficient programming language, and *vice versa*.

9.1.1 Quantitative Temporal Logics

Hooman and Widom (1989) present a compositional proof system relating an `occam`-like language to a quantitative temporal logic, similar to the one developed by Koymans and de Roever (1983). Although the system description language is somewhat limited, it is clear that quantitative temporal logics are useful assertion languages; Jackson (1990) shows how such a logic may be employed as a specification language for timed CSP. It would be interesting to see the proof system applied in the development of a large, complex system.

Shasha *et al.* (1983) use a quantitative temporal logic to prove the correctness of a carrier-sense broadcast protocol, similar to the one described in chapter seven. By assuming a simplified version of the service provided by the physical layer, and an internal specification of the data link layer, the authors are able to establish that certain desirable properties hold of the network. The sketch proof provided is similar to the rigorous justification of the data link service presented in chapter seven.

In terms of complexity of specification, and support for formal reasoning, there is little to choose between quantitative temporal logic and the notation presented in this thesis. However, the structuring mechanisms of timed CSP, and the exclusive treatment of communication, are of some advantage when large systems are considered. We have yet to see a large-scale application of quantitative temporal logic to the hierarchical development of complex real-time systems.

9.1.2 Timed process algebras

In recent years, a variety of process algebras have been developed for the analysis of timed systems. These algebras may be classified (loosely) according to the methods adopted for specification and proof.

The bisimulation approach. Processes are given an operational semantics—the meaning of a process is given by a tree of possible transitions, describing the possible executions of the process. Processes are considered to be equivalent iff their execution trees are *bisimilar*. A bisimulation is a relation between tree structures: two nodes correspond if the sets of subsequent transitions are equivalent. The notion of equivalence depends upon the flavour of bisimilarity employed. The bisimulation approach has been adopted by Moller and Tofts (1990), Wang (1990), Liang Chen (1991), Nicollin *et al.* (1990), and Hansson (1991).

The testing approach. Processes are given an operational semantics, but equivalence is not defined by relations on synchronisation trees. Instead, processes are characterised by their possible interactions with testing processes. Two processes are equivalent under a certain class of testing process if no test from this class can distinguish them. Furthermore, a process P may be said to refine another process Q if it passes every test that Q passes. A specification consists of a process S and a relation R, which must hold between S and any proposed implementation. The testing approach has been adopted by Hennessy and Regan (1991).

The algebraic approach. Process equivalence is defined by a complete set of algebraic laws. A specification is a term in the process algebra, and a proposed implementation may be verified using laws which define a refinement relation. This approach is often used in conjunction with either testing or bisimulation equivalence. Given a complete axiomatisation for the operational equivalence, both algebraic and operational techniques may be applied. The algebraic approach has been adopted by Baeten and Bergstra (1991) and Liang Chen (1991).

The denotational approach. Processes are associated with elements of a denotational domain; two processes are equivalent if they are associated with the same object. A specification is a predicate upon elements of the denotational domain, and a process satisfies a specification if the defining predicate holds of its semantics. The denotational approach has been adopted by Jeffrey (1992), Ortega-Mallen and de Frutos-Escrig (1991), Boucher and Gerth (1987), Hooman (1991), and Zwarico (1986).

9.1.3 A uniform theory

In this thesis, we have used denotational semantic models to support a timed theory of specification and verification. This provides for a convenient separation of processes and specifications. A specification language can be given an interpretation in the denotational domain, and used to capture system requirements in a property-oriented fashion.

In the bisimulation approach, specifications are terms in the process algebra, or properties of execution trees. In the first case, processes are proved correct by establishing that the semantics of the process is bisimilar to the semantics of the specification. In the second, we must establish that the semantics of the process has the specified property. These properties may be expressed in graph-theoretic terms, or within a modal logic such as the logic of Hennessy and Milner (1985).

The practice of using a process algebra to capture requirements is more successful at higher levels of abstraction. As more information is added to the semantics of the language, using processes in this way leads to over-specification—additional requirements are placed upon the implementation—or complicated expressions which are difficult to relate to the original intention.

Further, it is difficult to combine processes which represent requirements in an intuitive and compositional manner; the result of combining two such processes may not correspond to the desired combination of requirements. This problem is eliminated by the use of a denotational semantic model for specification. The nature of denotational semantics guarantees compositionality.

We will often wish to examine the behaviour of the same process at different levels of abstraction. Using an operational semantics, this may be done by considering different notions of process equivalence. With a denotational approach, a different semantic model is required. So far, the theory of CSP described in this thesis is the only one in which different denotational models may be used in same specification. Reed's hierarchy supports a uniform theory of program verification at several levels of abstraction.

9.2 FUTURE WORK

9.2.1 Traces and causality

It is now apparent that the universal delay constant δ may be eliminated from the language of timed CSP. In this thesis, we have shown that it may be removed from the semantics of recursion, if sufficient care is taken to avoid unguarded recursions. If we remove the trace equivalence axiom

$$(s, X) \in S \wedge s \cong w \Rightarrow (w, X) \in S$$

from the definition of the timed failures model, then we may eliminate the constant δ from the semantics of the sequential composition and timing operators. By adopting a more abstract view of timed observations—in which the order of simultaneous events is important—we obtain a simpler, more consistent semantics for the language.

In the revised language, $WAIT$ is no longer a primitive process. We can remove the delay constant δ from the semantics of the timeout operator, and define $WAIT$ by syntactic equivalence:

$$WAIT\ t \quad \widehat{=} \quad STOP \overset{t}{\triangleright} SKIP$$

Furthermore, the elimination law for interleaved parallel combination is restored:

$$a \rightarrow STOP \ ||| \ b \rightarrow STOP \quad \equiv \quad \begin{array}{l} (a \rightarrow b \rightarrow STOP) \\ \Box \\ (b \rightarrow a \rightarrow STOP) \end{array}$$

The removal of δ allows us to establish a closer relation with the untimed models of CSP, facilitating timed refinement of processes.

9.2.2 Infinite observations

The standard models of CSP are based upon finite observations. Within these models, we have only a set of finite approximations to the behaviour of a process over the entire time domain. For most applications, this presents no difficulties—finite approximations are perfectly adequate. However, if we wish to address issues like eventuality, fairness, and unbounded nondeterminism, we require a more sophisticated treatment of infinite observations. An infinite timed model would:

- guarantee finite variability without the use of the bounded speed condition. We could dispense with any restriction upon the use of the indexed choice operators. We could also obtain the result that, for any specification S, there is a least deterministic implementation P which satisfies S.

- allow us to define a specification language, with the temporal logic concepts of *always* and *eventually*.

- support a theory of timed refinement from the untimed failures model. Offers and refusals recorded in untimed CSP are based upon eventualities: we consider an event to be refused if it is eventually refused forever. Infinite refusal sets would allow us to express this condition, and thus establish a refinement relation between timed and untimed failure models.

- permit the analysis of timed fairness requirements.

The only disadvantage of such a model would be the complexity of the fixed point theory required to give a suitable semantics to recursive processes.

9.2.3 Further refinements

Probabilistic models. The existing timed theory lacks any mechanism for reasoning about probabilistic aspects of system behaviour. Such a mechanism would allow us to analyse the performance of communication protocols. However, a semantic model which allows us to formalise statements such as *the system responds within 5 time units, with a probability of 0.5* will be complex indeed. Although substantial progress has been made towards an untimed probabilistic model for CSP, by Seidel (1990), little has been done to combine probability and time. This is an area for future research.

Simulated time. Another area for research is the development of a simulated time model for CSP: a real-time model which permits unguarded recursive definitions. Such a model would support a useful set of algebraic laws for timed processes: e.g., we would be able to define a unit for parallel composition. These laws may be useful in establishing the correctness of compilers for a language with timing constructs, which must simulate the flow of time.

Implementation language. If the development method described in this thesis is to support formal reasoning at every stage of the development process, we must bridge the gap between the system description language and executable code. We are fortunate in that there exists a powerful programming language based upon CSP, the `occam` language defined by Inmos (1988). A refinement relation could be established between a subset of CSP and a subset of occam. To provide a formal basis for this refinement relation, we would need to give a timed failures semantics to the `occam` language.

Tool support. If we wish timed CSP to be adopted by industrial users, it is essential that the development process is supported by reliable software tools—to manipulate formal specifications, and to assist in verification—we cannot expect methods to reach maturity without leaving their home environment.

9.3 CONCLUSIONS

We have presented a formal method for the specification and development of real-time systems. This method supports both formal and rigorous reasoning at every stage of system development, and is applicable to systems of a realistic size. With or without the improvements suggested in the previous section, the method should prove a useful tool for improving both safety and reliability.

To assess the applicability of the method, consider the role of a formal method in systems development: initially, a set of informal requirements describing the intended behaviour of a system are translated into an abstract formal specification; this specification is then gradually refined towards some final implementation. If each refinement step is verified, then we may be certain that any behaviour of the implementation will be consistent with the original specification. However, as Barringer (1987) points out:

- the gap between informal requirements and formal specification means that there is no guarantee that the system performs as originally intended;
- as soon as realistically sized systems are considered, shortcuts have to be taken; the number of formal proofs required is just far too large.

These are valid criticisms, and must be addressed if our development method is to be of any practical use.

The specification language formulated in chapters four and six is an attempt to answer the first of these criticisms. If the intended behaviour of the system may be described in terms of the observation and availability of some set of communication events, then this language may be used to capture the system requirements in a clear and comprehensible fashion. Once the requirements have been formalised, the specification language may be used to reason about system properties, and to communicate the details of the design to others. At this stage of the development process, we will often detect inconsistencies and ambiguities in the original requirements. Even if the development is completed informally, the production of a formal specification will have improved the safety and reliability of the system.

The proof system introduced in chapter five provides a formal link between the specification language and the system description language. Given an implementation of a system component, we may use the inference rules presented in chapter five to establish that it behaves as expected. The compositional nature of the proof system supports the hierarchical development of large, complex systems: we may reason about the behaviour of each component in isolation.

The second criticism is more difficult to answer; real-time systems are complicated entities, and the proof obligations are necessarily complex. The theory of timed refinement presented in chapter five can be used to reduce any proof obligations which correspond to untimed safety conditions: if we can show that these requirements are satisfied in Reed's untimed traces model, then we may conclude that they are also satisfied in the context of the timed failures model.

The treatment of scheduling and abstraction introduced in chapter six yields another method of reducing the complexity of proof obligations. By separating the concerns of scheduling and concealment, we are able to present our requirements in a clear and structured fashion, as illustrated by the development method for hierarchical protocols described at the beginning of chapter seven.

Even with the features described above, when we come to apply our development method to systems of a realistic size, we may find that the number of formal proofs required is still uncomfortably large. However, we may replace many of these proofs with rigorous mathematical arguments, and still be reasonably sure that our implementation is correct. Where doubts remain, we may increase the degree of formality until the truth, or falsity, of the argument becomes apparent.

THANKS

For inspiration, friendship, practical assistance, and legal advice during the preparation of this thesis:

Greg Abowd, Laurence Arnold, Geoff Barrett, Howard Barringer, Alexandra Barros, Jose Barros, Helen Bevan, Ray Bevan, Matthew Blakstad, Steve Brookes, Sally Brown, Meghan Burke, Marlies Burlet, Mark Bush, Carole Cadwalladr, Sue Charlett, Ching-Hua Chow, Antonia Clark, Steve Clarke, Peter Coesmans, Katie Cooke, Damian Cugley, Naiem Dathi, Will Davies, Kate Davis, Vicky Elphicke, Susan Even, Mike Field, Antonia Foster, Paul Gardiner, Dave Gavaghan, Hugh Gazzard, Jeremy Gibbons, Steve Giess, Michael Goldsmith, Sally Goodliffe, Amy Greenwald, Joshua Guttman, Malcolm Harper, Guy Hart-Davis, Michele Hart-Davis, Alison Harvey, Claire Henderson, Michael Hinchey, Robyn Hitchcock, Tony Hoare, Iain Houston, John Iwnicki, Dave Jackson, Jeremy Jacob, Steve Jarvis, Alan Jeffrey, Liz Johns, Geraint Jones, Mathai Joseph, Mike Kalougin, Andrew Kay, Steve King, Alice King-Farlow, Nick Lawrence, Jo Leggett, Gavin Lowe, Florence Maraninchi, Lionel Mason, Sebastian Masso, David Mayers, Quentin Miller, Colin Millerchip, Robin Milner, Mike Mislove, Charlie Morcom, Carroll Morgan, David Murphy, Andrew Newman, Colin O'Halloran, Duncan Oliver, Ian Page, Monica Payne, Joy Reed, Mike Reed, Dave Penkower, Amir Pnueli, Phil Richards, Gordon Riddell, Alexandra Robert, Willem-Paul de Roever, Bill Roscoe, Anne Ryan, Bryan Scattergood, Elizabeth Schneider, Steve Schneider, Brian Scott, Jenni Scott, Jess Search, Karen Seidel, Julie Sheppard, Elizabeth Shimmin, Jane Sinclair, Ib Sørensen, Mike Spivey, Richard Stamper, Joe Stoy, Rebecca Sudworth, Bernard Sufrin, Wilson Sutherland, Anna Sutton, Ann Sweeney, Jacqui Thornton, David Tranah, Anna-Lisa Westergreen, Tim White, Jack Wileden, Rob Woiccak, Ken Wood, and Jim Woodcock.

REFERENCES

Baeten and Bergstra (1989)

J. C. M. Baeten and J. A. Bergstra, *Real time process algebra,* Report P8916, Programming Research Group, University of Amsterdam

Baeten and Bergstra (1991)

J. C. M. Baeten and J. A. Bergstra, *Real time process algebra,* Formal Aspects of Computing, Volume 3, Number 2

Barringer (1987)

H. Barringer, *The use of temporal logic in the compositional specification of concurrent systems,* in *Temporal Logics and their Applications,* Academic Press

Barringer *et al.* (1984)

H. Barringer, R. Kuiper, and A. Pnueli, *Now you may compose temporal logic specifications,* Proceedings of the Sixteenth ACM Symposium on Theory of Computing

Barringer *et al.* (1985)

H. Barringer, R. Kuiper, and A. Pnueli, *A compositional temporal approach to a CSP-like language,* in *Formal Models in Programming* E. J. Neuhold and G. Chroust (eds.), North-Holland

Berry and Gonthier (1988)

G. Berry and G. Gonthier, *The Esterel synchronous programming language: design, semantics, implementation,* Rapports de Recherche 842, INRIA Sophia-Antipolis

Berry (1989)

G. Berry, *Real time programming: special purpose or general purpose languages,* in *Information Processing 89,* G. X. Ritter (ed.), North-Holland

Brookes (1983)

S. D. Brookes, *A model for communicating sequential processes*, Oxford University D.Phil thesis

Bergstra and Klop (1984)

J. A. Bergstra and J. W. Klop, *Process algebra for synchronous communication*, Information and Control 60

Brinch Hansen (1975)

Per Brinch Hansen, *Concurrent pascal report*, Technical Report CIT–IS–TR–17, California Institute of Technology

Boucher and Gerth (1987)

A. Boucher and R. Gerth, *A timed model for extended communicating sequential processes*, Proceedings of ICALP '87, Springer LNCS 267

Davies and Schneider (1989)

J. Davies and S. A. Schneider, *Factorising proofs in timed CSP*, Proceedings of the Fifth Conference on the Mathematical Foundations of Programming Semantics, Springer LNCS 439

Enderton (1977)

H. B. Enderton, *Elements of Set Theory*, Academic Press

Hansson (1991)

H. A. Hansson, *Time and probability in formal design of distributed systems*, doctoral dissertation, Uppsala University

Hennessy and Milner (1985)

M. Hennessy and R. Milner, *Algebraic laws for nondeterminism and concurrency*, Journal of the ACM 32

Hennessy and Regan (1990)

M. Hennessy and T. Regan, *A Temporal Process Algebra*, Technical Report 2–90, University of Sussex

Hennessy and Regan (1991)

M. Hennessy and T. Regan, *A process algebra for timed systems*, Technical Report 5–91, School of Cognitive and Computing Sciences, University of Sussex

Hoare (1978)

C. A. R. Hoare, *Communicating sequential processes*, Communications of the ACM volume 21 number 8

Hoare (1985)
C. A. R. Hoare, *Communicating Sequential Processes,* Prentice-Hall

Hooman and de Roever (1989)
J. J. M. Hooman and W. P. de Roever, *Design and verification in real-time distributed computing: an introduction to compositional methods,* Proceedings of the Ninth International Symposium on Protocol Specification, Testing and Verification, North-Holland

Hooman and Widom (1989)
J. J. M. Hooman and J. Widom, *A temporal-logic-based compositional proof system for real-time message passing,* Proceedings of PARLE 89, Springer LNCS 366

Hooman (1990)
J. Hooman, *Compositional proof systems for real-time distributed message passing,* ESPRIT BRA–3096 (SPEC) deliverable, Eindhoven University of Technology

Hooman (1991)
J. Hooman, *Specification and compositional verification of real-time systems,* Springer LNCS 558

Inmos (1988)
Inmos Limited, *Occam 2 Reference Manual,* Prentice-Hall

Jackson (1990)
D. M. Jackson, *A temporal logic for timed CSP,* Programming Research Group Technical Report TR–5–90, Oxford University

Jahanian and Mok (1986)
F. Jahanian and A. K. Mok, *Safety analysis of timing properties in real-time systems,* IEEE Transactions on Software Engineering, SE–12

Jeffrey (1990)
A. S. Jeffrey, *Discrete timed CSP*, Programming Methodology Group, Chalmers University of Technology

Jeffrey (1992)
A. S. Jeffrey, *Observation spaces and timed processes,* Oxford University D.Phil thesis

Jones (1982)
G. Jones, *A timed model of communicating processes,* Oxford University D.Phil thesis

Joseph and Goswami (1988)

M. Joseph and A. Goswami, *Formal description of real-time systems: a review*, Research Report 129, Department of Computer Science, University of Warwick

Koymans and de Roever (1983)

R. Koymans and W. P. de Roever, *Examples of a real-time temporal logic specification* in *The Analysis of Concurrent Systems*, Springer LNCS 207

Lamport (1977)

L. Lamport, *Proving the correctness of multiprocess programs*, Transactions on Software Engineering 3

Liang Chen (1991)

Liang Chen, *An interleaving model for real-time systems*, LFCS report series, ECS-LFCS-91-184, University of Edinburgh

Milner (1980)

R. Milner, *A Calculus of Communicating Systems*, Springer LNCS 94

Milner (1983)

R. Milner, *Calculi for synchrony and asynchrony*, Theoretical Computer Science 25

Milner (1989)

R. Milner, *Communication and Concurrency*, Prentice-Hall

Moller and Tofts (1990)

F. Moller and C. Tofts, *A temporal calculus of communicating systems*, Proceedings of CONCUR 90, Springer LNCS 458

Nicollin *et al.* (1990)

X. Nicollin, J.-L. Richier, J. Sifakis and J. Voiron, *ATP: an algebra for timed processes*, Proceedings of the IFIP Working Conference on Programming Concepts and Methods

Ortega-Mallen and de Frutos-Escrig (1991)

Y. Ortega-Mallen and D. de Frutos-Escrig, *A complete proof system for timed observations*, Proceedings of TAPSOFT 91, Springer LNCS 493

Quemada and Fernandez (1987)

J. Quemada and A. Fernandez, *Introduction of quantitative relative time into LOTOS*, in *Protocol Specification, Testing and Verification VII*, H. Rudin and C. H. West (eds.), North Holland

Reed and Roscoe (1986)
G. M. Reed and A. W. Roscoe, *A timed model for communicating sequential processes,* Proceedings of ICALP '86, Springer LNCS 226; Theoretical Computer Science 58

Reed and Roscoe (1987)
G. M. Reed and A. W. Roscoe, *Metric spaces as models for real-time concurrency,* Proceedings of the Third Workshop on the Mathematical Foundations of Programming Language Semantics, LNCS 298

Reed (1988)
G. M. Reed, *A uniform mathematical theory for real-time distributed computing,* Oxford University D.Phil thesis

Roscoe (1982)
A. W. Roscoe, *A mathematical theory of communicating processes,* Oxford University D.Phil thesis

Schneider (1989)
S. A. Schneider, *Correctness and communication in real-time systems,* Oxford University D.Phil thesis

Schneider (1991)
S. A. Schneider, *An operational semantics for timed CSP,* Programming Research Group Technical Report TR–1–91, Oxford University

Seidel (1990)
K. Seidel, *Probabilistic CSP: work in progress,* Programming Research Group, Oxford University

Shasha *et al.* (1983)
D. E. Shasha, A. Pnueli, and W. Ewald, *Temporal verification of carrier-sense local area network protocols,* Proceedings of the 11th ACM Symposium on the Principles of Programming Languages

Sutherland (1975)
W. A. Sutherland, *Introduction to Metric and Topological Spaces,* Oxford University Press

Tanenbaum (1981)
A. S. Tanenbaum, *Computer Networks,* Prentice-Hall International

Wang (1990)
Wang Yi, *Real-time behaviour of asynchronous agents,* Proceedings of CONCUR 90, Springer LNCS 458

Woodcock (1990)

J. C. P. Woodcock, *Using Z,* Lecture Notes, Programming Research Group, Oxford University

Xerox (1980)

The Ethernet Specification, available from the Xerox Corporation, reprinted in ACM Computer Communication Review

Zwarico (1986)

A. E. Zwarico, *A formal model of real-time computing,* University of Pennsylvania Technical Report